JUSTIFICATION
BY FAITH

JUSTIFICATION BY FAITH

Do the Sixteenth-Century Condemnations Still Apply

Edited by Karl Lehmann

Translated by Michael Root & William G. Rusch

with Original Essays by

Michael Root and William G. Rusch

and J. Francis Stafford

Continuum • New York

1999

The Continuum Publishing Company
370 Lexington Avenue
New York, NY 10017

Originally published in German under the title
*Lehrverurteilungen—kirchentrennend? II: Materialien zu
den Lehrverurteilungen und zur Theologie der
Rechtfertigung*
© Verlag Herder, Freiburg im Breisgau 1989

English translation copyright © 1997
by The Continuum Publishing Company

Printed in the United States of America

Library of Congress Cataloging-in-Publication Data

Materialien zu den Lehrverurteilungen und zur Theologie der
    Rechtfertigung. English.
    Justification by faith: do the sixteenth-century condemnations
still apply? / edited by Karl Lehmann ; translated and with an
original essay by Michael Root and William G. Rusch.
        p.   cm.
    Essays from the work of the Ecumenical Study Group
(Germany)
    Includes bibliographical references.
    ISBN 0-8264-0896-6
    1. Excommunication. 2. Justification. 3. Reformation.
    4. Counter-Reformation. 5. Theology, Doctrinal. 6. Christian
union. 7. Lutheran Church—Relations—Catholic Church. 8.
Catholic Church—Relations—Lutheran Church. I. Lehmann,
Karl, 1936-   . II. Ökumenischer Arbeitskreis Evangelischer und
Katholischer Theologen (Germany)   III. Title.
BX9.5.E97M3913   1996
280'. 042—dc20   96-8821
                                                              CIP

Contents

Preface

In Europe considerable scholarly attention has been devoted to the question of whether or not the sixteenth century condemnations between Lutherans and Roman Catholics on the doctrine of justification could be declared nonapplicable. Such an inquiry may seem at first hand pedantic. In fact its answer could have direct implications for the churches involved, and indeed for a larger ecumenical audience.

Most of the literature on this significant ecumenical topic exists only in German. Thus the purposes of this volume are to make this discussion available to an English-reading audience and to indicate its specific relevance to the North American context.

The first two chapters are new essays particularly addressed to the American scene. The remaining eight essays are English translations of major contributions to the European debate.

The editors wish to thank The Continuum Publishing Group for its willingness to publish this collection and to note with deep appreciation their collaboration with Norman A. Hjelm without whose assistance this volume would not have been possible.

Michael Root
William G. Rusch

Abbreviations

Abbreviations of German journal titles follow the *Abkürzungsverzeichnis* of the *Theologische Realenzyklopädie*.

AE   *Luther's Works*, American Edition, edited by Jaroslav Pelikan and Helmut Lehmann (St. Louis: Concordia; Philadelphia: Fortress, 19558-86.

Apol   "Apology of the Augsburg Confession," BC

BC   *The Book of Concord. The Confessions of the Evangelical Lutheran Church*, translated and edited by Theodore G. Tappert (Philadelphia: Fortress, 1959).

BSLK   *Die Bekenntnisschriften der Evangelisch-Lutherischen Kirche* (Göttingen: 1930).

CA   "Augsburg Confession" (Confessio Augustana)

CCC   *Catechism of the Catholic Church* (Washington: NCCB, 1994)

CIC   *Code of Canon Law*, Latin-English Edition (Washington: Canon Law Society of America, 1983).

Cl   *Luthers Werke in Auswahl*, edited by O. Clemen (Berlin: 1930-35).

Condemnations   *The Condemnations of the Reformation Era? Do They Still Divide?*, edited by Karl Lehmann & Wolfhart Pannenberg (Minneapolis: Fortress, 1990).

CR   *Corpus Reformatorum* (Berlin: 1834ff).

CSEL   *Corpus scriptorum ecclesiasticorum Latinorum* (Vienna: 1866ff).

CT   *Concilium Tridentinum* (Freiburg i. Br.: 1901ff).

Dz   *Enchiridion symbolorum definitionum et declarationum de rebus fidei et morum*, 37th ed., edited by Heinrich Denzinger & Peter Hünermann (Freiburg i. Br.: Herder, 1991).

Ed. pr	"Editio princeps" of the CA
EKD	Evangelische Kirche in Deutschland - Evangelical Church in Germany
ELCA	Evangelical Lutheran Church in America
Epit	"Epitome," FC, BC
FC	"Formula of Concord," BC
LWF	Lutheran World Federation
MSA	*Ph. Melanchthons Werke in Auswahl*, edited by R. Stupperich (Gütersloh: 1951ff).
MySal	*Mysterium Salutis. Grundriss heilsgeschichtlicher Dogmatik* (Einsiedeln: 1965-1976).
ND	*The Christian Faith in the Doctrinal Documents of the Catholic Church*, edited by J. Neuner and J. Dupuis (New York: Alba House, 1982).
NPNF	*A Select Library of the Nicene and Post-Nicene Fathers of the Christian Church*, edited by Philip Schaff (Rpt, Grand Rapids: Eerdmans, 1956).
PCPCU	Pontifical Council for Promoting Christian Unity
PL	*Patrologiae cursus completus. Series Latina*, edited by J.-P. Migne (Paris: 1841ff).
RGG	*Die Religion in Geschichte und Gegenwart*, 3rd ed. (Tübingen: 1956ff).
SA	"Smalcald Articles," BC
SD	"Solid Declaration," FC, BC
Tr	"Treatise on the Power and Primacy of the Pope," BC.
WA	*Werke*, Martin Luther, Weimarer Ausgabe (Weimar: Böhlau, 1883ff).

Chapter One

Can the Sixteenth Century Condemnations on Justification be Declared Nonapplicable?

An Introduction

Michael Root & William G. Rusch

1. JUSTIFICATION, CONDEMNATIONS, AND COMMUNION

HOW ARE SINNERS found acceptable by a just God? This question was at the center of the Reformation. For some, it was the question upon which everything hung; for others, it was one of a group of central questions; for almost no one was it inconsequential. As Western Christendom divided, the churches rejected and condemned misunderstandings of justification they believed undermined the very foundations of Christian faith. They clearly thought they were condemning the teachings of other churches.

These condemnations remain a formal and material obstacle for closer relations between the Roman Catholic Church and the Lutheran and other churches shaped by the Reformation. Can churches enter into significantly closer fellowship if each still condemns the teaching of the other on as central a matter as the nature of Christian salvation? Beyond the question of the condemnations themselves, have the differences over justification either disappeared or come to be seen as no longer church-dividing?

In the ecumenical dialogues of the last thirty years, much attention has been given to justification. The essays collected in this volume derive from the latest phase of the discussion. Following a visit of Pope John Paul II to Germany in 1980, a Joint Ecumenical Commission was formed of Roman Catholic, and Protestant (Lutheran, Reformed, and United) church leaders in what was then West Germany to explore the preconditions for closer relations between the churches. One precondition for such relations would be an understanding or declaration that the various doctrinal condemnations promulgated in different ways on both sides during the century of the Reformation no longer in fact apply to the other church. Such a declaration has been an important part of the Leuenberg Agreement establishing church fellowship among the Lutheran, Reformed, and United churches in Europe. The Joint Commission asked the Ecumenical Study Group, a group of scholars which had been meeting since soon after the Second World War, to carry out a thorough historical and theological investigation of the Reformation era condemnations with the purpose of showing whether or not these condemnations are applicable to the partner church today.

The results of their study were published in 1986 in German and in 1990 in English under the title *The Condemnations of the Reformation Era: Do They Still Divide?*[1] It addressed the condemnations in the Lutheran and Reformed Confessions and from the Council of Trent in three areas: justification, sacraments, and ordained ministry. As is described below, this study and various other dialogues results have now moved the Roman Catholic Church and the Lutheran churches within the Lutheran World Federation (LWF) to consider the possibility of declaring the Reformation era condemnations in relation to justification non-applicable to the partner church of today.[2] Such a declaration would be based on more than the German discussion. It would be a culmination of work within and beyond the international, European, and North American dialogues. The German discussion forms the immediate background, however, of the present efforts.

2. THE SUPPORTING ESSAYS

The German publication of the *Condemnations* study was followed in 1989 and 1990 by the publication of two volumes of supporting essays from the work of the Ecumenical Study Group, each running to over 350 pages.[3] Like the study itself, the studies addressed the general ecumenical problem of condemnations and the specific themes of justification, sacraments, and ordained ministry. The present volume represents a selection of the essays that directly related to the possibility of declaring the condemnations on justification non-applicable.[4] Also included in this volume is an essay by Archbishop J. Francis Stafford, co-chair of the Lutheran-Catholic Coordinating Committee (US), which has been studying the condemnations. He places the possible declaration of non-applicability in the context of Catholic tradition and the ecumenical commitments of the Catholic Church and provides eloquent testimony to the significance of the issues involved.

2.1. Context-Setting Essays

The first three essays set the context of the discussion. Wolfhart Pannenberg and Karl Lehmann, the Lutheran and Catholic Theological Directors of the Ecumenical Study Group at that time, set the procedural and methodological context of the Study Group's work. **Pannenberg** describes the origin, course, and results of the Group's study. He summarizes the results in relation to all three topics the Group analyzed. This summary lets us see how the results on justification fit into the total study. Of particular importance is Pannenberg's argument that the churches can declare the condemnations on justification non-applicable although other issues (e.g., the papacy) remain controversial, even church-dividing. On the one hand, this conclusion means we can proceed with this step even if dispute continues on other questions. On the other hand, it means that full fellowship or communion will not immediately follow from this action. Lifting these condemnations is *a* precondition of communion, not the full and sufficient condition for communion.

In his discussion of justification, Pannenberg also presents a criterion for deciding whether a difference on some question justifies a condemnation and is thus church-dividing. Differences need not be church-dividing if "what one side lifts up is neither rejected nor overlooked and neglected by the other side, despite differing thought-forms." Decisive for the conclusion that the real differences between Lutherans and Catholics on justification need not be church-dividing is the experience of many dialogues that neither side in fact rejects or neglects what the other lifts up as of decisive importance.

Lehmann further elaborates the underlying assumptions and method of the study. The entire project works from the hypothesis of a "basic consensus" among Lutherans and Catholics on the nature of the gospel. Such a basic consensus is not yet the sort of "integral consensus" Catholics and many Lutherans see as needed for church fellowship. It represents, however, a common sense of the fundamental meaning of the gospel, and thus of justification.

If such a basic consensus exists, then the existing mutual condemnations on justification are inappropriate, not in the sense that what they condemn is not to be rejected, but rather in the sense that the partner church does not in fact teach what was condemned in the way it was condemned. The testing of the applicability of the doctrinal condemnations on justification is thus also a test of the existence of this basic consensus.

How could the conclusion be reached that the condemnations do not today apply to the partner church? Both historical research and contemporary ecumenical experience are important. Historical research must ask precisely what was rejected and why. Condemnations, even more than positive statements of doctrine, are shaped by the context in which they were formulated. What did those who framed the condemnations in fact know of the actual teachings of the other side? What were they seeking to defend against in rejecting this or that statement?

This historical knowledge must be joined with present ecumenical experience of the partner. Have we come to know one another as brothers and sisters in the same faith? Do we experience the effects of a basis consensus in our understandings of the gospel?

Lehmann's judgments are carefully differentiated. We cannot simply say that all condemnations in all areas do not apply. We may need more nuanced categories to describe ways in which condemnations may apply to certain aspects or expressions of a doctrine or practice, but not to others, or not to the doctrine itself. We may need a more comprehensive "hermeneutic of condemnations," something the Study Group did not try to produce. The historical "step backward" the concern with the sixteenth century condemnations represents will be an ecumenical step forward if it is a turn toward the basics of the faith in which we sense we are one.

The essay from Harding **Meyer** sets the discussion of justification in the *Condemnations* study into the context of the treatment of justification in the wide range of other ecumenical dialogues of the last thirty years. While his focus is on dialogues involving Lutherans, he also takes note of other dialogues that have addressed justification, most notably the international Anglican-Catholic dialogue.

Meyer notes that justification has been discussed in three ways in the dialogues: as a specific theme within theology, which he calls the dogmatic discussion; as a criterion by which all the church's teaching and practice is to be judged, which he calls the criteriological discussion; and as a criterion in its specific application to various church teachings and practices, which he calls the criteriological-applicative discussion. In this essay he addresses only the first two aspects of the discussion as it has occurred in the ecumenical dialogues.

The most important results of his survey relate to the nature and extent of the agreement reached and the similarity of the conclusions of the *Condemnations* study to those reached in many other dialogues. While the dialogues reveal a distinctive Lutheran insistence on the forensic and external or imputative, rather than effective and internal, character of justification, they also have uniformly concluded that differences are not "a divisive opposition in content, but a divergence in viewpoint, accent or concern." He sees the dialogues utilizing precisely the standard proposed by Pannenberg: neither side denies or overlooks what the other affirms as essential and central.

The dialogues, especially and importantly the Lutheran-Catholic dialogues, have also been able to agree on the criteriological status of that about which justification speaks, the gospel of our gracious salvation in Jesus Christ. It is agreed that the message of justification, although not any particular detailed doctrine of justification, is the heart of the gospel which serves as the measure of all that the church says and does. The differences that the dialogues have not overcome do not relate to the criteriological status of justification, but to the third aspect of the discussion, the criteriological-applicative, in which the specific applications of the criterion are examined.

Meyer notes that, while the discussion of justification in the *Condemnations* study often differs from other dialogues because of its mandated focus on the condemnations, its conclusions are substantively in line with those widely reached elsewhere. In fact, he finds these conclusions so widely agreed and solidly based that they should now be seen as "dialogue-definitive," as firm bases upon which actions and further discussion can be based without the need to return to these questions ever anew. The official declaration of the non-applicability of the condemnations on justification would be step in this direction.

2.2. Essays on the Lutheran Condemnations
A second group of essays deal with the condemnations on justification in the Lutheran confessions. The essay by Gunther **Wenz** (of which only the half relating to justification is here translated) addresses both the authority of the confessions and the condemnations on justification within them.[5]

He argues that, while the entire Book of Concord (the collection of the Lutheran confessions) needs to be taken into account, the centrality of the Augsburg Confession as the lens through which the totality is read needs also to be affirmed. This hermeneutical judgment is important for the

Condemnations study, because the CA, in harmony with all the confessions, but in a more explicit way, affirms the intention of the Reformation to teach the catholic faith shared with the ancient church. The authority of the confessions themselves is a function of their right interpretation of the gospel, normatively found in the Scriptures and from which the church has always lived.

After an analysis of the sense in which justification is the center and limit of the Lutheran confession (cp. the similar discussion by Meyer on justification as criterion), Wenz surveys the condemnations in the Book of Concord that relate to justification. The special merit of his presentation is his delineation of the understanding of justification, consistently held in the different confessions, which found expression in the condemnations. He thus makes clear what the Lutherans were condemning and why they thought it must be condemned. In the process, he shows that while the Lutheran understanding of justification did find its center in the belief that we have our righteousness only *extra nos,* in Christ, the Lutherans never held that justification could be separated from internal regeneration and renewal. They were not asserting what many Catholics feared.

Condemnations in the individual Lutheran confessions are then analyzed by Vinzenz Pfnür and Friedrich Beisser. **Pfnür** deals with the confessions of the 1530s: the Augsburg Confession (CA), its Apology, and the Smalcald Articles. By a careful textual analysis of the CA, writings from Luther, and texts from Gabriel Biel, the influential late medieval nominalist theologian, Pfnür demonstrates that the target of the Lutheran condemnations on justification in these early texts was the position of Biel. While the opinions of Biel were shared by many, they were not normative Catholic teaching. Similarly, the CA's condemnations of the teaching that sacraments can justify *ex opere operato*, i.e., simply by being performed, is seen to relate to a position of Biel's, but not to normative Catholic teaching. On the sacrament of penance, the crucial context for many of the discussions of justification in the early years of the Reformation, Pfnür again shows that the CA was attacking a position held by some late medieval theologians, but not by the Catholic church itself. Pfnür's general conclusion is that the condemnations in the early confessions were aimed at extreme positions and did not, then or now, apply to the official teaching of the Catholic church.

Beisser surveys the more numerous and precise condemnations relating to justification in the Formula of Concord (FC). Since the FC was primarily concerned with intra-Lutheran disputes, only a limited number of its condemnations potentially relate to the Catholic Church, although among these some are explicitly addressed against "papists," "monks," or "scholastics." In his careful survey of the FC, he confirms much of the analysis of Wenz, especially in relation to the continuing Catholic intent of Lutheranism and to the nature of the Lutheran understanding of justification. Lutherans continued to insist that the righteousness of the Christian was always in Christ and thus not a function of the Christian's renewal, but they also consistently understood justification and renewal as inextricably connected. The question for the FC was not whether renewal inexorably accompanies justification, but whether renewal makes its own independent and necessary contribution to justification.

Beisser notes that the oft repeated opinion (repeated even in footnotes contemporary editors have added to the FC) that certain condemnations in fact describe positions put forward by the Council of Trent is in many cases unjustified. For example, in relation to a possible contribution to justification by a human will freed by grace, he argues that Trent takes no clear position on precisely the opinion the FC condemns. His final conclusion is not undifferentiated; he notes that further investigation (perhaps moving beyond the strictly historical investigation he has carried out) is needed to decide the relation of Catholic teaching to a few of the FC's condemnations, especially as they relate to the possible contribution to justification of the Christian who has received grace.

2.3. Essays on the Catholic Condemnations

The supporting essays on the Catholic condemnations face a task at once easier and more difficult: easier because only one text must be dealt with, the decree on justification of the Council of Trent; more difficult, because the condemnations in this text are far more numerous than those in the Lutheran confessions. The essays by Erwin Iserloh and Otto Hermann Pesch both deal with Trent, but in complementary ways.

Iserloh deals with the more general question of how Trent reached its conclusions on Reformation teachings and how these conclusions are to be read. He notes the variety of sources the Council fathers had before them and the interest of some, such as Cardinal Pole of England, for the Reformation understanding of justification to be carefully considered rather than immediately and entirely rejected. Iserloh's conclusion, however, is that Trent often condemned propositions or ideas taken from Reformation writings without a sense of their context. Often they did not understand the condemned proposition in the same way as did the Reformers who had put it forward.

Iserloh also comments on the form of the Trent's decree. Unlike a number of earlier councils, Trent only condemned certain teachings; it did not name and condemn individuals it believed held these teachings. One reason for this procedure was the desire to keep the door open to the Protestants. Iserloh also stresses the hermeneutical and canonical importance of the condemnations.

Read strictly, the condemnations form the defined teaching of the council. The importance of the preceding chapters cannot be denied, but that importance must not hermeneutically outweigh the canons.

Iserloh's general consideration is followed by **Pesch**'s careful examination of each of Trent's canons on justification. Of each canon, Pesch asks four questions: what position was the canon meant to reject? Did the canon successfully exclude the position it was meant to reject? Does it describe the teachings of the Reformation churches today? If so, what is the significance of the difference the canon represents? Pesch's article thus is a detailed example of the hermeneutic of doctrine upon which the larger study rests.

Pesch's presentation is particularly rich and difficult to summarize. Two conclusions of his study should here be emphasized. First, although Trent wished to reject certain aspects of Reformation teaching on justification, they also wanted to affirm an unambiguous Augustinian rejection of any form of Pelagianism and they did not want to take a position on certain medieval debates on issues related to grace. As a result, some of their condemnations were finally phrased in a way that rejects only extreme positions not officially taught by the Reformation churches.

Second, while Pesch believes that Catholic and Reformation understandings of justification are opposed on few, if any, matters of substance, he also shows how they do utilize different, mutually exclusive languages to state their convictions. These differences are not trivial, but do they justify condemnation and church division? He puts the matter clearly: does each side find its own rules of speech on this question so indispensable that they cannot acknowledge that those who speak differently have also spoken of the event of justification in an appropriate way?

2.4. What the Essays Accomplish

The supporting essays translated here were not written to provide a comprehensive argument for the Justification section of the *Condemnations* study or for the proposal to declare the condemnations on justification non-applicable. Most were written in the course of the study and retain many of the characteristics of documents for a work in progress. What do the essays in fact give us?

First, they should remove any suspicion that the proposal to declare the condemnations on justification non-applicable rests on a devaluation of doctrine or of the doctrinal traditions of the involved churches. The essays testify to the seriousness with which both sides have taken the doctrinal results of the Reformation era.

Second, the essays provide a resource for those who are concerned about specific issues or texts which the *Condemnations* study could not address in detail within the forty pages it devotes to justification. In the essays here translated, virtually all the condemnations on justification in the Lutheran confessions and in the decree on justification from the Council of Trent are handled in some way.

Finally, while it was not the intent of the essays to outline a shared understanding of justification, they give a powerful witness that such a shared understanding exists. A careful reading of the essays by Wenz, Meyer, and Pesch would uncover an extensive agreement on the nature of our salvation and righteousness in Christ. We can declare the condemnations non-applicable not just because of detailed considerations about this or that passage in this or that text, but far more because we have come to see how deeply we agree on central matters of the faith.

3. DEVELOPMENTS IN THE UNITED STATES AND ON THE WORLD LEVEL

3.1. The Lutheran-Roman Catholic Dialogue in the United States

The origins of the dialogue in the United States can be traced back to 1963. The actual dialogue began in 1965 and continued its work on a regular basis until 1992 when a deliberate hiatus was caused so that the work of the dialogue could be evaluated and a new series begun. Members churches of the Lutheran World Federation (LWF) in the United States and the Lutheran Church-Missouri Synod sponsored the dialogue with the United States National Conference of Catholic Bishops.[6]

Although it is not clear whether the goal of the dialogue was ever formally defined, in fact the dialogue explored the theological differences between the two churches to discover to what degree these differences that divided the churches in the past still remain obstacles to fuller communion.

From the beginning the dialogue worked with the assumption that it should start with areas where there is probably broad agreement and then move on to areas that have been more controversial or divisive. Thus the dialogue took up the topics of the Nicene Creed, baptism, Eucharist, ministry, papal primacy, and teaching authority. In the opinion of many, the dialogue identified convergences and consensus of varying degrees on these subjects.

From 1979 until 1983 the dialogue engaged in the study of justification by faith.[7] Members of the dialogue noted that this topic, although alluded to or touched upon earlier in the dialogue, had never been addressed in its own right.

The prominent role of this doctrine in the sixteenth century disputes required the dialogue to investigate this theme.

In their Common Statement the dialogue members declared that they shared the affirmation that the entire hope of justification and salvation rests on Christ Jesus and on the gospel whereby the good news of God's merciful action in Christ is made known. The dialogue report recognized that differences in thought structure play a considerable role in causing tension between the Catholic and Lutheran views of justification. Yet it stated that in the light of convergences which exist, Lutherans and Catholics can acknowledge the legitimacy of concerns that come to expression in different ways and that theological disagreements about the structures of thought, though serious, need not be church dividing.[8]

At the same time as the US dialogue, a bilateral on the world level was taking place between the LWF and the Secretariat for Promoting Christian Unity of the Vatican (now the Pontifical Council for Promoting Christian Unity—PCPCU). It began its work in 1967. In 1972 this dialogue issued its report on "The Gospel and the Church," the so-called Malta Report. This document disclosed a wide range of convergences on questions that had been regarded as church dividing since the sixteenth century. These included the gospel, Tradition, and justification.

In regard to the last topic, the Malta Report indicated that a far-reaching consensus is developing. Catholic theologians stress in reference to justification that God's gift of salvation to the believer is unconditional as far as human accomplishments are concerned. Lutheran theologians emphasize that the event of justification is not limited to individual forgiveness of sins, and they do not see in it a purely external declaration of the justification of the sinner. Rather an encompassing reality basic to the new life of the believer is involved.[9]

After attention to the Eucharist, ministry, and models of unity, the international dialogue in 1986 took up the theme of the church and justification.[10] This was done to test the claim of a "far-reaching consensus" on justification.

In 1993 the international dialogue released its report, *Church and Justification*. This text lays out the basic convictions that Catholics and Lutherans share about the church and justification, so that one may not speak about a fundamental conflict or opposition between justification and the church. The dialogue claimed that this is quite compatible with the role of justification in seeing that all the church's institutions contribute to the church's abiding in the truth of the gospel which alone creates and sustains the church.[11]

Harding Meyer, a Lutheran participant, described the work of the dialogue. According to him, the consensus on justification should be characterized as "nuanced consensus." This means that between Lutherans and Roman Catholics there is not an identical form of the doctrine of justification. Rather there are two different concepts or doctrines of justification that correspond to each other.[12]

Thus by 1993 both the US dialogue and the international dialogue were maintaining that a consensus exists between Catholics and Lutherans over the doctrine that played a central role in their division in the sixteenth century.

Also by this time the sponsoring churches had begun the process of formal evaluation of dialogue work. Such critique, even if somewhat slow in coming, is a welcome part of the reception process in which the churches must engage. Often these attempts at response disclose that the churches are entering into a new area of work. They have difficulty in seeing these dialogue reports as ecumenical texts that require a new perspective on the respective churches' teachings.

In 1986 the former American Lutheran Church (ALC) responded to *Justification by Faith* through its Inter-Church Relations Committee.[13] This response questions the depth of consensus in the text, arguing that the participants cannot together affirm the sola fide. The former Lutheran Church in America (LCA) responded through its convention."[14] On the whole more positive, it asked for a more precise definition of the phrase "fundamental consensus in the gospel." The response requests that the basic consensus be tested further in church life, teaching, practice, and structures. If the consensus is not widened, the agreement will need to be "reconsidered," an important word that was carefully selected.

The Evangelical Lutheran Church in America (ELCA), formed in 1987 from the ALC, LCA, and the Association of Evangelical Lutheran Churches, made its own response in 1991.[15] More nuanced, it affirmed the claimed "fundamental consensus" in the gospel, noting the agreement both on the content of the doctrine and on its role as a criterion of church teaching and practice. Disagreement remained in the concrete application of the criterion. The response explicitly noted the German *Condemnations* study, which it saw as a confirmation of the American results.

The response of the US Conference of Catholic Bishops came in 1990.[16] The response sees the dialogue's Common Statement as a movement beyond partial agreements on particular truths, but also pointed out areas that still needed further work, e.g., justification as a hermeneutical principle.

Thus by the early 1990s the results of Lutheran-Roman Catholic dialogue in the United States and on the world level were claiming a consensus on the doctrine of justification by faith through grace. These dialogue results were by and large being confirmed by the sponsoring churches in their responses. The challenge was clearly how to move forward with this consensus.

3.2. The Condemnations on Justification

At the time of the Reformation, Lutherans and Roman Catholics developed different and often antithetical expressions of doctrine in such areas as justification, the sacraments, and the ministry. These differences reached the highest degree of escalation in doctrinal condemnations expressed in official texts such as, for Lutherans, *The Book of Concord* and, for Roman Catholics, the decrees of the Council of Trent. Such condemnations declare the differences concerning specific doctrines are of such serious nature as to divide the Church and for succeeding generations they obviously present obstacles to ecumenical advance. Such condemnations are not merely matters of historical or academic interest; they continue to shape the identity of both the Lutheran and Roman Catholic churches and thus are causative of deep division.[17]

The concrete consequence of these condemnations has become clear in dialogues of the present generation. As early as 1980, when Pope John Paul II visited Germany and carried on discussions with Lutheran Bishop Eduard Lohse regarding ecumenical issues, it became clear that the condemnations of the sixteenth century stood in the way of common witness by Roman Catholics and Lutherans. Largely as a result of that discussion official ecumenical groups in Germany took up the matter of the condemnations to test their applicability in the current situation. This work by Lutheran and Roman Catholic theologians led to the publication in 1985 of the volume which subsequently appeared in English in 1990 under the title, *The Condemnations of the Reformation: Do They Still Divide?*[18]

In this study the churches involved were asked "to express in a binding form that the sixteenth-century condemnations no longer apply to today's partner; inasmuch as its doctrine is not determined by the error which the condemnation wished to avert. Even where no full consensus has yet been achieved in all the questions involved, the ancient antithesis have been softened." It is perhaps not surprising that this German study provoked intense discussion, especially among Lutherans.[19]

The various streams of discussion—German, American, international— concerning both justification as such and the matter of the condemnations began to come together in the early 1990s. The LWF and the Vatican's PCPCU were considering ways of responding to and continuing the dialogue on the international level; the lengthy and fruitful North American dialogue was at the point of evaluating what had been accomplished. Three factors seemed clear:

the national and international dialogues claimed a convergence and, in some areas, a consensus on justification; the German *Condemnations* study recommended a statement of the inapplicability of some condemnations in relation to the present partner, and progress was not uniform in relation to all the topics condemned in the sixteenth century.

In 1992 the Department for Ecumenical Affairs of the Evangelical Lutheran Church in America (ELCA) under the leadership of its then Director and one of the authors of the present essays, William G. Rusch, began to focus on the possibility of building on the consensus which seemed to be approaching. This focus had several immediate advantages. It drew on the German, American, and international dialogue results, all of which had addressed justification; it recognized that the German *Condemnations* study had achieved its greatest progress in relation to justification; it centered on the critical issue that caused the split of the western church in the sixteenth century, viz., justification; and it held the promise that if agreement could be found here by official action of the churches, a new context would be created for future Lutheran-Roman Catholic dialogue. It was foreseen that if the churches could state on an official and binding level that they had reached a consensus on justification it would also prove possible for them to declare that the condemnations on justification in both the Lutheran confessions and the decrees of the Council of Trent no longer applied to the present-day partners.

Plans in the United States crystallized during a series of discussions and meetings in 1992 and 1993 involving the ELCA and the LWF as well as both Lutherans and Catholics. In February 1993 the creation of a U.S. Lutheran-Roman Catholic Joint Coordinating Committee to pursue both the feasibility of a joint declaration on the condemnations dealing with justification and the next phase of overall U.S. Lutheran-Roman Catholic dialogue was authorized. In March 1993 Bishop Pierre Duprey, Secretary of the PCPCU of the Vatican, and Professor Harding Meyer of the LWF-related Institute for Ecumenical Research at Strasbourg, France, addressed the ELCA Conference of Bishops, agreeing that it should be possible for the Lutheran and Roman Catholic churches today to declare a consensus on justification and the inapplicability of the sixteenth century condemnations today.[20]

In the same month, March 1993, the U.S. National Committee of the LWF, a group identical with the governing body of the ELCA's Department for Ecumenical Affairs, voted to seek the advice of the LWF on various ecumenical proposals before the ELCA, including the possibility of declaring the condemnations related to justification not applicable to the contemporary Roman Catholic Church. This action was communicated directly in late March 1993 to the General Secretary of the Lutheran World Federation in Geneva, Gunnar Staalsett.

At its June 1993 meeting in Kristiansand, Norway, the Council of the LWF, on recommendation from its Standing Committee for Ecumenical Affairs, acted to establish a process to consider "lifting: the condemnations on justification. This process would include sharing texts and information with the Federation's member churches, requesting them to study and react to the proposal. The action also committed the LWF to summarize the process and to be the *locus* for a culminating affirmation by the global Lutheran communion.

The LWF Council action stressed the need to work as closely as possible with the Roman Catholic Church. The Vatican's PCPCU was already in the process of evaluating the German Ecumenical Study Group's *Condemnations* study. Its evaluation, although unofficial and never published, disclosed general agreement with the work of the Ecumenical Study Group's work, especially in relation to the doctrine of justification, concluding that the condemnations of the sixteenth century must henceforth be seen in a new perspective. In response to the LWF, the PCPCU declared itself ready to work toward the possible declaration concerning the inapplicability today of the condemnations in question. The target date of 1997 was set for such a declaration. That year is the 50th anniversary of the Lutheran World Federation and the 450th anniversary of the Roman Catholic condemnations of Lutheran teaching on justification by the Council of Trent. Additionally, both the LWF and the ELCA are to hold assemblies in 1997.

Since 1993, work at the international level has concentrated on the production of a brief "Joint Declaration" which would summarize the results of the dialogues on justification and apply them to the relevant doctrinal condemnations. Such a Declaration would serve as the lens that could bring the various earlier statements into a sharper, more immediately perceptible focus. An initial draft was produced in March 1994 by a Task Force of Roman Catholic and Lutheran theologians meeting in Geneva. The penultimate paragraph of this draft stated, "Therefore we are in a position to declare that mutual doctrinal condemnations regarding the doctrine of justification no longer apply to the partner today."

In the United States, this 1994 draft was studied by the Lutheran-Roman Catholic Coordinating Committee. Discussions in that committee have shown the importance of the move to a consideration of the condemnations. No longer is discussion abstract; official church actions are now contemplated. While support for the declaration of the non-applicability has been widespread, hard questions are also being asked and proposals for amendments have been made.This process, in regard to the 1994 statement, was pursued in Lutheran churches throughout the world and, obviously, by the Roman Catholic Church through its own channels. A revised Declaration was released in late Spring 1996 for study by the churches prior to anticipated action in 1997.

Both the Lutheran and Catholic churches are now exploring new ecumenical territory. All agree that ecumenical rapprochement requires agreement , by some form of declaration, that the condemnations of the past do not today apply. For Rome such a declaration would be a new sort of step. The lifting of the excommunications between Rome and Constantinople in 1965 was of a different nature. On the Lutheran side, some precedent exists for such a declaration in the 1973 Lutheran-Reformed "Leuenberg Agreement" in Europe. There is, further, a difficult problem for Lutherans in the coordination of responses from the many Lutheran churches around the world. At most the LWF can articulate a consensus of its member churches. In Germany, where the present volume originated, complications have arisen concerning the relation between the international process, coordinated by the LWF, and the responses in Germany to the earlier *Condemnations* study. The 1997 goal for a global "Joint Declaration on the Doctrine of Justification" now apparently cannot be met. All agree, however, that the subject matter is more important than the calendar.

4. PRACTICAL IMPLICATIONS

The above description portrays a process that could be viewed as theologically dense and bureaucratically cumbersome. It could at once raise the question of whether there is any immediate or practical benefit of all of this for the vast majority of Lutheran and Roman Catholic Christians.

First, it must be underscored that the Joint Declaration is not the end in itself. Rather, through the Declaration, the Lutheran and Roman Catholic churches would be stating that in regard to the doctrine of justification their confessional differences would no longer be exclusive alternatives, but rather they would be differentiated accents of the same Christian faith. The churches would move from controversial polemics of the past into an enriching dialogue of the future.

This would be a major ecumenical step. It could renew ecumenical energies at a time when this is obviously needed. But it would not be an initiative which would lead immediately to full communion between Lutherans and Catholics. Rather a new context would be provided for further dialogue aiming at such communion. Although many topics would still require discussion and resolution on the road to full unity, a decisive step would have occurred. Lutherans and Roman Catholics would have a greater assurance that they are both in fact confessing the same Christian faith and they would have begun the process of removing the condemnations of the past.

While much in the discussion of this topic is indeed abstract at first glance, it does have direct implications for the churches. Teaching about justification determines the identity of the churches. These condemnations, whether or not they are always recognized on the practical level, stand in the way of fuller cooperation and visible unity between Roman Catholics and Lutherans. These differences cannot simply be overlooked if Lutheran and Catholic Christians are to realize as a gift the unity Christ wishes for the Church. Other agreements between Lutherans and Roman Catholics will be meaningless without a genuine agreement on justification. Such a declaration about the condemnations on justification would move both churches a long way toward such an agreement. It would indicate that on basic Gospel teaching Catholics and Lutherans no longer reject and condemn each other. This would be true in spite of the statements in their defining documents, e.g. Confessions and conciliar decisions.

The Joint Declaration would further mean that the confessional commitments of Lutheran pastors at ordination would not reject official Roman Catholic teaching about justification. Roman Catholic priests in pledging acceptance of the official teaching of their church on justification would no longer be rejecting Lutheran teaching about justification.

A further implication would be that Lutherans and Catholics would be able to dialogue about their remaining doctrinal differences in a new context. They would have a solid basis of common teaching to address the social and ethical issues of the day.

Lutheran and Roman Catholic congregations with proper authorization would be able more easily to engage in appropriate forms of common worship (services of the Word), evangelism, mission, catechetical instruction, Bible study and Christian education. Materials already exist from the Vatican and LWF for joint congregational bible study on the theme of justification.

All these results of the official acceptance by the churches of a Joint Declaration on justification that declared the condemnations non-applicable could deepen the common foundation shared by Catholics and Lutherans, so that new building can occur. It should become obvious to all that agreement on justification and the inapplicability of the condemnations on this issue do matter. Disagreements and condemnations stand in the way of more practical cooperation, prevent fuller recognition, and even the claim of theological consensus in other areas.

With the acceptance of the Joint Declaration, a new symbol of unity would be created. Even if full communion would not yet be reached, a context of love between churches would be established. Official action on the Declaration becomes a fundamental presupposition for the progressive solution of the remaining differences. It is an important stage on the way to the restoration of communion between separated churches.[21]

These are the reasons why the following collection of critical essays is being published in English for the first time. The editors of this volume hope that the availability of this scholarship to an English-reading audience will facilitate a responsible process of reception within the churches.

5. SELECTED BIBLIOGRAPHY

"An Evaluation of the Lutheran-Catholic Statement Justification by Faith—The Roman Catholic Bishops of the United States," *Lutheran Quarterly,* 5, 1991, 1:63-71.

Anderson, H. George; Murphy, T. Austin; and Joseph A. Burgess; eds. *Justification by Faith: Lutherans and Catholics in Dialogue VII.* Minneapolis: Augsburg Publishing House, 1985.

Church and Justification: Understanding the Church in the Light of the Doctrine of Justification. Geneva: The Lutheran World Federation, 1994.

Duprey, Pierre, "The Condemnations of the 16th Century on Justification: Do They Still Apply Today?" with response by Harding Meyer, *Occasional Papers Contributing to 1997 Decisions.* Chicago: Department for Ecumenical Affairs, ELCA, 1995.

Lange, Dietz, ed., *Outmoded Condemnations? Antithesis Between the Council of Trent and the Reformation on Justification, the Sacrament and the Ministry—Then and Now.* Fort Wayne: Luther Academy, 1992; originally published as *Überholte Verurteilungen?.* Göttingen: Vanderhoeck & Ruprecht, 1991.

Lehmann, Karl and Pannenberg, Wolfhart, eds. *The Condemnations of the Reformation Era: Do They Still Divide?* Minneapolis: Fortress Press, 1990, esp. 1-69.

"Malta Report," in *Growth in Agreement,* edited by Harding Meyer and Vischer. New York: Paulist Press, 1984, 167-189.

Mutual Condemnations: What Are They?. Chicago: Department for Ecumenical Affairs, ELCA, n.d.

Response to Justification by Faith. Chicago: Department for Ecumenical Affairs, ELCA, 1991.

Tanner, Norman P., ed., *Decrees of the Ecumenical Councils.* Washington: Georgetown University Press, 1990, Vol. II, 679-681.

Notes:

1. Lehmann, Karl and Wolfhart Pannenberg, eds., *Condemnations of the Reformation: Do They Still Divide?*, trans. by Margaret Kohl (Minneapolis: Fortress Press, 1990). The German original appears as *Lehrverurteilungen— kirchentrennend?* (Freiburg i.B.: Herder; Göttingen: Vandenhoeck & Ruprecht, 1988).

2. Some explanation needs to be given of the Catholic-Lutheran and more general Catholic-Protestant character of the discussions and the process surrounding them. The Protestant partner in the Joint Ecumenical Commission was the Evangelical Church in Germany, which includes all the Protestant territorial churches or *Landeskirchen* in Germany (Lutheran, United, and Reformed), although Lutherans constitute the majority. The Ecumenical Study Group which actually carried out the study had been a Catholic-Lutheran group; for this study it was expanded to include Reformed members. As Otto Hermann Pesch has noted, however, through a series of accidents the discussion in the sub-group on justification for the most part took place without significant Reformed participation. The section of *Condemnations* that deals with justification thus often reads like a Catholic-Lutheran dialogue. Since the publication of *Condemnations,* while the process in Germany has continued to involve the entire EKD, internationally it has been the Lutheran and Catholic communions which have taken up the discussion. The volume of supporting essays from which the essays in this volume come did include a short (six page) essay on justification in the Reformed confessions, especially the Heidelberg Catechism, and its relation to the Council of Trent.

3. *Lehrverurteilungen—kirchentrennend?*, Vol 2: Materialien zu den Lehrverurteilungen und zur Theologie der Rechtfertigung, edited by Karl Lehmann, and Vol. 3, Materialien zur Lehre von den Sakramenten und vom kirchlichen Amt, edited by Wolfhart Pannenberg (Freiburg i.B.: Herder; Göttingen: Vandenhoeck & Ruprecht, 1989-90).

4. The essays by Pannenberg, Lehmann, and Wenz come from the section of the first volume of essays which deals with the larger question of re-evaluating the condemnations. The others come from the section on justification. The section on justification includes, besides the essays translated here, essays by Karl Kertelge on justification in Paul, by Gerhard Goeters on justification in the Reformed confessions, by Bernhard Lohse on confession and penance in the Lutheran Reformation, and by Otto Hermann Pesch on the course of the discussions within the sub-group that produced the justification section of *Condemnations.*

5. In later sections, he deals with condemnations relating to the Eucharist and with the status of condemnations within the Lutheran Confessions, especially within the Formula of Concord.

6. For a more complete discussion of the early history of this dialogue, see William G. Rusch, *Ecumenism—A Movement Toward Church Unity* (Philadelphia: Fortress Press, 1985), 80-85.

7. After completing its work on justification in the fall of 1983, the dialogue turned

to the topic of sanctification and the role of the saints, and Scripture and Tradition. This work was published as H. George Anderson, J. Francis Stafford, and Joseph A. Burgess, eds., *Lutherans and Catholics in Dialogue VIII: The One Mediator, The Saints and Mary* (Minneapolis: Augsburg Publishing House, 1992), and Harold C. Skillrud, J. Francis Stafford, Daniel F. Martensen, eds., *Lutherans and Catholics in Dialogue IX: Scripture and Tradition* (Minneapolis: Augsburg Publishing House, 1995). Both volumes are significant, but they do not relate directly to the discussion of the condemnations on justification.

8.   H. George Anderson, T. Austin Murphy, and Joseph A. Burgess, eds., *Lutherans and Catholics in Dialogue VII: Justification by Faith* (Minneapolis: Augsburg Publishing House, 1985), esp. 16.

9.   Harding Meyer and Lucas Vischer, eds., *Growth in Agreement* (New York and Geneva: Paulist Press and World Council of Churches, 1984), 174.

10.   For fuller discussions of the international Lutheran-Roman Catholic dialogue see Rusch, Ecumenism, 85-88, and Heinz-Albert Raem, "The Third Phase of Lutheran/Catholic Dialogue (1986-1993)" in *One In Christ* 30 (1994):310-327.

11.   *Church and Justification* (Geneva: The Lutheran World Federation, 1994), 115.

12.   See material quoted by Raem, "The Third Phase", pp. 315-318.

13.   This document appears never to have been published. It exists in typescript as "A Statement of the Inter-Church Relations Committee of the American Lutheran Church to The Lutheran/Roman Catholic Dialogue on Justification" (Minneapolis, 1986).

14.   "A Response to Justification by Faith" in *Ecumenical Documents of the Lutheran Church in America, 1982-1987* (New York: Department for Ecumenical Relations, Lutheran Church in America, 1987).

15.   For the text of "The Response to Justification by Faith of the Evangelical Lutheran Church", see Thomas Rausch, "Responses to the US Lutheran-Roman Catholic Statement on Justification," in *One In Christ 29* (1993), 342-349. For the record it should be noted that Rausch also publishes part of a response from the Lutheran Church-Missouri Synod from 1992. This document does not play any role in the subsequent discussion in the United States about a consensus on justification and thus a declaration of the inapplicability of certain condemnations on justification from the sixteenth century. Rausch was apparently not aware of the two earlier Lutheran responses.

16.   The text of "An Evaluation of the Lutheran-Catholic Statement Justification by Faith" appears in Rausch, op. cit., 333-353.

17.   Cf. Genischen, Hans-Werner, *We Condemn: How Luther and 16th Century Lutheranism Condemned False Doctrine* (St. Louis: Concordia Publishing House, 1967), esp. Ch. 3; and in this volume Wenz, Günther, "Damnamus? The Condemnations in the Confessions of the Lutheran Church as a Problem for the Ecumenical Dialogue between the Lutheran and Roman Catholic Churches," p. 99 below.

18. Cf. p. 18, Note 1, above.

19. The most important criticism came from the Lutheran members of the Protestant theological faculty at Göttingen, translated as "An Opinion on *The Condemnations of the Reformation Era*. Part One: Justification." *Lutheran Quarterly* 5 (1991): 1-62. The responses from various Protestant church committees are in *Lehrverurteilungen im Gespräch: Die ersten offiziellen Stellungnahmen aus den evangelischen Kirchen in Deutschland* (Göttingen: Vandenhoeck & Ruprecht, 1993). The response of the Ecumenical Study Group to these responses is in Wolfhart Pannenberg and Theodor Schneider, eds., *Lehrverurteilungen—kirchentrennend? IV* (Göttingen: Vandenhoeck & Ruprecht and Freiburg im Breisgau: Herder, 1994), esp. Appendix D for an overview of the literature. The common official response of the German Protestant churches, passed in late 1994, is in "Gemeinsame Stellungnahme der Arnoldshainer Konferenz, der Vereinigten Kirche und das Deutschen National komitees des Lutherischen Weltburndes zum Dokument 'Lehrverurteilungen—kirchen-trennend?'." *Ökumenische Rundschau* 44 (1995): 99-102

20. Duprey, Pierre: *The Condemnations of the 16th Century on Justification: Do They Still Apply Today?* with response by Harding Meyer, in Occasional Papers Contributing to 1997 Decisions (Chicago: Dept. for Ecumenical Affairs, ELCA, 1995).

21. For a further treatment of these ideas, see William G. Rusch, "Should Catholics and Lutherans Continue to Condemn One Another?: What is at Stake in 1997?" in *Pro Ecclesia* (V,3) Summer 1996, 282-91.

Chapter Two

The Significance of the Proposed
Joint Declaration

J. Francis Stafford

A S PRESENTLY ENVISAGED, the proposed Joint Declaration on the
Doctrine of Justification between the Lutheran World Federation and
the Roman Catholic Church seeks to bring together in an eight page
summary the results of four major Lutheran/Roman Catholic reports published
since 1972. These include the following: the 1972 Malta Report, "The Gospel
and the Church"; the 1983 USA document *Justification by Faith*; the 1986
German ecumenical study, *The Condemnations of the Reformation Era: Do
They Still Divide?*; and *Church and Justification: Understanding the Church in
the Light of the Doctrine of Justification*, 1994, under the aegis of the Lutheran
World Federation and the Pontifical Council for Promoting Christian Unity.
Since 1997 is the 450th anniversary of the promulgation of the Decree on
Justification by the Council of Trent (January 13, 1547), the hope has been to
issue the Joint Declaration in that year.

Presently, the proposed Joint Declaration is not an official statement of the
two international bodies mentioned above. Although drafted under the auspices
and at their initiative, it has not yet been approved definitively by them, nor is
the present draft, by definition, the final product. Both Rome and Geneva are
insisting upon consultation within their respective academic and pastoral
communities.

Nevertheless, even the prospect of issuing such a declaration requires
Christians to set aside time for reflection, discussion, and prayer. Many

Protestants originally defined their "protest" against the Catholic Church on this issue. The Declaration would signal a development within these communities and between them. The doctrine of justification has been a divisive issue between Roman Catholics and Protestants for over 450 years. A new ecclesial self-awareness would emerge among all Christians, if the document should be eventually approved.

From a Catholic perspective, the four reports are the fruit of the Second Vatican Council. A little over thirty years ago the Council concluded its work. Its four constitutions, nine decrees, and three declarations, encouraged the participation of the Catholic Church in ecumenical and interfaith dialogue. Since then, unprecedented and unexpected progress has been made. As the four documents attest, giant steps in addressing past divisions have been made. A Joint Declaration on Justification by two official world-wide bodies would be a unique fruit of the Council.

These developments call for a close study of the doctrines of those Churches and communities stemming from the Reformation. Such themes include forensic justification, the sinfulness of the justified, the sufficiency of faith, the notion of merit, the theology of satisfaction, and the concrete norm of Christian ethics. The bilaterals have been the chief means for the Catholic Church's engagement in examining and assessing them.

In these momentous times, Catholics will need to make an extra effort to orient themselves. Strong doses of study, reflection, and prayer will be required. Catholics will find themselves in some unusual intellectual inquiries. And they may even need to make a kind of comprehensive examination of conscience. For the most part, Catholics have not been accustomed to reflect upon the act of justification. Nor have they, until recently, dealt with it in an explicit catechesis. Yet, their biblical roots are filled with praise for God's glory perceived through the grace of justification.

Catholics might begin their reflections with a study of justification presented in the 1994 *Catechism of the Catholic Church* (*CCC*). They might find it useful to compare the *CCC*'s presentation with that of the *Roman Catechism* (*RC*) produced in 1566. *RC*'s brevity on justification may come as a surprise to them.

Catholics might also be assisted in their study by noting how far back Catholic reflection on this matter has stretched, and how much development there has been since 1566. The Roman Catechism summarizes Catholic belief from the Council of Trent. The Catechism of the Catholic Church summarizes the whole tradition, including the teachings of the Second Vatican Council and developments since then.

An example may be helpful. The *RC*'s index mentions "justification" only once. It is found where the form of the Sacrament of Penance is dealt with. (Incidentally, the Sacrament of Penance was the occasion which precipitated Luther's reflections on justification while still an Augustinian monk.) The *RC* states that priests of the New Testament "have this power [i.e. the power not only to declare the forgiveness of sins, but actually to forgive sins], of course, as the ministers of God, who alone is the source of grace and justification" (263).

In the *RC*'s index on faith, another reference to justification can be found—in the explanation of the fifth article of the creed, Jesus's descent into hell and his resurrection. "Furthermore, he rose with the purpose of confirming our faith, which is necessary for our justification. For the resurrection of Christ from the dead by his own power gives our faith its principal argument for his divinity" (71).

In this text, *RC* presents faith in a somewhat abstract manner. Following the lead of the Council of Trent, *RC* teaches that hope and charity are intimately connected with faith (259). This inner nexus among the three theological virtues has been an integral part of the Church's response to Luther's teaching. If Catholics want to know how and why their Church may be approaching "a common understanding" with Lutherans on justification, reflection and prayer must be directed to Trent's teaching on this nexus. They also need to note the progress made in New Testament exegesis on justification, sometimes within the bilateral dialogues themselves (e.g. 1 Cor.1:30; Rom.6:6f; 7:4; Rom.5:5; 8:23; Gal.3:2-5; 2 Cor.5:5). As the authors of *Condemnations* said, "New Testament exegesis has initiated a step forward to which we cannot ascribe too great an importance, because it has taken the rigidity out of the old disputes" (48).

At the same time, Catholics should reflect on the decisive role which Lutherans attach to the doctrine of justification. Luther said, "If this article stands, the church stands; if it falls, the church falls." The German ecumenical study group wrote, "According to Protestant interpretation, the faith that clings unconditionally to God's promise in Word and Sacrament is sufficient for righteousness before God, so that the renewal of the human being, without which there can be no faith, does not in itself make any contribution to justification" *(Condemnations,* 52). Focus needs to be given to the exchange, which is like a "lightning-flash", whereby one's guilt passes over to Christ. The Book of Concord, which contains "the Confessions of the Evangelical Lutheran Church", states that the faith involved in justification is an act of unconditional trust in the merciful God. The Augsburg Confession says that Lutherans "mean such true faith as believes that we receive grace and forgiveness of sin through Christ" (CA 20,23). And later in the Apology, one reads, "So whenever mercy is spoken of, faith in the promise must be added.

This faith produces a sure hope, for it rests on the Word and commandment of God" (Apol 4.346).

Reflection on Catholic and Lutheran teachings has led these same German scholars to conclude: "[I]f we translate from one language to another, then Protestant talk about justification through faith corresponds to Catholic talk about justification through grace; and on the other hand, Protestant doctrine understands substantially under the one word 'faith' what Catholic doctrine (following 1 Cor.13:13) sums up in the triad of 'faith, hope and love.' "

The *CCC* is key for Catholics to come to an understanding of the Church's teaching on justification today. Its treatment is more extensive and systematic than that found in *RC*. Significantly, one discovers the theme of justification and grace (1987-2009) in Part III, Life in Christ. Here a beautiful text is woven from Sacred Scriptures, the Fathers of the Church, the Council of Trent, and St. Therese of Lisieux. The *CCC* places emphasis on the act of justification from the perspective of faith — faith working through charity. Again, it highlights the scriptural basis. Its teaching is an enrichment and development. Nor can it be interpreted in any way to be a repudiation of Trent or of the *RC*. Rather, it is a development of their doctrine in light of the Church's long tradition and reflection on what has taken place over the past 450 years. The new *Catechism* is the "new light" in which one can read the controversies of the sixteenth century.

In the future the teaching of the great tradition on justification will increasingly become a part of the catechesis of the Catholic people. This will require a further renewal of *lectio divina* wherein "the Word of God is so read and reflected upon that it becomes prayer" (*CCC* 1178). A deeper reading of the letters of St. Paul and the Gospel of St. John will be needed. Such a spiritual renewal would be an immense blessing from God; it would have emerged within the Catholic Church as a result of sustained readings of the bible with Lutheran Christians.

The chief aim of the proposed Declaration is to state that the sixteenth century condemnations, insofar as they relate to the doctrine of justification, no longer apply to Lutherans and to Catholics. Whether the two international communities will find the conclusions persuasive rests finally on the validity of the work done both by the Ecumenical Group of Protestant and Catholic Theologians in Germany in *The Condemnations of the Reformation Era—Do They Still Divide?* and by the various national and international bilateral dialogues. The Joint Declaration would affirm "the soundness of past work."

I am the Catholic Co-chairman of the Lutheran-Roman Catholic Coordinating Committee in the USA. I support the proposed Declaration and the Joint Response to it from the USA Coordinating Committee. At the same time, however, it is important to note that three Roman Catholic members of the Committee, including myself, recommended "that the final form of the Joint Declaration be expanded to show more clearly from the extensive work of the dialogues how Roman Catholic and Lutheran teaching on preparation for justification, the faith of unrepentant sinners, and satisfaction (Trent canons 4, 28, and 30) are not incompatible." For myself, clarification on these three issues is essential to warrant the general conclusion of the proposed Joint Declaration that none of the condemnations of the sixteenth century on justification still applies to either party.

Even if these three issues are clarified, one may still wonder how such an unequivocal judgment could be reached with the heavy burden of centuries of controversy still with us. Catholics may be very uneasy because such a conclusion may imply that the religious leaders of the sixteenth century were mistaken. More specifically, they may reasonably ask whether the Council of Trent was in error when it condemned some doctrines on justification which appear to have had Lutheran Christians in mind.

This objection was vigorously and forthrightly addressed by the Ecumenical Working Group of Protestant and Catholic Theologians in Germany, *The Condemnations of the Reformation Era—Do They Still Divide?*. Its respected editors, Karl Lehmann and Wolfhart Pannenberg, deal with this subject in the opening paragraph of the preface: "It has been generally accepted that doctrinal differences were the essential reason for the disintegration of the Western church into different denominations. At the same time, it must be pointed out that other elements contributed to the division of the churches in the sixteenth century, not differences of doctrine alone. Political, cultural, social, and economic factors were involved, as well as the laws that go to maintain any already existing institutions. Nor must we forget the part played by individual human characteristics."

In the Introduction, the authors share another important insight. It illuminates the theological climate in which these controversies first unfolded. "No less important for an understanding and evaluation of the Reformation was the more precise distinction between the mental approach of patristic and medieval Latin writers and the late scholasticism which Luther studied and which was his main target of attack." Catholic theologians have moved a long way from the nominalism of Gabriel Biel whose texts the young Luther used at the Erfurt cloister and university. These texts, so characteristic of the treatment of grace in late medieval Scholastic theology, had only tenuous roots in the scriptural and patristic sources of justification.

It should be clear to Catholics that the Tridentine conciliar canons are true; but it is also true that such Church condemnations are "enunciated ... in terms

that bear the traces of [the changeable conceptions of a given epoch]"
(Declaration of the Congregation for the Doctrine of the Faith, *Mysterium
Fidei*, June 24, 1973, sec. 5). So the question arises whether the condemnations
still apply. At the very least, one must admit that Lutherans and Roman
Catholics today cannot stand with the same agendas with which their ancestors
confronted one another in the sixteenth century. They live in a dramatically
changed ecumenical situation. Among other things, Lutherans and Roman
Catholics no longer perceive one another as adversaries. Both agree that the
baptized have become truly incorporated into the crucified and glorified Christ
(*Unitatis Redintegratio*, 22).

In this context, another insight of the German ecumenical group was
helpful. One of the keys they used in interpreting the individual condemnations
was this: on the one hand, the Reformers were concerned with and emphasized
the profound sense of sin and the attendant human misery. On the other, the
Catholics placed their emphasis upon the regenerative power of God. In these
differences, I am reminded of Pascal's reflection on man's situation and his
emphasis on the experience of faith: "In a word, man knows that he is
wretched. He is wretched, because he is so; but he is really great because he
knows it" (*Pensées* 416).

The authors of the document *Justification by Faith* addressed these two
concerns with the help of modern biblical studies. Its originality consists in the
acknowledgement that the term "justifying" is recognized as having two
meanings, "counting righteous" and "making righteous." Cardinal Newman
had pointed out that justification includes under its meaning both God's
justifying and man's being justified. "To be saved one must be judged righteous
and be righteous" (156). The same document underlines that Christians "are all
called to pass from the alienation and oppression of sin to freedom and
fellowship with God in the Holy Spirit" (161). A Catholic reading of the phrase
"the fellowship with God and the Holy Spirit" would recognize here the
doctrine of "the indwelling of the Holy Spirit."

In his recent encyclical letter, *Ut Unum Sint*, Pope John Paul II presented
an hermeneutical principle for understanding and evaluating some of the
controversies of the sixteenth century. In affirming ecumenical dialogues as a
means of resolving age-old disagreements between divided Christians, he
writes, "In this regard, ecumenical dialogue, which prompts the parties
involved to question each other and to explain their positions to each other,
makes surprising discoveries possible. Intolerant polemics and controversies
have made incompatible assertions out of what really was the result of two
different ways of looking at the same reality. Nowadays, we need to find the
formula which, by capturing the reality in its entirety, will enable us to move

beyond partial readings and eliminate false interpretations" (38).

For the past twenty-four years, I have been involved in various bilateral discussions as a Catholic Co-chairman. These included Oriental Orthodox, Methodists, and Lutherans. I can attest to the significance the Pope attaches to ecumenical dialogues.

The response to the Proposed Declaration by the Lutheran-Roman Catholic Coordinating Committee in the USA has been helpful. It emphasized the "new light" in which the sixteenth century anathemas must be examined. This means a candid reappraisal of "over 400 years of subsequent developments in each of our traditions. It reflects the ecumenical impact of events like the Second Vatican Council. It makes use of biblical and theological studies, often done together in dialogues. It should not be viewed as mere reflection of a period in history that relativizes doctrine. But it is consonant with the treatment of condemnations in other dialogues like the US Lutheran-Reformed and Roman Catholic-Assyrian" (6). I wish to comment from personal experience on the last point. For several years, I co-chaired the USA Catholic/Oriental Orthodox dialogue. In my heart I know "the great joy" of Pope John Paul II on the occasion of the "signing of the Christological declaration with the Assyrian patriarch of the East, His Holiness Mar Dinkha IV, who for this purpose chose to visit with me in Rome in November, 1994. Taking into account the different theological formulations, we were able to profess together the true faith in Christ" (*Ut Unum Sint*, 62).

Many Roman Catholics and Lutherans are surprised by the fact that the last official dialogue on divisive doctrines took place in 1541 at the Diet of Regensburg—455 years ago! It was convened by the Holy Roman Emperor Charles V, and the agreement reached by the two sides was on justification. Unfortunately, the subsequent opposition of Martin Luther and of Cardinal Caraffa, neither of whom was present for the discussions, as well as political rivalries, prevented any reunion from being effected. From that time forward into the twentieth century, the two sides were irreconcilable. Only the opening of the Second Vatican Council in 1962 broke the back of the hostility. In the meantime, the interminable wars between Christians did incalculable harm to the mission of Christ. The secularization of the West began as a reaction to the religious intolerance of the sixteenth and subsequent centuries.

For me the most significant step was the 1983 agreement between Lutherans and Roman Catholics in the USA. It was made in that breakthrough formula on justification with Christ as its corner-stone. "Our entire hope of justification and salvation rests on Christ Jesus and on the gospel whereby the good news of God's merciful action in Christ is made known; we do not place our ultimate trust in anything other than God's promise and saving work in

Christ" (157). These are glorious words, worthy to lead the two communities into a rediscovered unity during the third millennium. Christ's love and surrender "even unto death" is the manifestation of God's absolute love for us. His mission, his task was to take upon himself the sin of the world, to be so dispossessed out of love for his Father that he was willing to bear the sins of others. Faith means to surrender to the love that has sacrificed itself for us.

The 1983 affirmation has had a profound impact on the lives of many Catholics and Lutherans. As Co-chairman of the USA dialogue, I learned much about Christ, grace, and faith by meditating upon this text. Both sides have insisted in season and out upon the essentially Christological foundation of justification. Such emphasis will serve only to reinforce the centrality of Christ in the live of Christians. The sinner's justification through faith in Christ's death means that faith in Christ will be directed to the incomprehensibility of God's love. "For God so loved the world that he gave his only Son, that whoever believes in him should not perish but have eternal life" (John 3:16).

The doctrine of Christ's vicarious death and our faith in him as savior must be central in any effort at renewal among Christians. It is on this criterion that a judgment is made whether a theology is simply an anthropology or is an authentic expression of a Christology.

From his earliest Catholic days to his death, Luther built up his theology from the elements provided by the passion and death of Christ. The "common agreement" will be a catalyst for deeper reflection upon these mysteries. In the future, Lutherans and Roman Catholics together may wish to explore the theology of the *sub contrario* by which means that God discloses himself in the very act of concealment. My initial insight into this took place from a comparative reading of both John of the Cross and Luther. Hans Urs von Balthasar has explored the *sub contrario* in his classic overview of Good Friday, Holy Saturday, and Easter Sunday.

For some time, I have felt that it would be very useful to explore Luther's understanding of the *sub contrario* while studying the teachings of some Catholic saints. The latter always point away from themselves to love, the love of God revealed in the pierced heart of his Son. The experience of possessing God by being abandoned by him has struck me as a common element in the writings of Roman Catholics like Catherine of Sienna, Rose of Lima, the great Teresa, John of the Cross, and little Therese.

Before concluding, I wish to mention two friends, both of whom contributed to ecumenism since 1961 and to the process leading to 1997. Both are deceased. They influenced my life and ministry.

The Most Rev. T. Austin Murphy was Auxiliary to the Archbishop of Baltimore (1962-1984). From 1965 to 1984 he served as the Catholic Co-chairman of the Lutheran/Roman Catholic Dialogue in the USA and was my immediate predecessor. During that time, he made major contributions to the first seven rounds of this dialogue. I have first-hand knowledge of estimates of his work. Undoubtedly, one of his legacies is the monumental breakthrough in the seventh round, *Justification by Faith*. A Lutheran participant offered me his assessment of Bishop Murphy: "His thoughtful, consistent, even-handed and patient leadership contributed significantly to the creation and success of that document."

Lawrence Cardinal Shehan, the twelfth Archbishop of Baltimore (1961 to 1974), is the other friend whom the Catholic ecumenical and interfaith movements consider to be a founding father. He was one of the early pioneers. In 1962 he established the first Archdiocesan Commission for Christian Unity in the USA. He was later invited to become a member of the Vatican Secretariat for the Promotion of Christian Unity under the presidency of Cardinal Augustin Bea, S.J. He became instrumental in moving ahead the conciliar Declaration, *Nostra Aetate*, and gaining its eventual approval. He was also instrumental in involving Bishop Murphy in the dialogue with Lutherans. I had the privilege of accompanying him on a number of visits to synagogues and Protestant churches. In 1973 he was Papal Legate for Pope Paul VI at the International Eucharistic Congress in Melbourne. In that capacity, he was particularly at ease and effective in his relations with the ecumenical and interfaith communities.

For these two men and their contributions to the ecumenical and interfaith movements, I wish to express my deepest respect and admiration. May they rest in peace.

Chapter Three

Can the Mutual Condemnations between Rome and the Reformation Churches Be Lifted?

Wolfhart Pannenberg

A T THE MAY 1985 synod of the Evangelical Church in Germany (EKD) in Berlin-Spandau, Bishop Scheele of Würzburg, responsible for ecumenical affairs for the German Catholic Bishops Conference, reported on the work of the Evangelical-Catholic Joint Commission.

This Commission had been appointed after the 1980 visit of the Pope to Germany, which included a meeting in Mainz of the Pope with representatives of the EKD. The Commission had been asked to clarify the presuppositions for three church actions suggested to the Pope by the Chair of the Council of the EKD, Bishop Eduard Lohse: the possibility of common ecumenical worship, even on Sundays; common pastoral care for confessionally mixed marriages; and the authorization of mutual eucharistic hospitality. From the beginning, it was clear that this last theme brought with it the problem of church fellowship in its full breadth. Press reports of Bishop Scheele's speech dwelt on the disappointment that the Commission had achieved no breakthrough in relation to these three practical steps. It was said that the theologians had only come a bit closer to working through the mutual condemnations which each church had laid upon the doctrine of the other during the sixteenth century.

One would not gather from the press reports that these theological clarifications concern unavoidable presuppositions for progress in the practical relations between the churches. Churches which condemn each other in their normative doctrinal documents cannot undertake mutual eucharistic hospitality, an expression of church fellowship, unless these condemnations have been revised. It is certainly true that the development of a spirit of ecumenical cooperation has moved the churches beyond the attitudes to each other expressed in the condemnations of the sixteenth century. For members of both churches, the commonalities in Christian faith far outweigh the oppositions of the past. For the most part, these oppositions are understood today only by theologians. Nevertheless, neither church can declare that its earlier doctrinal statements are simply obsolete and thus can be dropped from the present discussion. Such action would amount to a disrespect for the normative character of church teaching in general. Such an attitude is not acceptable to either church. Not only for Rome, but also for the Reformation churches, doctrine, i.e., the doctrine of the gospel, is the foundation of the unity of the church. Only after a conscientious examination of the doctrinal disagreements which led to the condemnations of Reformation teaching by the Council of Trent and to the condemnations of the Catholic positions by the Reformation confessions can we perhaps move beyond the opposition spelled out in the still normative church documents. Then perhaps we can also move forward on the practical questions in relation to which the churches seem to be so intransigent.

In recent decades theologians of both churches have been much concerned with the themes that have been at the center of controversy since the time of the Reformation: the doctrine of justification and the authority of scripture, the Lord's Supper and ministry, Word and sacrament. Many individual theologians as well as study commissions created by the churches have sought to dispel mutual misunderstandings and to formulate common conceptions from a contemporary perspective. For example, the international Roman Catholic/Lutheran Joint Commission produced studies on "The Eucharist (1978) and "The Ministry in the Church" (1981), which were preceded by a general assessment entitled "The Gospel and the Church" (1972). Similar dialogues have taken place between the World Alliance of Reformed Churches and the Roman Catholic Church, leading in 1977 to an initial, comprehensive overview of the agreements and problems between the two churches. On problems of eucharistic doctrine, the doctrine of ministry, and authority in the church, results in many respects comparable to those of the Lutheran/Roman Catholic dialogue have also been achieved in dialogues between Rome and other churches, especially in the dialogue with the Anglicans. Similar results had been produced already by dialogues at the national level, especially the Lutheran/Catholic dialogue in the USA. Parallel to these bilateral efforts, the Faith and Order Commission of the World Council of Churches in Lima in 1982 completed its statement "Baptism, Eucharist, and Ministry." Recently such efforts at formulating common conceptions of formerly church-dividing themes have been labeled "convergence ecumenism." To this label is easily joined the suspicion that the commonality is an illusion, superficially covering deeper differences.

In many respects, the detailed theological work does not merit such suspicion. Nevertheless, the normative doctrinal documents of the churches still contain the old oppositions, sharply expressed in the mutual condemnations. The perspectives on church-dividing issues developed in the ecumenical convergence work of the last decades now needs to be applied explicitly to the churches' mutual condemnations. Then we can ascertain to what extent these condemnations can be upheld from a contemporary outlook. We must also test to what extent even at that time the opposing sides really engaged each other, where they relied on historically conditioned and now superseded conceptions of the controverted issues, where simple mutual misunderstanding was involved, and to what extent the condemnations still apply to the contemporary Catholic or Evangelical partner or can be formally judged to be no longer relevant.

In 1981 the Joint Commission of the two churches in Germany commissioned a mixed (Catholic, Lutheran, Reformed) commission of theologians to examine these questions in relation to the churches' mutual condemnations pronounced at the time of the Reformation. To understand the dimensions of this task, one must recognize that the decrees of the Council of Trent alone involve over 130 condemnations. Contemporary research has already shown that these judgments do not all carry the same weight, not even according to their own self-understanding. Not all of them concern doctrinal truths in a strict sense. Many are of a more disciplinary nature, directed at alleged presumptuous disrespect among Protestants for ecclesiastical customs and rules of speech. Since the persons addressed remain unnamed throughout, one must attempt to establish in each case which Reformation assertions the council fathers had in mind. Such a reconstruction is sometimes possible on the basis of collections of Reformation statements put together for the council fathers.

Naturally, in such collections the contexts of the relevant sentences are consistently lacking, so one must test whether the council's understanding of these sentences corresponded to their sense in their original contexts. In addition, the condemnations often refer to several Reformation assertions, so that one must ask whether the council intended to condemn each individual assertion or whether the condemnation is directed at the total picture which results from their combination. These are only some of the difficulties with which the study of the Tridentine condemnations must deal. Astonishingly, this preparatory work had been carried out only to a very limited degree. Beyond the clear and precise consideration of the condemnations themselves, one needed to investigate the theological background of both the teachings of the council and the contrasting Reformation conceptions, as each is seen by contemporary research. Then one could compare contemporary judgments of the controverted issues with earlier conceptions. Corresponding questions had also, of course, to be raised in connection with the condemnations in the Reformation confessions. They are not as numerous as those from Trent and not always explicitly formulated as condemnations. But when, e.g., Reformation statements repeatedly describe the pope as antichrist or the mass as accursed idolatry, a condemnation is naturally implied. As was not the case with Trent, the addressee is usually explicitly stated. The interpretation of such statements is not, however, thus made easier in all respects. To some extent, the possibility disappears that existed with the Tridentine canons, of simply showing that certain Reformation conceptions in fact do not come under the condemned teaching. When condemnations are explicitly directed against another church, as often is the case in the Reformation confessions, an explicit correction is required when a substantially mistaken statement of a condemned idea is found.

The Ecumenical Study Group of theologians appointed by the Joint Commission of both churches completed its study of the condemnations in spring 1985 and delivered the results to the Commission. Its report is a document of just under 200 pages. This served as the basis for the report to the Synod of the EKD by Bishop Scheele, himself a member of the theologian's Study Group, and form the foundation of the opinion delivered to the churches by the Joint Commission itself. The visit to Rome of Bishop Lohse, Chair of the Council of the EKD and co-chair of the Joint Commission, may have helped personally inform the Pope about the state of the analysis and the new assessment of the churches' mutual condemnations.

In 1986 the final theological document of the Study Group was published and taken up for study within the German churches. Within Germany alone, of course, final conclusions on these matters cannot be drawn. On the Catholic side, the question will need to be taken up on the world level. On the evangelical side, the council of the EKD will need to hand on to its member churches the question of a possible lifting of the condemnations directed against Rome, for only the member churches are authorized to deal with confessional questions. Presumably, the Synod of the Leuenberg Agreement [encompassing Lutheran, Reformed, and United churches in Europe] will also take up the matter. In addition, the Lutheran World Federation and World Alliance of Reformed Churches and their member churches will need to be involved. On both the catholic and evangelical sides, one must reckon with a process that will take years.

Something now needs to be said about the content, character, and results of the report of the Joint Commission. Then some reflections will be made on the relative importance of its theme for the process of ecumenical understanding between Rome and the Reformation churches.

The theological report groups the condemnations under three comprehensive categories: justification, the doctrine of the sacraments, and ministry. Their consideration is preceded by an introduction which briefly discusses the necessity of a testing of the mutual condemnations. It goes on to discuss in more detail the changes in theology and church life that have transformed the controversial situation of the Reformation period and which both demand and make possible this testing. It is emphasized that the oppositions of the past must not be trivialized. The claim of church teaching to abiding validity must not be neglected, notwithstanding present insights into the historically conditioned character of its formulations. Positive doctrinal assertions cannot be simply separated from delimitations over against error; the positive statement was itself formulated in response to the rejected conception. One cannot simply hold on to the positive teaching while giving up the delimitation, i.e., the corresponding condemnation; each conditions the other. Nevertheless, the condemnations are historically conditioned in a special way by being bound to the controversial situation of their time. They are "case-specific" in a different way than the positive statement of the faith, which claims a general validity beyond its particular time, even if in a historically conditioned language that will always require new interpretations. Thus common engagement with the positive content of the doctrinal statements can contribute to the result that the condemnations of the past "do not apply" to the present partner "because their doctrine is not determined by the error the old condemnation sought to block" (Ecumenical Study Committee of the United Evangelical-Lutheran Church of Germany).

In light of such insights, judgments about who was addressed by the condemnations will also change. This result is very important for ecumenical understanding, because each of the contemporary churches understands itself as bound by loyalty to the faith of its forebears. Although the Reformation churches are in principle always ready to test their doctrinal statements against Holy Scripture, they have not in fact reckoned with the necessity of a total revision of their doctrinal foundation, above all not in relation to the controversies of the past. Nonetheless, insufficiencies in the formulations of both sides can today be recognized and agreed upon. Since in the past neither side recognized these insufficiencies, a common material understanding now seems possible which earlier was beyond reach. An instructive example here is the doctrine of sacrifice in connection with the celebration of the Lord's Supper. The Reformation saw in the Catholic doctrine of eucharistic sacrifice a denial of the unique character of the sacrifice of Christ and presumed an intention to complete Christ's sacrifice through the liturgical act of the priest. Thus the mass was accused of works-righteousness and idolatry. The Catholic side felt itself misunderstood, but could not find an appropriate and unmistakable way to state that the priest and congregation participate through the Eucharist in the sacrifice of Christ by "remembering" his death, as Paul says. The close connection between the real presence of Christ in the Eucharist and the presence of his sacrifice into which the celebrants are drawn can be better understood and described by contemporary perspectives so that in this central question no church-dividing opposition need anymore exist.

The chapter on the *doctrine of justification* which follows the Introduction brings together the most important controversial points of the sixteenth century—controversies over the corruption of human nature through sin and over the assessment of concupiscence as itself sin or only an occasion and effect of sin, over the Lutheran assertion of human passivity in justification, over the opposition between an "external" imputation of the righteous of Christ to the sinner and an "internal" transformation of the person by grace, over the Reformation formula of justification *sola fide* and the emphasis on faith's certainty of salvation, and over the necessity of good works and their meritorious character. Point by point it is shown that these opposition were caused in part by misunderstandings, in part by deep seated differences in forms of thought and expression. Usually both are found together. For example, differing answers to the question whether the baptized could be considered sinners were drawn from the differing understandings of the relation between concupiscence and sin. Both sides agreed that concupiscence was present in the baptized Christian. The difference was that the Lutheran side, appealing to Augustine's usage, called it sin, while Trent avoided this designation.

Another example can be found in the differing understandings of the concept "faith," which led to sharply contrasting formulations of the significance of faith for justification. If one understands faith as the assent to church doctrine that must stand at the beginning of the process of justification, then talk of justification by faith *alone* seems naturally excluded.

The Reformation use of this formula, however, presupposes a different concept of faith: faith as trust in the promise of Christ, through which the person is joined to Christ and gains the fullness of salvation. A glaring example of misunderstanding due to differing forms of expression is Trent's rejection of the Reformation teaching of faith's certainty of salvation. The rejection was directed at a false self-assurance of one's own salvation. Luther also battled against such *securitas carnis*. The Council did not have in view Luther's actual teaching of certainty of salvation as obedient trust in the promise of God. Nevertheless, it does not suffice to speak only of misunderstandings. Behind them lie differing terminologies and material perspectives, in particular, differing anthropologies. These appear especially in the opposition between Trent's conception of justification as a qualitative change in the human soul itself and the Reformation doctrine of justification *extra nos* in God's judgment upon us. But, according to Luther, believers participate in the righteousness of Christ that exists outside of them.

This righteousness does not remain simply external; rather, in faith persons are drawn outside themselves and transplanted into Christ. For the Catholic conception, persons are transformed by grace not in separation from Christ, but rather in connection with Christ. When this is noted, the remaining disagreements about our access to the event of justification no longer permit mutual condemnations. The existence of deep seated differences must be conceded. They can lose their church-dividing significance, however, and become a mere difference between theological schools if we bear in mind that what one side lifts up is neither rejected nor overlooked and neglected by the other side, despite differing thought-forms.

The case is similar with the concepts of faith; with the differing understandings of the interrelation of faith, baptism, and penance; and with the concept of merit. A series of open questions remains in relation to the sacrament of penance, especially in connection with the priest's power to absolve and with the understanding of satisfaction and merit. Nevertheless, differing answers to these questions can hardly justify mutual condemnation.

The chapter on justification is followed by a large chapter on the doctrine of the sacraments. That it is the most comprehensive chapter of the report is understandable in light of the many condemnations to be dealt with. The first section deals with the general doctrine of sacraments, with its controverted questions about their institution and number. A second, more comprehensive section deals with oppositions over the doctrine of the Eucharist. Shorter discussions of confirmation, marriage, and the anointing of the sick then follow.

On the general doctrine of the sacraments, some misunderstandings within the sixteenth century oppositions were corrected and some differences were seen as superseded in view of convergences that have occurred since then. Disparate conceptions still exist in the understanding of the institution of the sacraments by Christ (which both churches emphasize), in the understanding of the concept of sign, and in the description of the working of grace in the sacraments. Nevertheless, such "far reaching agreement" exists in the understanding of the actions themselves and their effects that the weight of the still existing repudiations is diminished.

With the Eucharist, we can today affirm that the theological controversies of the past have been "so fully dealt with" that "the grounds for mutual condemnations do not apply." Remaining differences relate more to the practice of the eucharistic celebration and to eucharistic piety, although even in these areas "decisive convergences" have occurred on communion under both species and on the relation of the presence of Christ to the right use (*usus*) of the sacrament according to its institution. Questions still requiring clarification exist above all in relation to the treatment of unconsumed elements after the Eucharist.

With confirmation, a new context for discussion has been created by insight into its close connection to baptism. The possibility now appears of an agreed judgment about the controversies of the Reformation period and also a "factually appropriate harmonization with regard to the contemporary theory and practice of the churches." As a result, the different conceptions and forms of confirmation need not longer stand "in church-dividing contradiction."

The debates of the sixteenth century over what was called "extreme unction" also appear today "in a new light" because of better knowledge of the history of the anointing of the sick and its relations to the charisma of healing. The Second Vatican Council took into account the Reformation criticism of the interpretation of the apostolic anointing of the sick reported in James 5:14f as a sacrament for the dying. Both the Reformation rejection of the then prevalent conception and practice and Trent's canon in their defense have today become obsolete. It still remains open, however, whether the evangelical churches recognize a special action of anointing the sick. Such a special action might be the visitation of the sick by the pastor, with pastoral conversation, Bible reading, and prayer. Whether here a comparable act is found on the evangelical side depends on whether the emphasis in the anointing of the sick falls on the prayer at the sickbed or on the act of anointing as such.

The confessional differences in the understanding of marriage concern above all the question whether it belongs only to the order of creation or also to the order of salvation. Already in 1976 a study commission of the Roman Catholic and Evangelical churches came to the conclusion that marriage is to be viewed as a covenant which is related to the covenant of God with humanity in Jesus Christ. Further discussions are needed, however, to show whether on this basis one can arrive at a common interpretation of Eph. 5:21-32 in its significance for the understanding of marriage. Significant differences also exist between the confessional traditions in relation to divorce and in the valuation of the single state. For the evangelical conception also, divorce does not correspond to the will of God in creation, and the possibility of singleness in celibacy is recognized by Luther and Calvin, as well as the Lutheran Confessions, as a special gift of God's grace. Despite deep differences in doctrine and practice, especially over divorce, the churches are not in these questions "irreconcilably divided from one another." The question is thus asked whether, because of these differences, condemnations "need to remain in force with church-dividing effect."

It is striking that in the final theological report on the mutual condemnations, the still existing differences over the understanding of marriage and the practical consequences of these differences were judged as less resolved than the other, more central, controversial questions. This was also true in comparison with the discussions over ministerial office in the report's final chapter. The report states that today a high degree of agreement exists in relation to the differentiation of ministerial office from the priesthood of all believers.

This agreement follows greater emphasis among Catholics on the task of the proclamation of the Word and the removal of the controversial character of the orientation toward eucharistic sacrifice by agreement on this theme in the context of the Lord's Supper. Neither the Lutheran confessions nor Calvin fundamentally rejected the sacramentality of ordination. They demanded only a reform of the rite and theology of ordination corresponding to original apostolic practice. The Roman Catholic understanding of ordination now orients itself to the laying on of hands rather than, as before, toward the handing over of the chalice and paten. This new orientation removes the occasions for Luther's critique, which denied the biblical basis for this action and which was the target of the relevant canons of the Council of Trent. In relation to the effect of ordination, a higher degree of agreement exists in view of the common affirmation of the uniqueness and unrepeatability of the action than the differences in theological language, especially in the controversy over the concept *character indelibilis*, would lead one to believe. In terms of its substance, the Reformation understanding of office is not touched by the corresponding Tridentine condemnations.

Greater differences exist in relation to the Catholic conception of the structuring of ministry into the three levels of deacon, presbyter, and bishop. Over against this understanding, the Reformation churches maintained an original unity of the offices of pastor and bishop. This question was much discussed on the Catholic side during the Middle Ages and has still not been unambiguously clarified. Since the Reformation churches (at any rate, the Lutheran) do not simply reject a subordination of pastors to a regional episcopacy, but rather are ready to grant the latter's validity as a churchly ordinance (even if not commanded by Christ himself), they are not touched by the corresponding Tridentine condemnations. Also the authority to ordain can thus be reserved to the bishops. The Reformation churches departed from this rule only under an appeal to an emergency situation that existed for them in the sixteenth century. The practice of ordination in the evangelical churches up to the present is based on the emergency order created at that time. If the Catholic Church would grant the validity of these arguments, then the condemnations of the Council of Trent against the nonepiscopal (and thus noncanonical) ordinations in the Reformation churches could lose their church-dividing character.

The sharpest condemnations from the Reformation side were directed against the papacy. The designation of the pope as Antichrist is to be understood as conditioned by the controversial situation of the time. This judgment was even at that time "materially unjustified in relation to a more precise evaluation of papal self-understanding," since the popes of the Reformation period did not claim to be able to disregard the authority of Scripture, although they seemed to their opponents to do so. After the explicit assertion by the Second Vatican Council of the subordination of the church's teaching office to the authority of the Word of God, an agreement on a universal office of unity within Christendom is thinkable. In relation to such an office both the historical claims of the Roman bishops as well as the functions of ecumenical councils would need to be considered. The Reformation has "never fundamentally excluded" an office for the preservation of Christian unity at the level of all Christendom. In relation to the doctrines of the two Vatican councils, "significant differences still" exist. The final report on the mutual condemnations does not describe these differences in greater detail.

In addition to the Reformation controversy over the exegetical basis for the Roman primacy in the references to Peter in the New Testament and to reservations about the claim advanced by Vatican I for a universal primacy of jurisdiction and an infallibility of papal doctrinal decisions, there is also an issue already referred to in the introduction to the document concerning the relation of the magisterium to the interpretation of Scripture within theology and to the reception of the magisterium's statements by the faithful: there exists "as yet no explicit consensus about the critical function of Scripture over against the formation of the church's tradition." Here lies an unresolved problem in the Constitution on Revelation of the Second Vatican Council, as was already emphasized at that time by Joseph Ratzinger in his commentary on the Constitution.

The report on the condemnations does not deal with the claims of the Roman Catholic Church in connection with the teaching office of the pope. In these details the 1981 Final Report of the Anglican-Roman Catholic Dialogue went much further. The reticence in relation to these questions in the context of a treatment the condemnations that stand between the churches presupposes the expectation that an agreement on the papacy should not be a condition for an agreement to set aside the Reformation period condemnations between Rome and the Reformation churches. The mutual condemnations between Rome and the Orthodox Churches have been lifted without a prior agreement on the place of the papacy in the total church.

In the reconsideration of the mutual condemnations stemming from the Reformation period, it is initially only a matter of the Reformation churches and Rome reaching that level of ecumenical mutuality which today exists between Rome and the Eastern Orthodox churches. This requires that the mutual condemnations cease to be effective and also that the designation of the pope as Antichrist by formally withdrawn. A positive agreement on the authority of the pope throughout the church is not required for this. This question cannot be settled in a bilateral discussion between Rome and the Protestants; the participation of the orthodox Churches would also be necessary. The original territories of the Reformation stood under more than just the universal ecclesial authority of the pope, which in a certain sense was always more program than reality if it was meant to imply more than a primacy of honor of Rome among the other patriarchs and bishops of Christendom. The original territories of the Reformation also stood under the jurisdiction of the pope as patriarch of the West, and this was a much more solid historical reality. This patriarchal power of the pope cannot today be again established in relation to the Protestant churches. A recognition of the papacy and its universal claims by the Protestant churches ecumenically should not be sought prior to an understanding on this question that also includes the Eastern Orthodox churches. The Anglican churches have perhaps already gone too far in this direction. These questions belong within the structure of discussions including the Orthodox churches. Presumably solutions that are acceptable to the Orthodox churches will also be acceptable to the Reformation churches. As far as the Reformation churches are involved, however, such discussions are only conceivable if they proceed from the same starting point as now exists between Rome and the Orthodox churches. That point will be reached when the mutual condemnations cease to be effective.

We are concerned here only with a relatively limited step on the way to full unity. The full unity of the churches will not be reached immediately with the lifting of the condemnations. But just for this reason such a step is realistically conceivable. The ecclesiastical committees and responsible persons who must make this decision can, clearly conscious of its limited nature, more easily bear the weight of the involved responsibility.

If the decision to lift the mutual condemnations between the Reformation churches and Rome is made by the responsible authorities on both sides, more than just the questions connected with the papacy will then need further clarification. The final report on the condemnations names a number of substantive themes about which no full consensus has been reached. Differences requiring further clarification remain over the two basic models of the event of justification, over the relation between baptism and penance, over the theology and practical form of the sacrament of penance, in the area of eucharistic piety, over the relation between confirmation and baptism, in relation to the signification of anointing in confirmation and the anointing of the sick, over the relation between marriage and the saving mystery of Christ, and over the canonical provisions on divorce, but also over the general doctrine of the sacraments in relation to the institution and number of sacraments, and finally over the doctrine of ministry in relation to the degree of the presbyter's participation in the authority of the episcopal office. Agreement on these matters is still not complete. The extent of the achieved agreement, however, is such that the question needs to be raised for examination and decision, whether the remaining differences still have a church-dividing character. The judgment of the theological Study Group is that they do not, but the decisive judgment on this question must be made by the responsible church authorities, not by theologians. Fortunately, not all theological differences have a church-dividing effect. Between Rome and the Orthodox churches, for example, there exist differences over the relation between baptism and confirmation and over the dependence of the validity of baptism on church fellowship. Especially in their consequences for churchly life, these differences are more decisive than most of the remaining differences between the Reformation churches and Rome.

It is important to recognize that all existing doctrinal differences need not be settled to full mutual satisfaction in order to find that the lifting or declaring ineffective of the mutual condemnations is well founded and called for. A whole series of confessional doctrinal differences and differences of piety which have led to opposition between the churches remained undiscussed in the study of mutual condemnations because they neither formed "the real ground of division" nor could "justify by themselves its continuation." Here belong such themes as monasticism and priestly celibacy, the veneration of the saints, as well as Mariology. It is hardly conceivable that we must live in divided churches because of differences over these questions if we have achieved an agreement on the central oppositions from the Reformation period so extensive that the maintenance of the old condemnations in the latter areas appears no longer justified.

A final word on the condemnations themselves. They do not become trivial if their church-dividing effect is annulled. They will not be simply stricken from the binding doctrinal documents of the churches. Rather they will still have the significance of a healthy warning not only for Christians belonging to the other confessional tradition, but also for members of one's own. With both the Council of Trent as well as the Reformation confessions, condemnations were directed against one-sided statements which both churches should today judge as reductions of their own understanding of the faith. These mutual condemnations should warn members of both churches against again understanding and expressing their own traditions in a way that reignites the oppositions now surmountable by new theological developments and thereby gives a new relevance to the old condemnations.

Chapter Four

Is the "Step Backward" Ecumenical Progress?

Introduction to the Method and
Hermeneutics of the Study

Karl Lehmann

U NTIL NOW, DOCUMENTS of "Growth in Agreement" stood in the forefront of the ecumenical dialogue between Lutheran and Catholic Christians. The way ahead pointed toward increasing agreement. Moreover, the contrasting doctrinal condemnations had been already treated, if only selectively and case by case. The study by the Ecumenical Study Group of Protestant and Catholic theologians, *The Condemnations of the Reformation Era: Do They Still Divide?*, whose background and creation may be assumed here,[1] began with the commission to treat the official mutual condemnations in their context and to raise the question whether the doctrinal condemnations of the sixteenth century still concern the present day partner. The statement of the problem and the direction of the investigation by this study appear to be turned exclusively backward. For many this means a step backward, namely, into the sixteenth century, whose problems are scarcely understandable to many present day believers. The ecumenical process would not be oriented forward to further progress, but it would mark time and be entangled in the difficult to penetrate undergrowth of the questions of the sixteenth century and come to a stand still. Then the enterprise would soon become a step backward. Not a few who regard the mandate of the Ecumenical Study Group as meaningful and necessary are worried whether the situation of ecumenism could not in fact get worse if an official reception of the "reassessment" of the doctrinal condemnations should not be successful.

In this context the question of method and hermeneutics of the study of the doctrinal condemnations should again be taken up. The following reflections have occupied the author from the beginning on the basis of his joint responsibility and work. Thus they became elements of the common procedure and were the basis of the first interpretation of the study. Therefore they belong in a report on the group's work as a structural element of the whole. They are a constituent part of the material published in this volume although they have been again in part revised.[2] For the sake of documentation, no effort was made to deal with works which appeared after the publication of the study. Here it is first and especially a question of working out the particular method.

I.

O n the basis of its mandate, the Joint Ecumenical Commission proceeded from the presupposition that the joint witness of the churches should be strengthened and that "new realities" have arisen between the churches. The old massive disagreement in fact no longer exists.[3] The judgments, which in the sixteenth century were promulgated by one church against another and which belong to the sum of their binding teaching, stand in contrast to these joint statements of faith. Whether one shares this description of the situation and assessment of the ecumenical dialogue—at least in its outline—is already rather decisive for the evaluation of this study. These presuppositions have been corroborated in various convergence texts. This is especially true for the documents of the Lutheran/Roman Catholic conversation "The Gospel and the Church," "The Eucharist," "Ministry," "Ways to Community," and "Facing Unity." The fundamental assumption has been confirmed by many arguments especially in the research on the Augsburg Confession on the occasion of its 450th anniversary. Although the church division of the sixteenth century was great and in many areas produced directly exclusive and thus irreconcilable antitheses, the division did not extend to the deepest root. Precisely the studies of the Confessio Augustana have shown that, beyond the link of the Holy Scripture and the confessions of the ancient church, more in common from the comprehensive tradition of the faith binds the churches together than divides them.

Such an assessment has in principle, and certainly in a guarded form, found its entry into official documents. We here only need to recall the address of Pope John Paul II on the 450th anniversary of the Augsburg Confession: "We are the more grateful that today we see with even greater clearness that at that time, even if there was no success in building a bridge, the storms of the age spared important piers of that bridge. The intense and long-standing dialogue with the Lutheran Church, called for and made possible by the Second Vatican Council, has enabled us to discover how great and solid are the common foundations of our Christian faith."[4]

Christians could only discover this deeper mutuality because Protestants and Catholics became better acquainted with each other, dismantled common prejudices, or at least could diminish them, and could again clearly articulate agreement in the fundamental truths of the faith. Thus the language of a "basic consensus" or "fundamental consensus" arose. This includes a mutuality in the sustaining elements of the Christian faith, but it is not identical with a consensus in the comprehensive sense (sometimes not falsely but unsuitably named "total consensus"). Thus a "basic consensus" does not yet mean—this is often overlooked—an integral consensus of the sort, e.g., which is and must exist as an expression of church fellowship in the Catholic understanding. When we can formulate in disputed questions only a partial agreement and individual diverging elements, the concepts of "partial consensus" and "difference" are developed. Even where no consensus is reached, not infrequently there are common perspectives, which, without detriment to the still open questions, point toward and already hint at the possibility of an agreement that might later be achievable ("convergences").

These instruments of ecumenical dialogue on the one hand are familiar to each expert and almost obvious. On the other hand, the concepts are not always sufficiently explained and in part are also intensely disputed. This is true in recent time especially for the meaning and significance of the concept of convergence. In the discussion of the last decade, especially in the German-speaking area, a further category has appeared, which speaks of a "basic difference". This concept, which is not very clear and often little related to the categories explained above, supposes that between the Catholic Church and the churches of the Reformation there is finally, despite all the mutualities in individual affirmations, a still unworked through difference in the fundamental understanding of the faith, e.g. in the basic concept of Christianity, in the stance of Christian existence, in the fundamental comprehension of salvation, in the mediation of salvation, even in the definition of God and Jesus Christ. The concept "basic difference" is met in ecumenical documents not as a fixed technical term, but it determines the basic approach to ecumenical conversation of not a few theologians. The less clear the matter is, so much more influential and uncontrolled becomes the acceptance of such a basic difference. It is not wrong to assert that in the immediately past years the acceptance—often not well thought through—of such a basic difference has increased, or at least been more openly stated. The discussion of this concept is by no means yet closed.

Already the mandate, but also the process and its execution, proceeds from the view that ecumenical conversation has reached a "basic consensus," although its scope and significance is not defined. At least it can be established that the hypothesis of the existence of such a basic consensus belongs to the presuppositions for even a meaningful beginning to the study. Whoever, whether implicitly or explicitly, proceeds from the contrary assumption of a "basic difference" will be able from such a viewpoint to agree with details of the study, but will more likely hesitate in principle about it as a whole.

II.

F rom this background the total weight of the mandated task first becomes recognizable. Remaining impediments stand in the way of the further development of consensus and a common witness of faith. In order to confirm this, it was necessary to keep always before our eyes the present condition of ecumenical conversation. A study of the applicability to the contemporary partner of earlier doctrinal condemnations cannot be limited to historical research, but must include in its context present perceptions. If this cannot occur comprehensively, present perceptions must at least be active as ferment and catalyst in the "reassessment" of the doctrinal condemnations in relation to their present applicability. There is no doubt that the historically oriented reassessment of the doctrinal condemnations and the examination of the present reception of ecumenical texts involve mutual critical challenges, but this can be a positive stimulus. In this sense both dimensions of the mandate belong together, even if the engagement with ecumenical documents is not always and everywhere made explicit.

The thematizing of the doctrinal condemnations must take place on the basis of several concerns. The mandate had already expressed the untested assumption that the doctrinal condemnations would by general opinion not be applicable to the contemporary partner. However, this cannot remain a mere "private conviction but it must be established by the churches as binding."[5] Because of its seriousness for the faith of the church and out of truthfulness towards the confession, this matter cannot remain a vague presumption, even if it were widely shared. Naturally in previous ecumenical conversations individual doctrinal condemnations have been have been more exactly investigated, but for the most part this occurred only sporadically and, e.g. in view of the Council of Trent, relatively accidentally. A great number of the condemnations have been handled neither collectively nor individually. This is true for theological scholarship and also for ecumenical dialogue. In the long run, however, we cannot overlook that many condemnations of the sixteenth century stand opposed to the repeatedly posited "basic consensus". For years ecumenical discussion has thus, so to speak, placed the condemnations in brackets. For various reasons, one treats them with reserve. But now it is necessary that they be taken up directly, and thus thematically and systematically.

It is also a requirement of ecumenical honesty to accept this task. The doctrinal condemnations belong to the binding confessions of the respective churches, although with different weight. As long as no official "reassessment" occurs, such statements must be handed on. This holds at least for theological doctrine. It would be insincere simply to ignore the condemnations. Often in the past they have been passed over in silence out of a variety of motives: some consider the classical doctrinal condemnations as antiquated and no longer worth discussion; others believed the progress of ecumenism accomplished this "reassessment" as if automatically; not a few would like to leave "the purification of the past" to a later phase of ecumenical conversation. Such attitudes are no solution, at least in the long run. The doctrinal condemnations have a continuing weight for the churches. No Catholic theologian can, e.g., by him or herself remove the binding character of such statements or, even more, annul them. On the Reformation side, especially in its Lutheran form, there is a solemn commitment to the confessional writings that is not to be overlooked. Thus with the ordination to the clergy occurs the so-called "charge" on the basis of the individual confessional writings, often enumerated by name. Even more recent ordination rites do not depart from this custom. What sense would it have for someone to make a commitment to the totality of the confessional writings and also to their doctrinal condemnations, and at the same time almost completely to ignore them? Thus an elementary honesty in relation to the accepted heritage of the church, and also in relation to one's own behavior in the present and toward the conversation partner, requires a detailed engagement with the condemnations in their concrete binding character.

In this context it is also necessary to be conscious of the theological character of the condemnations. The doctrinal condemnations go back to the usage in the New Testament of "anathema". Therefore they are also named "anathematismen". By "anathema" is meant condemnation of a person. Ancient Christianity had perceived early the necessity of marking off the limits of fellowship. It was not only a disciplinary measure, but concerned an eschatological word of judgment. It was applied to an attitude which injured the foundations of the community and would be punished at the end by God's judgment. Thus the formula in 1Cor.16:22 ("Who loves not the Lord, let him be anathema") is encountered as a component of the entrance liturgy of the Eucharist. Those who teach or perform what is condemned are by the formula (cf. also 1 Corinthians 11:27; Galatians 1:8ff; 3:13; 1 Corinthians 12:3; Romans 9:3; Revelation 23:14) excluded from the fellowship of the church, and especially from participation in the Eucharist, in the name of God and with holy authority. The New Testament "anathema" already binds together the claim of truth, a defense against error, and a decision about membership in the church. Whether it is a question of "principles of holy law" may remain open. The legal components and the authority of the church related to them are in any case not be overlooked. As there are different forms in the confessional statements and dogmas (e.g. creed, doxology, doctrinal text), so also the doctrinal condemnations developed in different ways. As recent research on the Council of Trent proves, the "anathema" can contain different nuances of meaning. In the doctrinal condemnations that are expressly, properly, and consciously executed, it is in any case a question of the highest degree of God's truth and of the serious consequences of an intentional divergence from it. The misjudgment of a truth of revelation which is thereby punished is so scandalous that only an exclusion from fellowship represents the suitable answer. Our difficult term "condemnation," a word that has become difficult to understand, suitably expresses this structure, even if its complete meaning to a large extent escapes our notice.

Condemnations are thus not expressed because of a humanly based quarrel, but are theologically legitimate only if they are based on the foundation of ultimately binding teaching and valid practice of the faith. Therefore church fellowship is also affected by the condemnations, which historically was handled in rather differentiated ways. The clear and strict "damnamus" stands and falls with a contrast in teaching that touches the foundation of faith and the Gospel. In this sense the decisions of the churches in the sixteenth century are in fact spiritual judgments, however strange they may sometimes appear to us today.

If we visualize the original status and the full meaning of the doctrinal condemnations, then we cannot simply and indifferently pass by them. Above all, the question arises how such condemnations can still exist if a basic consensus is assumed. Or do the doctrinal condemnations remain as concrete formulations of an unbridgeable basic difference? If there is a basic consensus, however, then we must seriously ask whether in its light we must not understand and evaluate many of the condemnations in new ways. Ecumenical dialogue is no longer permitted to avoid this challenge.

III.

When we recognize the total weight of this task and accept it, the difficulties of an appropriate investigation do not become smaller. The Joint Ecumenical Commission, in giving the assignment, pronounced already a serious warning when it emphasized that the intended "reassessment" did not involve a "frivolous relation to our own history. On the contrary it means that, accepting our own history, we also accept the new insights that have meanwhile emerged, new challenges and new experiences."[6] Even if we remain conscious of the changed situation of Christendom in the world and of new theological insights, the doctrinal condemnations cannot be comprehended as merely historical ballast, rubble of history to be cleared off, bits of now meaningless memory from the era of church divisions. Something of continuing validity and binding character comes to expression in the doctrinal condemnations also for contemporary Christians. "Indeed we must gratefully recognize that the separated churches have drawn life and strength from the spiritual heritage of that era. Just because we are convinced of the truth of these statements, they remain for us worthy of reflection. We must therefore think about them afresh, making them our own in a new way in order to understand more profoundly and fully, in a situation that has in many respects changed, statements that were expressed in a historically conditioned and limited way."[7]

The task of a "reassessment" and the conviction of the continuing validity of the doctrinal condemnations form a basic hermeneutical problem of the study. With the publication of the text, it was consciously stated already in the "Introduction": "The task the Ecumenical Study Group was given and which it has fulfilled brings us face to face with a fundamental contradiction. On the one hand the creeds and dogmas of the church retain their validity. Yet on the other hand they are supposed to lose their force, inasmuch as they no longer apply to the present state of doctrine in the other church."[8] It cannot be the intention of the study to correct the doctrinal condemnations spoken by the fathers in the faith. It would also make no sense to agree that the common confession is valid, but the condemnations are outdated.

Here one must carefully attend to the question posed: do the doctrinal condemnations still touch the present partner. It is not a matter simply of confronting the doctrinal condemnations of the past with each other, specified through our present historical knowledge. The path from the binding doctrinal expressions of the sixteenth century through the reception of this teaching and finally to the present situation must repeatedly be traveled and measured. Perhaps one might better say that the present teaching is no longer determined by the error against which the earlier rejection sought to defend.[9]

About such a procedure, the question is repeatedly asked: why is such a weighty distinction made between the past condemnations and the doctrine or partner of today? Especially if the doctrinal statements involved at that time belong to the basic elements of the faith of a church, then we must presume a continuous identity incompatible with such decisive differences between then and now, despite the distance of time. Obviously we are no longer dealing with the unaltered doctrinal positions of the sixteenth century. In spite of all continuity, we have experienced the Enlightenment and critical reflection, Idealism and historical thought as well as new insights from other sciences. Therefore a historical distance does exist to that which occurred in the sixteenth century. In the understanding of the doctrinal condemnations bridges must first be built and different horizons must be brought together. This fundamental situation has greater consequences for the doctrinal condemnations than for other areas within the confessional statements. On the whole, the condemnations are subjected more strongly to the historical conditions and limitations of human speech than are confessional statements. They are more directly related to concrete situations and these are often reconstructed only with difficulty; they are often strongly codetermined by a concrete polemic and argument. Often the subsequent period is not fully aware of these situations. It becomes more easily possible for the condemnations to become detached from this limited context and to exceed their reach and range of validity. There are many examples of this in the history of the interpretation of the decisions of the Council of Trent and of the doctrinal condemnations in the Confessions.

We could fulfill the mandate of the study only with the help of new insights gained from theological scholarship and ecumenical experience. On the one hand, historical knowledge makes possible the step back into the controversies of that time: we frequently can see much more exactly the occasion, presuppositions, situation, and limitations of a dispute. History alone, however, is still not enough, despite its indispensability. New insights from biblical research, the results of renewed patristic study, the history of doctrine and the councils, but especially systematic reflections have enriched the spectrum of thought forms, widened the area of discussion, and relaxed the opposing positions of the past. All these perspectives allowed the differences of the sixteenth century to appear in a new light. These elements were decisive in the dialogue. These methodological possibilities do not need to be enumerated here again in detail. This has taken place already in the "Introduction" to the *Condemnations* text[10] and in the "Final Report of the Joint Ecumenical Commission on the Examination of the Sixteenth-Century Condemnations."[11] In addition, these perspectives have been repeatedly formulated elsewhere.[12] Whoever for whatever reason cannot or does not wish to accept these insights in their methodological as also in their substantive aspects, will have difficulty agreeing with the study's procedures and accepting its results.

Such a statement is carefully considered, but it must be seen in its limits. The impression could easily be given that, with our present questions and knowledge, we are far above that which was thought and expressed in the era of church division. The scholarly possibilities available to us today can enrich us, but they should not lead to a self-confident arrogance. This warning has several motives. First, we are dealing historically with problems where, on the bases of text and situation, statements can sometimes be made with high certainty, but sometimes only with probability or even as conjecture. Legitimate differences of opinion are possible. In addition, scholarship in the area of the interpretation of dogma and confession is extremely helpful, but it reaches here an inner limitation. The law of relativization is inherent within the historical question: everything is placed in mutual interrelation and appears in its multiform dependence. Much thereby becomes plausible and explainable, but the aspect of normativity and validity can be lost. At the end stands historicism. We must recognize soberly these tendencies and temptations. At the same time, a contrary tendency arises from the study's mandate and method: the formulations are historically conditioned and limited, but they do not thereby lose their claim as dogma and confession to say something valid for the present and the future. This question makes us modest for it asks us whether we measure up to the earlier intellectual and spiritual experiences and whether we take sufficient effort to understand them. There is no reason for any form of intellectual or spiritual arrogance.

Here lies a final reason why scholarly knowledge is indispensable for carrying out the mandate. At the same time, however, experience from ecumenical conversation of the present leads to the insight that there is between the partners, bound to their respective doctrinal condemnations, a new mutuality which makes possible the rapprochement in the "reassessment" of the condemnations. There is a new lack of prejudice between the partners, which has laid a new foundation for such tasks. This is what is meant when one speaks in ecumenical conversation of a "basic consensus". If many questions are still insoluble, this new relationship produces the real possibility of reading the doctrinal condemnations of the sixteenth century in an unprejudiced way and of evaluating them anew, without simply giving them up. As we proceed through many stages of scholarly knowledge and processes of reception, we should not in the midst of these reflections forget an ultimate immediacy of experience, namely, that separated Christians have preserved more in common than they previously recognized and that they are more bound together in their commonality than they are separated in their difference.

The significance of the consequences of the method described are scarcely to be overestimated: the intellectual space in which the earlier formulations are to be understood becomes much broader; frequently one can mean the same thing with different words, and even something different with the same words; alternative possibilities of response become discernible. Only when one follows the multidimensional logic of the matter will the results become evident.

Nevertheless, we must be clear that questions remain. They have already been indicated. Basically it is the problem of the relation between truth and method, truth and history, truth and language. Closely connected is the relation between truth and tradition. This problem has been touched on in the study. Nevertheless, it was not the study's task to address this extensively still unresolved basic question explicitly in addition to its other tasks.

In the framework of the study, however, the approach to a solution is sufficiently given. For the Catholic theologian, recent hermeneutics of doctrine has provided sufficiently reliable instruments and procedures to tackle the task of an interpretation of the earlier doctrinal condemnations in relation to the present. Against this background the Ecumenical Study Group of Protestant and Catholic theologians set up as a methodological instrument the following individual steps toward an answer to the question whether the doctrinal condemnations of the sixteenth century still concern the present partner:

1. First one must examine against whom a particular doctrinal condemnation is directed. In many controversies this is not self-evident, but it must be explicitly determined.

2. By means of historical investigation, one must examine whether a condemnation correctly touches the position of the partner at that time, whether the opposing side at that time in fact taught what was condemned, and whether the condemnations in this sense are justified. The comprehensive teaching is to be kept in view from which sharp sentences, extreme formulations, and misunderstood remarks might have been selected in a one-sided manner. Polemic can seduce one to do this.

3. The condemnations, however, are not to be interpreted only historically.

They belong—even if with differing qualities—to the confession or dogma of the church. The doctrinal decisions live on in the churches that are presently in conversation with one another. Thus the question is unavoidable, whether the present partner still so teaches. Does an earlier doctrinal condemnation touch the position the partner takes today?

4. From the comparison of both points of view, the historical look backward and the analysis of the present teaching position, the question is raised whether the formulations of that time are still today justifiable in all points. Thereby the question is asked whether the partner churches still today are the addressees of the condemnation.

5. If an earlier condemnation still touches the present position of the partner, then it must be investigated with care, what status and what importance does the actually remaining difference have? A distinction must be made between those differences in the teaching and practice of a church which concern foundations of the church's being and those which indicate a legitimate variety in the faith and ordered life of a church. The specification of church-dividing and non church-dividing differences which results is not a simple matter. The criteria involved are also those of the being of the church and of church fellowship. This important question in involved in the attempted reassessment of the doctrinal condemnations.

IV.

In carrying out the project, the Ecumenical Study Group could find no models which could directly serve as a pattern and measure for its own task. In the framework of this paper only two documents should be mentioned, each of which has it own rather different proximity to this study.

The question of the "reassessment" of the doctrinal condemnations recalls the procedure and discussion in reference to the "Leuenberg Agreement." This Agreement of Reformation churches in Europe is a text adopted in a final form in 1973, which sought to realize a "church fellowship" on the European level among Lutheran, Reformed and United churches, the Bohemian Brethren and the church of the Waldensians.[13] The Leuenberg Agreement contains tensions similar to the project on the doctrinal condemnations in that, on the one hand, the sixteenth century condemnations between Lutherans and Reformed could not be withdrawn but remained valid in the confessions of the churches. On the other hand, the relevant partners were to be expressly excluded from the condemnations if they accepted the Agreement. Thus the condemnations of the sixteenth century do not touch the present doctrinal position of the partners.

The Leuenberg Agreement is already appealed to in a letter from Bishop Lohse and Cardinal Ratzinger of June 1981, the first official description of the mandate, when it says, "The path entered upon the Leuenberg Agreement between the Lutheran and Reformed churches ought to find a corresponding continuation between the Protestant churches and the Roman Catholic Church."[14]

The similarity of the question posed within the Leuenberg Agreement to the task of the "reassessment" of the doctrinal condemnations was clear from the first. Still the Leuenberg Agreement played an astonishingly small role as a model and in the course of the negotiations was mentioned relatively rarely by name. Obviously it was known among the members of the Ecumenical Study Group. Some had even participated in the process of its development and reception. Nevertheless, we must see the considerable difference from the Leuenberg Agreement.

1. From the beginning, no "concord" was intended which would represent a binding agreement and re-establish church fellowship. Such a concord could only be developed later at its own pace. The investigations of the Ecumenical Study Group on the doctrinal condemnations could be in the best of cases only a preparatory work.

2. The Reformation churches did indeed break church fellowship with one another. Occasionally they have accused one another of not even understanding correctly the Reformation and its significance. Nevertheless, they have often understood themselves only as theological schools within the Reformation. The Lutheran and Reformed churches belong to the same type. The relation between the Reformation churches and the Roman Catholic Church has a fundamentally different structure.

3. The position of the Reformation, and especially Reformed, churches to the confessional writings is different from the commitment of the Catholic Church to its dogmatic doctrinal decisions. From the beginning, the "relativizing" of the confessions by the Reformation conversation partner has been stronger, through their relation to scripture and the historically conditioned character of their statements. Such a "relativizing" is not possible in the Catholic area. Nevertheless the Catholic theologian has in the modern hermeneutic of dogma an instrumentality which can bind continuity and change together in a very differentiated way.

4. Especially in the Lutheran churches, the Leuenberg Agreement encountered vehement protest precisely because of the relation between confession and history and between claims of truth and topical "relativizing." The Catholic theologians knew about the fundamental dilemma. Therefore it

appeared less appropriate to see in the insoluble difficulties of the Leuenberg Concord something like an exemplary model.

Because of these differences, the Leuenberg Agreement played the methodological role of a kind of initial ignition in the work of the Ecumenical Study Group, but as the work progressed, it had practically no influence on the findings. Many points of contact result from the proximity to the historical-critical method and from the general procedure in ecumenical dialogue. We must still ask, however, how far the condemnations study has fundamentally and convincingly overcome the inner aporia of the Leuenberg Agreement.

A second example is taken from the conversation between the Roman Catholic Church and the churches of the East. It is a question of the "restoration of love" of December 7, 1965. The lifting of the sentences of excommunication has a great spiritual proximity to the mandate to "reassess" the condemnations. Even if through no sacramental church fellowship has yet arisen, the lifting of the excommunication of 1054 has a deep ecclesial effect.

In the common explanation of Pope Paul VI and Patriarch Athenagoras, it is stated:

> Nothing can be done to change the fact that these events were what they were in that particularly disturbed period of history. But now that a calmer and fairer judgment has been made about them, it is important to recognize the excesses by which they were marked and which brought in their train consequences which, as far as we can judge went beyond what was intended, or foreseen by those responsible.... Being certain that they are expressing the common desire for justice and the unanimous feeling of charity of their faithful people..., Pope Paul VI and Patriarch Athenagoras I with his synod declare in mutual agreement:
>
> a) that they regret the offending words, the baseless reproaches, and blameworthy symbolic acts which on both sides marked or accompanied the sad events of this time;
>
> b) that in the same way they regret and remove from memory and from the midst of the Church the sentences of excommunication which followed, the remembrance of which acts right up to our own times as an obstacle to our mutual approach in charity, and they condemn these to oblivion;
>
> c) that they deplore, finally, the troublesome precedents and the further happenings which under the influence of various factors, including misunderstanding and distrust on both sides, eventually led to a real rupture of ecclesial communion.[15]

It is thus a question of changing the attitude to the past in order to bring forth a new present and future. Memory gives to the past a dangerous power also in the historical present and permits deadly dangers from the poison of the past to flow into the present. Thus we would like to purify the memory, to leave the past in God's hands in order to be released for the preparation of a better future.[16] The lifting of the doctrinal condemnations is an important presupposition of the proper goal, the restoration of love. Through the lifting of the sentences of excommunication, the symbol of separation is destroyed. Even if ecclesial communion is not yet reached, brotherly love between the churches is thus revived. It is, as a fundamental presupposition for the progressive solution of the still existing differences, the most important stage on the entire way to the restoration of love.

The "purification of memory" is indeed described by the words of forgetting. But this forgetting is more than a silence without consequences. The "purification of memory" is rather an act of mutual pardon. This is not only an official and canonical or unofficial and spiritual act, but it is at its kernel an intensification of and further approach toward ecclesial communion. The weight with which events such as the anathemas of 1054 stand in the history of the church is now radically altered. The new qualification of history means also a new appraisal of the present. The churches can no longer give play among themselves to the old poison, but must renew their memory from the very day of the lifting of the anathemas.

This lifting of anathemas has not yet reached the immediate goal: the full restoration of love in the form of eucharistic fellowship. But this example is a signpost for the further progress of the study of the condemnations. Even if we keep in mind the different relation of the church of the East to the Roman Catholic Church, the lifting of the anathemas of 1054 is the closest and most meaningful analogy to the aim of the "reassessment" of the doctrinal condemnations. The event of 1965 points to the future because it makes visible the comprehensive ecclesial context beyond the doctrinal condemnations and in a way includes it. As far as I can see, this analogy at no point played a role in the work of the condemnations study. Attention to the lifting of the excommunication of 1054 becomes all the more important when we ask what could be achieved progressively and by stages through the "lifting" of the doctrinal condemnations.

No more need be said about these examples. Their differing relations to the condemnations study has become clear despite the conciseness of the sketch. It is apparent that neither could be a direct model. The condemnations study had to find its own way among the many condemnations to its initial conclusions.

V.

The question of the method was not only a problem of procedure during the investigation, but it arises also in pondering and assessing the results. In this context the far too bold attempt to summarize concisely the results of the research need not be made. One should not forget that the sections within the *Condemnations* text are already extremely condensed syntheses of extensive chains of reasoning and analyses. Still less could the sections convey all the reasons and grounds for the argumentation. Much could only be made accessible in the form of additional materials, as it became available in volumes 5 and 6 of the series "Dialog der Kirchen". Summaries are necessary, but they are also dangerous and can lead astray. They possibly conceal the richness and differentiation within the results.

The "Final Report of the Joint Ecumenical Commission on the Examination of the Sixteenth-Century Condemnations" already attempts a summary.[17] Although the short texts are very differentiated, the Report almost necessarily runs the danger— at least in some formulations—of a generalizing summary, although the concrete picture is not so easily reduced to a common denominator. The "Final Report" was useful as the first public presentation on January 22, 1986 of the results of the work. However helpful as an introduction, however, it cannot replace the knowledge of the various sections of the *Condemnations* study. It was never intended that the "Final Report" be considered as the basis for the totality of further work or as an official synthesis of the results.

The sections of the study have brought to light results which will require comprehensive reflection in the future. The spectrum of the different evaluations of the extent to which individual sixteenth-century condemnations no longer touch the present partner is exceptionally great. We stand before an abundance of highly differentiated judgments, which even with repeated reading of the text are not easily reduced to some few denominators. Above all we lack a comprehensive hermeneutic for this work. The criteria and categories of previous ecumenical conversation are not sufficient. The available instrumentality is too simple and inadequate. The danger repeatedly arises of a reduction to a simple formula. e.g. all condemnations of the sixteenth century are only "misunderstandings", persons did not understood each other, they spoke at cross purposes. This was neither the historical state of affairs nor the way the individual sections make their judgments. We must repeatedly defend against such an evaluation of the study, whether from an extreme traditionalist or a progressive direction.

The Joint Ecumenical Commission and the Ecumenical Study Group (including the three working groups) have not carried out the final differentiated evaluation of the research. Perhaps this is just as well. The Ecumenical Study Group has fulfilled its task in direct, tangible work and brought to light many substantive insights. It is a lack, but also—at least for the first phase of the work—an advantage, that one has applied oneself over the years completely to the subject matter, without devoting too much time to a detached consideration of hermeneutical principles. Perhaps others, who have not participated in producing the results, could more freely and independently carry out such a hermeneutical reflection. It is also conceivable that the Ecumenical Study Group will itself investigate the results anew in this light in the course of future debates and reception.

The differentiated working through of the results is, in my opinion, an urgent desideratum of the future engagement with and exposition of the text. It is not possible in the framework of this contribution to fulfill this task. Still an sketch could be attempted, so that at least the direction toward a detailed answer becomes recognizable. Completeness and a detailed documentation is deliberately dispensed with.

By no means could all the condemnations be "lifted". No one can declare that the present partners are in general no longer struck by the past condemnations. Rather a very differentiated picture results.

1. Historical Perspectives

a) On both the Reformation and Catholic sides, there are condemnations which—as we recognize today—are not directed against the binding teaching of the church or against Reformation teachings, but are set against theological opinions, e.g. late Scholasticism or nominalism. Similarly there are condemnations from the Catholic side directed against relatively isolated individual sentences from lists of errors collected at second or even third hand to (cf. the contributions of Professor E. Iserloh and Professor V. Pfnür in this volume).

b) In this context we discover condemnations which refer to extreme positions and marginal statements of the opposing side. Not only are these almost necessarily open to misunderstanding through their own one-sidedness, but they easily become hardened into exclusive antitheses. Upon closer inspection such extreme positions are often not official church teaching, but personal theological opinion (e.g. even of Luther).

c) Many condemnations have a distinct "Sitz im Leben", e.g. in the contemporary practice of penance and indulgences as well as its critique. If we take them out of this context and understand them as principles, their original meaning is frequently overextended and overdrawn. For example, statements which are formulated in the struggle against abuses can only with care be converted into statements of principle.

d) It would not correspond to the seriousness of the past dispute to see everywhere only "theological shadow-boxing." Nevertheless, in spite of bitter polemic, it was not always and only a matter of ultimate objective difference. At least in some cases it was also a question of "wrangling over words" between combatants, as could be already then be ascertained (cf., e.g., Confessio Augustana and the Confutatio).

2. Hermeneutical Consequences

a) We can recognize today that many condemnations were formulated against extreme positions and pointed theses of the opponent which in their one-sided sharpness did not even then represent the comprehensive teaching. This is all the more true today.

b) In the formulations of the condemnations can be found one-sided emphases and occasionally also unclear formulations.

c) What sometimes was expressed in the past as a mutually exclusive antithesis can prove itself today as complementary in the light of an unprejudiced view of the total teaching and of broader possibilities of knowledge.

d) Missing doctrinal elements appear in other contexts and in other terminology.

e) Different approaches and stances toward the same comprehensive phenomena (cf., e.g., concupiscence) not only create confusing problems of definition, but also can in the end distort something held in common.

f) Opposed positions remain stuck sometimes in antitheses, appearing irreconcilable because they remain within the confines of a particular conceptuality, of limited forms of thought, conditioned by insurmountable constellations of the history of theology. One thinks here, e.g., of the shape of late medieval teaching about the Eucharist and its influence on the Reformation and Counter-reformation, especially in relation to the dispute over the sacrificial character of the Eucharist.

3. More Comprehensive Ways toward Reconciliation

a) With many antitheses it is necessary to move from the pointed and sometimes one-sided statements formulated in the condemnations back to the underlying intentions and "concerns." The genesis and structure of the doctrinal condemnations can be reconstructed on this basis, even and precisely when they relate to extreme positions. We must be careful, however, not to defuse objectively given antitheses on the basis of secondary motives.

b) Sometimes neither common judgment nor objective agreement is possible, but the respective intentions—if not yet the concepts and forms of thought—can possibly be recognized and better understood (cf. e.g., the problems of "passivity" and "cooperation" in the section on Justification). At the same time it is admitted that certain concepts of our own (e.g., "cooperation", "merit") are not free from obvious misunderstandings.

c) A frequently recurring formula states something important about mutual reproaches and rejections: Often the one side really does not advocate what the other side fears. We could demonstrate this in the mutual understanding of the relation between the principle "faith alone" and so-called "good works".

d) Frequently we can recognize that the different partners do not say yes and no to the same thing (cf.,e.g., the concept of merit). This requires then positive reassessment.

This can only be a first and rough survey which demonstrates the ramified network and the complex context of the investigations.

Beyond these more formal and hermeneutical reflections, the material results also must be carefully analyzed. Not many condemnations are unrestrictedly recommended for "lifting" in view of the present partner. Many problems remain where no full consensus or even no consensus at all was reached (cf. especially the basic questions in the understanding of Scripture, infallibility of the church, and the papacy). It would be indeed fatal if we were to remain fixed on the alternative "lifting" or "remaining difference". The value of the study consists precisely in the existence of many intermediate steps:

• Pointed and one-sided statements diminish;
• Differences can be reduced, antitheses can be broken down;
• Disputed questions, burdened by polemic, could be corrected and their tensions perhaps eased;
• The defusing of old antitheses can, under specific presuppositions, lead to the renunciation of the standard rejoinder of the past;
• Occasionally it is established that there is no longer a contradiction (cf., e.g., "the corruption of nature" in the Justification section);
• Sometimes a considerable convergence is reached (cf. the concept of concupiscence), which must be extended;
• Antitheses remain, but they are no longer exclusive, thus possibly no longer "church-dividing".

In addition and as something not to be overlooked, many convergences are provided with a condition which neither follows of itself nor is self-evident. A consensus in such cases is only then valid if the expressed condition in fact obtains (cf., e.g., the role of a biblically renewed concept of faith in the context of the "certainty of salvation" in the Justification section).

The spectrum is thus considerable. In addition, there enters into the study in general the already discussed presupposition: even if the present partner is no longer touched by the earlier condemnations, one cannot simply pass over the doctrinal decisions of the sixteenth century. We have already spoken about the hermeneutical problems. Many formulations in the investigations, that, e.g., the earlier doctrinal decisions are "dropped" or "lifted", are misleading and need case by case interpretation in the sense that they no longer concern the present partner. Such an explanation does not dissolve the binding character and the spiritual power of the doctrinal condemnations. The study specifically indicates in this connection that even if the doctrinal condemnations no longer concern the present partner, they retain an objective meaning for the present and the future. "This is not to say that today we could simply sweep aside the condemnations uttered at that earlier time. They are still important as salutary warnings, both for the members of the churches in which they were originally formulated, and for members of the other Christian confession in question. In each individual tradition, they warn us not to fall short of the clarifications already achieved in the sixteenth century in that particular church. In each given case, they warn members of the other church against interpreting and expressing their own tradition in such a way that antitheses that more recent theological development have made surmountable, break out anew, lending the rejections fresh topical force."[18]

The important question of the evaluation of the remaining oppositions remains. We have seen that in these oppositions very many nuanced gradations are revealed. If the oppositions are no longer of an exclusive kind, can be reduced, or for various reasons are no longer so sharp, etc., then a differentiation is needed in order to assess anew the weight of such oppositions. Doctrinal differences can remain which should not be obscured, but which no longer have or never had a church-dividing character. Differences remains which *by themselves* cannot justify continued church division. To this extent the fundamental difference is between church-dividing oppositions and those which lie below this line. Difficult questions repeatedly arise here in the course of study: To what extent are differences which remain really church-dividing? Are church-dividing effects allowed to continue even when it is no longer a serious question of exclusive doctrinal oppositions? Perhaps just here other problems also lie hidden. Talk of church-dividing effects or non-church-dividing oppositions presupposes a sufficiently common clarification of the being of the church and the criteria of its unity. This could not be accomplished, however, within the course of the Group's work, especially since it went beyond the given mandate. Certainly it is still worthwhile to investigate more exactly the talk of church-dividing and non-church-dividing oppositions. This is not possible, however, without the careful analysis of texts.

VI.

T he discussion of the study of the doctrinal condemnations has only slowly and hesitatingly begun. Whoever knows the genesis and process of consensus formation in the Ecumenical Study Group and its sub-groups is not surprised by this. The theological discussion by experts will have a great weight. Much will only become visible in the course of controversy. Such opinion building needs discourse and discussion if it does not wish to remain abstract. In light of the complexity and the differentiation of the material, it is certainly to be expected that on some points a wide-ranging spectrum of positions will be taken, not only on the basis of different theological perspectives, but also because of the difficulties of the strictly historical knowledge and of systematic assessment. It is desirable here that the ecumenical conversation and its results find a broader resonance. Sometimes expert theology gives the impression that it lives in two different cultures, on the one hand occupying itself intensively with ecumenical questions, and on the other reacting to ecumenical texts and questions with a significant indifference, even apathy. Precisely here is needed the judgment of experts who have themselves previously not participated in the studies.

What can we expect in the way of results? I would like to answer this question personally, without wanting to anticipate the reception process. It can only be dealt with in a small sketch.

1) If all the partners agree, we could declare that a series of doctrinal condemnations no longer concern the present partner. It remains to be clarified in detail which doctrinal statements these could be.

This official determination would be a great gain. Hindrances to a greater mutuality will be removed, stumbling blocks of ecumenical dialogue will no longer be in the way, and century-old wounds could be healed. Such a formal withdrawal in reference to the present partner could solemnly and publicly be carried out. This would be an analogy to the earlier declaration of condemnations, but also to the lifting of the excommunication of 1054 between Rome and Constantinople.

Consequently the participating churches must make well-aimed revisions of all catechisms, textbooks, and official statements. For the formation of theologians, religious teachers, and catechists this would be a great gain.

2) Even if synods and the church leadership should agree with the

investigations, it is of decisive importance that theological experts actually accept the officially received conclusions and establish them in their teaching. No theologian can simply write off the doctrinal condemnations of the sixteenth century without at least coming to terms with the results of the reception process. The theologians remain especially challenged to investigate more incisively the problems which are seen in the reception process to involve still unresolved difficulties and objections.

3) After a fruitful debate over the doctrinal condemnations, a step forward in the ecumenical conversation could also consist in an official delimitation of the obstacles which really exist between the churches. It is self-evident that even after these studies many open questions remain. It must be clarified whether the remaining differences do or do not have a church-dividing character. Such a delimitation would help give a more concentrated and well-aimed shape to future dialogue. Official doctrinal conversations concerning the remaining church-dividing differences would then become more urgent.

4) If in general or on individual points an official and mutual reception of the results of the study does not occur, the study can—if it is really attended to—lead to fruitful results: pointed assertions and extreme positions in the teaching can diminish; oppositions are reduced; polemically distorted questions of conflict are relaxed, if not yet solved; considerable convergences have become attainable, etc.

We cannot remain only with questions lying in the immediate orbit of the doctrinal condemnations of the sixteenth century. We have seen how everything must be repeatedly referred to the present partner. The clarifications that occurred in the meanwhile and the open questions of the ecumenical conversation cannot then in the long run be absent. One should not object that the study of the doctrinal condemnations have not more explicitly taken up these questions. Their study would have extensively widened the horizon and burst the given mandate. It is self-evident, however, that in a larger context especially the question about the church cannot be absent, which is made clear by every section of the study in its own way. This is necessary above all if ecumenical consequences which will lead further are drawn from the study. Only when an agreement about the being and the necessary structure of the church is attained can it be sufficiently clarified what the basic requirements must be for the unity of the church. The study has not expressed its opinion on the problem of the concept of unity, since this was not its assignment. But the unclarity of the concept "church-dividing/non-church-dividing differences" discloses how urgent this problem is. On this point further work must be done.

If agreement can be reached in the course of the process of reception, a very important partial goal on the way to full ecclesial communion would be attained. But ecclesial communion is more than merely theological speech. The churches must along the way manifest much more mutuality in their life and witness, internally and especially externally. In spite of cooperation at certain points, this still occurs too infrequently in view of the public character of the commission of the gospel. The churches do not live from the "doctrinal condemnations", nor even from their "reassessment", but from the Word of life, which they should helpfully proclaim to the world. Conversion always begins with themselves.

Common witness of faith and acts of love are also necessary because we cannot overlook the dangers of the overall enterprise. The reception process contains in itself a character of high venture and risk. Not only are theological results up for debate which cannot in such a form be worked out and debated every few years, but the introduction of a new stage of the ecumenical path is at stake. If the undertaking "doctrinal condemnations" completely fails, it could possibly prove more damaging than if it had not been begun. The "step back" can in fact become a set-back if it is deprived of the described support.

In fact we cannot remain with the addition of many details. Also with the question of the doctrinal condemnations it is a question of the whole. To this extent important and fundamental decisions are part of the reception process. In this conversation it must be shown whether the prior basic conviction can convincingly be upheld that there is a "basic consensus" between the churches. There are still not a few theologians on both sides who start from the premise that the accepted basic consensus is only an illusion of a common understanding of the faith. In reality there would exist amid all the detailed agreements a radical basic difference, which can be shown from the experience of God's work, through the understanding of Christian existence, up to the concept of the mediation of grace. In the end, even the relation of God and human beings in the events of salvation would be determined fundamentally differently by each side. The difference between the churches would exist at the root. We should not overrate such voices, but we also cannot overlook them. No taboo is allowed here. For the Catholic theologian this basic question becomes critical in the determination of the relationship between justification and the church. Still there is, in my opinion, at the center of the doctrine of justification the possibility of a firm basic consensus. But it is for many reasons very vulnerable. If a specific understanding of justification exclusively establishes itself and becomes the only theological principle, applied in a practical intent only critically-negatively, then the church and the mediation of grace within it can scarcely be understood adequately. Perhaps the more intensive occupation with the doctrinal condemnations forces some first clarifications.

The "step back" which was spoken of at the outset reveals itself as the return to the basic questions and as the approach to the sources. Only thus can the "step back" in the sense of the answer to the title of this contribution become true ecumenical progress, which even could introduce a new epoch of ecumenical conversation and a new relation. The "step back" also presupposes final decisions. The question of truth, the discovery of which all methods should promote, is the final challenge. The dispute about it should not lead to new doctrinal condemnations, but in the struggle for the truth of faith we must become neither compliant and timid nor obstinate and arrogant. Between these lies the selfless engagement for the truth and its freeing effect for all. This is a great responsibility. In it participate not only synods and church leadership, bishops and theologians, Roman authorities and the Lutheran World Federation, but also all Christians and especially those journalists who busy themselves with these not very contemporary and splendid, but nevertheless necessary and helpful, matters.

Notes

1. Cf. the introduction of the editors "The Origin and Growth of the Study," in Condemnations.

2. A section of these comments were first published under the title "Ist der 'Schritt zurück' ein ökumenischer Fortschritt? Die Aufarbeitung der gegensetigen Lehrverurteilungen der Kirchen: Ertrag und künftige Perspektiven aus katholischer Sicht," in *Ein Schritt zur Einheit der Kirchen: Können die gegenseitigen Lehrverurteilungen aufgehoben werden?*, by W.-D. Hauschild et al. (Regensburg, 1986) 127-147. The present essay also includes material from a lecture, "Die Verwerfungen in den reformatorischen Bekenntnisschriften und in den Lehrentscheidungen des Konzils von Trient: Treffen sie noch den heutigen Partner? Einführung in die Untersuchung und ihre Ergebnisse," which was presented at a study day on this topic at the spring meeting of the German Bishops' Conference, February 17-20, 1986, at Mallersdorff/Regensburg and which has remained unpublished. Both texts in part go back to earlier presentations which were formulated during the working out and publication of the entire project. Therefore some passages are found in a similar wording in the "Editors' Preface" (see nt. 1). Of course, much in the present synoptic presentation has been supplemented and deepened.

3. *Condemnations*, 168.

4. *LWF Report* 10 (1982): 59.

5. *Condemnations*, 169.

6. Op. cit., 168.

7. Op. cit., 20f.

8. Op. cit., 6f.

9. Cp. in another context the position of the Ecumenical Study Committee of the United Evangelical Lutheran Church in Germany, "Die Verwerfungen der Confessio Augustana und ihre gegenwärtige Bedeutung," Hanover 1980, Section V, no. 16.

10. *Condemnations*, 13-28.

11. Op. cit., 178.

12. Cf. K. Lehmann, *Signale der Zeit—Spuren des Heils* (Freiburg i.B.: 1983) 99-103; H. Fries & O. H. Pesch, *Streiten für die eine Kirche* (Munich: 1987).

13. Cf. on the history of the Leuenberg Agreement the comprehensive account by E. Schieffer, *Von Schauenburg nach Leuenberg: Entstehung und Bedeutung der Konkordie reformatorischer Kirchen in Europa*. Konfessionskundliche und kontroverstheologische Studien, 48 (Paderborn: 1983), with an appendix of documentation.

14. *Condemnations*, 169f.

15. *Toward the Healing of Schism*, Ecumenical Documents III (New York: Paulist Press, 1987) 127.

16. Cf. op. cit., ns. 94, 131, 123; and on the point, cf. further Joseph Ratzinger, *Principles of Catholic Theology: Building Stones for a Fundamental Theology* (San Francisco: Ignatius, 1987) 203-218.

17. *Condemnations*, 178-187.

18. Op. cit. 27.

Chapter Five

The Text "The Justification of the Sinner" in the Context of Previous Ecumenical Dialogues on Justification[1]

Harding Meyer

I N VIEW OF its central position in Lutheran thinking, one would expect
that the question of the witness and doctrine of justification would occupy
a special place in the ecumenical dialogues of the Lutheran churches with
other churches and would not be treated as simply one question among others.

The dialogues in fact meet this expectation. The endeavor toward
agreement in the understanding of justification has been given an appropriate
place in the dialogues of the Lutheran churches with other churches, even if not
in every regional or local dialogue. This is true:

in the dialogues with Reformed and Anglicans;
in the dialogues with Methodists and Catholics;
in the dialogues with Baptists, Old Catholics, and Orthodox.

1. LOCATION AND NATURE OF THE DISCUSSION OF JUSTIFICATION IN THE COURSE OF THE DIALOGUES

T he previous listing of dialogues intentionally formed three groups. This
grouping indicates that the location of the discussion of justification in the

course of the dialogues has varied. At some point, each of these dialogues addressed justification in a way that was recorded in their final reports. But the location of this discussion within the dialogue process and the degree of achieved agreement was not everywhere the same.

These differences are not accidental. Rather they indicate how the question of justification and of the doctrine of justification presents itself differently in the theological dialogue of Lutheranism with other churches depending on the respective partner. They also say something about the previous relation between the Lutheran church and the respective partner church and about the degree of achieved agreement.

1.1. The Dialogue with Reformed and Anglicans

In the dialogues beginning in the 1960s between *Lutheran and Reformed* the doctrine of justification was not as such initially addressed. The reason was obvious: no Lutheran-Reformed opposition existed or exists here. This was stated by the later Leuenberg Agreement (1973)[2] and was stated in a very similar way by the first North American dialogue (1966).[3]

This situation changes with the Leuenberg Agreement. Suddenly, the common assertions about the message of justification become the core of the total text.[4] The reason for the change was a shift in the goal of the dialogue. While earlier dialogues sought to work through existing controversial questions, the Leuenberg Agreement was concerned with the establishment of church fellowship. The doctrine of justification is here ascribed the appropriate significance and function according to Reformation convictions. In the common understanding of the gospel as message of justification—along with a corresponding common understanding and use of the sacraments—the effective basis is given for church fellowship.

In the continuation of the North American Lutheran-Reformed dialogue, the same can be observed. There also the question of the doctrine of justification became an explicit subject of discussion only when the third dialogue phase (1981-1983) turned to the realization of church fellowship.[5]

Similarly, in the *dialogue with Anglicans* justification was not at first explicitly discussed. Here again one finds the argument that the doctrine of justification as such is not controversial between Anglicans and Lutherans. Already in the first dialogue phase, however, it was indicated that a distinct discussion of the question of justification would be necessary as the dialogue proceeded further. The North American dialogue stated that if the "future unity" should be a "unity of common confession," then the central place in this confession would have to be occupied by a common understanding of the gospel, i.e., by precisely that which the doctrine of justification seeks to express.[6]

This discussion then occurred in the continuation of the Anglican-Lutheran dialogue. In the Report of the Anglican-Lutheran European Commission (1982), which stated that "there are no longer any serious obstacles on the way towards the establishment of full communion between our two Churches,"[7] it had previously confirmed and outlined a "common understanding" of justification as the first of its agreements"[8] The same was the case with the second phase of the North American dialogue (1976-1980), whose results led to the declaration of "interim Eucharist fellowship" (1982) and to a third dialogue phase with the declared goal of "full communion." Here also a "Joint Statement on Justification"[9] and a "Joint Statement on the Gospel"[10] are first in the series of consensus statements.

The discussion of the doctrine of justification in the dialogue with the Reformed and in the dialogue with the Anglicans thus has followed essentially the same pattern: corresponding to the conviction that justification neither is nor has been controversial with this partner, the doctrine of justification has been explicitly taken up only when the moment of the realization of communion has been reached. The treatment of justification here does not aim at overcoming doctrinal differences, but from the outset serves the definition of the consensus necessary for communion.

1.2 The Dialogue with Methodists and Catholics

The second group of dialogues is marked by a thematization of justification at the very beginning because theological controversy has especially focussed on this issue.

This is particularly apparent in the Lutheran-Methodist dialogue. On both the international and national (German) levels, the question of justification was taken up immediately after the discussion of the Bible and its authority.

The same is fundamentally true of the Catholic-Lutheran dialogue, although there matters present themselves in a more differentiated way.

In the international Catholic-Lutheran dialogue, the very first session up the justification question, along with the Scripture-Tradition problematic. The Malta Report (1972) devoted several sections to this topic. The central, repeated statement was that a "far reaching consensus" and a "far reaching agreement" existed in the understanding of justification and the doctrine of justification.[11] That the dialogue at that time did not investigate in detail questions about the doctrine of justification was the result of the conviction that these questions had already been essentially worked through by the theological and ecumenical research of the preceding years. They believed that here a broad consensus could be presupposed and confirmed, without the dialogue itself needing to work it through or extensively to reproduce it.

In its return to the topic of justification in the recent third phase of the international dialogue, the commission has not sought to address the question of justification as such. The concern is rather with "the question of the Church and the nature of its instrumentality in God's plan of salvation," a question which the Lutheran side in particular immediately interpreted as a question about "the reciprocal relations or implications of the understanding of justification and of the understanding of the church." It is recognized that "this question has been present in international Catholic-Lutheran dialogue from the beginning," but—and this is important—the question is now taken up in a new perspective shaped by the results which have been reached by the dialogues: the "question of the realization of Catholic-Lutheran communion,[12] especially as raised and investigated in the previous document of the dialogue, *Facing Unity* (1985). This means that the doctrine of justification will no longer be taken up only in relation to the clarification of controversial questions, but also in relation to the realization of communion. The perspective under which justification is discussed thus begins to shift in a way that brings it closer to the perspective in which justification has been handled in the dialogues with Reformed and Anglicans.

The same can be said, I believe, about the Catholic-Lutheran dialogue in the US, which only late, 15 years after its beginning, explicitly addressed the question of justification and then discussed it over a five year period (1978-1982). The reason for this late thematization was not that this problematic was bracketed as the most difficult of controversial themes and only discussed after working through preliminary controversial questions. As the Preface and Introduction to the text *Justification by Faith* show, the question of justification had "been touched upon or alluded to in previous sessions of the dialogue"[13] and the dialogue was thoroughly aware of and did not call into question the "far-reaching consensus" in the understanding of justification which the international dialogue had affirmed.[14] George Lindbeck, a member of the dialogue from its inception, has said the same: The conviction of an agreement in justification

> has been the basis of the dialogue between Lutheran and Roman Catholic churches in the last two decades. Those who proposed the American dialogue back in 1964 were persuaded that our churches, though widely separated on many issues, did share the same basic conviction that salvation through Jesus Christ is a free gift received in faith. If we had not believed that there was this fundamental unity underneath all our differences, there would have been no point in seeing how far it is now possible to overcome divisions on such secondary,

though vital, issues as the Lord's Supper, ministry, papacy, and infallibility.[15]

The explicit thematization of justification at a relatively late point in the dialogue process thus was not for the sake of overcoming a still existing disagreement and working out a yet to be achieved consensus. Rather, as the text states, it was for the sake of "a greater clarity about the way to understand and speak of justification."[16] The desire for "greater clarity" developed in a situation different from that of the beginning of the dialogue. In this new situation, the concern was not primarily centered on overcoming controversial, church-dividing questions, but rather on "proclaiming our common faith" and "joint proclamation of the message of justification."[17]

The US Catholic-Lutheran dialogue thus dealt with justification in a perspective comparable to that in which it was addressed in the dialogues with Reformed and Anglicans.

The section on justification in *Condemnations of the Reformation Era* also falls within this perspective. It is not only—along with the US dialogue report—the most detailed ecumenical document on justification, but also the specific approach of the total study, the testing of mutual and binding doctrinal condemnations, indicates that the concern was no longer just theological agreement, but already was, as the final report of the Joint Ecumenical Commission put it, "to delineate, deepen, and strengthen the degree of Christian fellowship and community between the churches that had been achieved."[18] As the Lutheran-Reformed Leuenberg discussions had already shown, binding doctrinal condemnations by their very nature become a problem only at an advanced point in the movement toward agreement, when, in contrast to earlier times, new and "growing ecumenical ties" press toward a "closer fellowship," one in which the churches will be officially committed to each other.[19] Just as in the international Catholic-Lutheran dialogue, so here the orientation is "toward the goal...to arrive at full community [*Gemeinschaft*], even if new and great tasks arise along this road."[20]

1.3. The Dialogue with Baptists, Old Catholics, and Orthodox

In this third group of dialogues, justification has not remained undiscussed, but it has not received the appropriate weight which it has received in the other dialogues.

Baptist-Lutheran dialogue began on the international level only in 1987.[21] The dialogue in West Germany (1980-81) spoke only briefly about "the justification of the godless by grace alone for the sake of Christ" in connection with the question "Baptism and Faith/Faith and Baptism.[22] The first common statement from the dialogue in the US (1979-81) begins with a section on the understanding of faith in which, first together and then above all from the Lutheran side, it speaks of "the gracious justification of God through faith in Christ." The emphasis, however, falls on questions about "the nature of that faith" and faith as "divine initiative and human response." The differences between Lutherans and Baptists in these matters were interpreted as "differences of emphasis" which derive from the different historical origins of Lutheranism and the Baptist movement.[23]

The brief agreement between the Evangelical Church in Germany (EKD) and the Diocese of the Old Catholics in Germany on a mutual invitation to participation in the Eucharist (1985) was not preceded by a true dialogue. It was developed at two sittings of a joint commission which drew upon other dialogue results. The section of the agreement which dealt with justification in a very concise consensus formulation was taken over almost verbatim from the Report of the Anglican-Lutheran European Commission.[24]

In the Lutheran-Orthodox dialogue, a full thematization of justification has so far run into difficulties, although this dialogue has been conducted for some time on various levels and in many places. The first discussion between the EKD and the Russian Orthodox Church (1959) offered a very tentative treatment of justification through faith.[25] Neither here nor in any other dialogue context, however, has this beginning been continued in a way that produced results. The doctrine and problematic of justification, especially as it developed in the Reformation, is seen by the Orthodox as closely tied to Western and Latin thought and to the history of Western theology and is experienced as unfamiliar, if not strange. The Communique, of the 1985 dialogue of the EKD with the Romanian Orthodox Church, which several times touches on justification, says that "assertions about justification, which are important for Western and especially Reformation theology, find hardly any anchorage in the Orthodox liturgy." For Orthodox thought and piety, "deification" (*theosis*) rather than justification is the content of the saving work of God in humanity."[26]

The one Lutheran-Orthodox dialogue which so far has produced a common official statement on justification is that between the Russian Orthodox Church and the Lutheran Church of Finland, "Salvation as Justification and Deification" (1977).[27]

1.4 The Threefold Mode of Discussing Justification

The central position which, from a Lutheran viewpoint, is to be ascribed to the doctrine of justification means that the form and manner of its treatment in ecumenical dialogue also takes a special shape.

Lutherans will expect that justification is treated in at least a *threefold manner or mode*:

• first, justification must be treated in its various aspects as a clearly outlined doctrinal topic (a "dogmatic" discussion);

• second, the question of the relative importance of the doctrine of justification—the question of its centrality and thus of its function as a criterion of all the church's preaching and teaching—must be directly and fundamentally discussed (a "criteriological" discussion);

• third, this criteriological function of the doctrine of justification must be thought through in relation to all other controversial questions and applied case by case (a "criteriological-applicative" discussion).

This may sound overly schematic. In fact, when one looks at the totality of dialogues so far, the doctrine of justification has been discussed in just this way. Of course, each of these modes of discussion is closely related to the others and none can be isolated.

In the following, only the first two modes of discussing justification will be depicted. A portrayal of the "criteriological-applicative" discussion will here have to be dispensed with.[28]

2. THE "DOGMATIC" DISCUSSION OF JUSTIFICATION

2.1 The Doctrine of Justification as Explication of the Gospel

In the discussion of the doctrine of justification in the dialogues, "gospel" is always the starting point and framing concept. The message of justification and the doctrine of justification are *explications of the gospel*. This usually explicit differentiation and interrelation of gospel and justification is fundamental. It forms so to speak the first layer of that which is said together about justification. In addition, "gospel" is then more broadly determined, in all cases Christologically and occasionally in relation to the Trinity.[29]

Both the differentiation and the interrelation of gospel and justification are important. The interrelation preserves the Christological ground of justification and protects it from a merely anthropological interpretation. The differentiation avoids an exclusive identification of gospel and justification as if the gospel of Jesus Christ could only be expressed in the terminology of justification. Such an identification would be biblically and theologically indefensible and have problematic consequences for the dialogue.

2.2 Consensus Formulas on Justification

For the most part, the message of justification as explication of the gospel is summarized in the dialogues in short, often formulaic statements.[30] They claim to state the consensus between the partners which exists or which has been reached in the course of the "dogmatic" discussion of the doctrine of justification. As expressions of achieved agreement—and not as the agreement itself—these consensus formulas should not be valued too highly. Nevertheless, they do more than simply arrange theological abstractions. In their formulations they are reminiscent of statements in confessions. They can thus be seen as part of the preliminary stage of the formation of an ecclesial confession, especially since their wording is also taken from confessions of the churches.

It is important that the true core of these formulas on justification consists of three elements which belong closely together and form a whole, even if their order can vary. There is a common affirmation of:

• the *complete graciousness of justification*, which is underlined in most texts by the use of "alone" and supplemented by the explicit rejection of a merited justification;

• *faith as the realization of justification*, by which one can assume that in the dialogue statements with Catholics, Anglicans, and Old Catholics, the "only" (by grace) relates grammatically and materially also to faith;

• the exclusive *foundation of justification in the saving act of God in Christ*.

It is thereby assured that the "dogmatic" consensus on justification summarized in these assertions agrees with the basic requirements for a right understanding of justification laid out in the Lutheran confessions. In the well known words of the Formula of Concord, "the only essential and necessary elements of justification are the grace of God, the merit of Christ, and faith which accepts these in the promise of the Gospel."[31] The dogmatic consensus on justification achieved or confirmed in the dialogues coincides also with the "freely justified for Christ's sake through faith" which is central for the article on justification in the Augsburg Confession (CA 4). On this basis, the consensus on the doctrine of justification "as such" (the dogmatic discussion) can be seen as valid.

It is important to note here that what is said in these formulas on justification in the Lutheran-Catholic and Lutheran-Methodist dialogues does not lag behind that which Lutherans have said with Reformed and Anglicans as the expression of an already existing consensus.

In this connection, the US document requires special mention. This text also emphasizes a formulaic consensus statement that our entire hope for and trust in salvation and justification rests on nothing other than Christ, his gospel, and God's promise.[32] This statement does not present itself as fully equivalent with the Reformation doctrine of justification in so far as it does not make use of the Reformation's concepts.[33] In this sense, it does not appear as a "consensus formula on justification" in the same formal sense as do those in the dialogue statements already discussed. Nevertheless, it claims to express the "central concern" of the Reformation doctrine of justification, and thus ultimately the "solus Christus,"[34] and to describe a "fundamental consensus on the gospel."[35] On the basis of this consensus, salvation and the justifying act of God can be expressed and interpreted in terms other than those of the Reformation without the difference in terminology destroying the unity reached in the fundamental consensus.[36]

The text of the Ecumenical Study Group which produced the *Condemnations* study offers no such summary "consensus formula on justification." In light of the specific task set for the group—testing the historical condemnations—such a formula is not to be expected. In any case, a description of the results of the dialogues on justification cannot only consider the consensus formulas. The agreement on justification which has been achieved in the dialogues is condensed in these formulas, but cannot be reduced to them.

2.3 The Specific Problem Areas

In relation to the individual problem areas which belong to the question of justification, the Catholic-Lutheran dialogue on justification offers the most comprehensive framework for organizing the debate over justification in the other dialogues. Among the Catholic-Lutheran dialogues, the Ecumenical Study Group offers the most detailed breakdown of the problematic of justification in its seven points, including its excursus on "Justification, Baptism, and Penance" with its discussion of the idea and practice of satisfaction.

The five problem areas set out and discussed by the American dialogue coincide with the corresponding points of the Ecumenical Study Group.[37] Only the question of the sinfulness of the justified is not as such thematized by the Ecumenical Study Group, but is rather taken up in the context of the forensic understanding of justification and, briefly, in the treatment of the concept of concupiscence.[38]

The three aspects of the justification problematic discussed in the Anglican-Catholic dialogue can also find a place in the framework set by the Ecumenical Study Group.[39] As a fourth point, this dialogue discusses the theme "The Church and Salvation,"[40] going beyond both the Ecumenical Study Group and the American dialogue. Here the dialogue steps outside the framework of the doctrine of justification as such and the strictly "dogmatic" discussion of justification and is already addressing the question of the ecclesiological implications and consequences of the doctrine of justification.

2.4. The Central Significance of the Question of Justification as "Forensic/external/proclamatory" Event or as "Effective/internal/transforming" Event

Obviously the results of the dogmatic discussion of justification cannot here be investigated in detail.[41] It is striking and worthy of note that one aspect of the problem has been taken up by all the dialogues and given a central place in the total structure of the discussion. It is the old question of the "forensic" understanding of justification, which in Lutheranism has possessed a character and weight as in no other confession. For the judgment of the total dialogue on justification, it seems to me important to be conscious of this particular "front" on which Lutheranism so to speak stands over against the rest of Christianity, even if the nature of this "over against" varies from case to case.

2.4.1. The Catholic-Lutheran Dialogue

In the Catholic-Lutheran dialogue, it is already stated in the Malta Report of 1972 that the consensus there described on the full graciousness and unconditionality of the gift of salvation does not imply or require an understanding of justification which is "limited to individual forgiveness of sins" and "a purely external declaration of the justification of the sinner." The consensus is rather that "the righteousness of God actualized in the Christ event is conveyed to the sinner through the message of justification as an encompassing reality basic to the new life of the believer."[42]

The US dialogue, which in fact begins with the question of forensic justification, and the Ecumenical Study Group deal in much greater detail with this problem and the agreement reached on it. In summary, the problem and the agreement present themselves in both dialogues in the following way:

On the *Lutheran* side, it is held that the graciousness and unconditionality of salvation are preserved by a forensically stamped understanding of justification: the justification of the sinner occurs as the gracious acquittal by God, who reckons the righteousness of Christ to the sinner, and in the faith of the person who accepts this promise. Righteousness is and remains a "reality on the side of God" (*iustitia aliena*), "outside of us" (*extra nos*), in which the person participates in the mode of faith.[43] Without underestimating or denying that justifying faith effects renewal and sanctification in the person, these effects of grace in the person are not counted as "parts of justification itself," but rather are understood as its "fruits."[44] It is feared that otherwise believers could again be thrown "back on their own resources."[45]

On the *Catholic* side, it is emphasized that justifying grace is not only an acquitting grace, but also a grace which is granted to the person interiorly, a renewing and transforming grace (*gratia infusa; gratia inhaerens; gratia gratum faciens*).[46] Without underestimating or denying the forensic aspect, one worries that justification understood only in forensic images and categories is exposed to the danger of disregarding the creative power of the grace of God in the person and of forgetting faith's praise of this life-renewing grace.[47]

The result is that the differences which are in fact present do not reach so far that one doctrinal position overlooks—not to mention denies—what the other emphasizes, or intends—not to mention argues for—what the other side fears.[48] The graciousness and unconditionality of salvation and the life-renewing power and sanctifying effect of grace are upheld on both sides, even if with different points of emphasis and from "different approaches."[49] These differences do give rise to mutual questions and warnings. They do not, however constitute "an antithesis which cuts through everything we have in common and makes mutual condemnation compellingly necessary."[50] This conclusion is confirmed through New Testament exegesis as well as through insights into the history of theology.[51]

As we have seen, the question of "forensic/external-effective/internal" justification is certainly not the only one the Lutheran-Catholic dialogue on justification has discussed, nor can the other questions be simply reduced to this common denominator. Nevertheless, at least in the judgment of the US dialogue, it appears that the total problematic is here especially concentrated. It contends that the differences in the understanding of justification between Catholics and Lutherans finally come together in a comprehensive difference that it characterizes with the concepts "transformational" and "proclamatory."[52] These concepts incorporate in a new and perhaps more adequate manner what was meant with the traditional concepts "effective" and "forensic"[53] and describe "two different sets of concerns" or "accents" or "emphases"[54] that do not oppose each other, but go together and can complement one another.

The Ecumenical Study Group did without such a brief summary of the total problem. It offered, however, two materially very full statements which evidently claim—similarly to the US dialogue—to characterize in a summary fashion the "varying concerns and emphases" while indicating their legitimacy and complementarity.[55] It would be perhaps a certain abridgement, but certainly no misrepresentation, if the so described concerns and emphases were labeled with the two characteristics used in the US dialogue.

When one surveys the dialogues of Lutherans with other churches from this perspective, the problematic concentrates itself even more clearly on this question of "forensic (external)"-"effective (internal)" justification than it does in the Catholic-Lutheran dialogue with its richness of problems and aspects.

2.4.2. The Lutheran-Reformed Dialogue

The Lutheran-Reformed dialogue in the US (1966) speaks of the different ways in which Lutherans and Reformed differentiate and interrelate "justification" and "sanctification." This difference does not call into question the consensus on the doctrine of justification, since "each tradition has sought to preserve the wholeness of the gospel as including the forgiveness of sins and the renewal of life."[56]

The Leuenberg Agreement goes a step further. It describes justification so that the aspect of renewal and sanctification is included:

> Through his word, God by his Holy Spirit calls all men to repent and believe, and assures the believing sinner of his righteousness in Jesus Christ. Whoever puts his trust in the gospel is justified in God's sight for the sake of Jesus Christ, and set free from the accusation of the law. In daily repentance and renewal, he lives within the fellowship in praise of God and in service to others, in the assurance that God will bring his kingdom in all its fullness. In this way, God creates new life, and plants in the midst of the world the seed of a new humanity.[57]

Because "justification" in the Leuenberg Agreement did not mean "an isolated doctrinal theme which could be differentiated in some way from sanctification, but rather a total interpretation of the saving act in Christ," it became possible for the Reformed "to acknowledge the central relative importance of the article of justification."[58]

2.4.3. The Lutheran-Anglican Dialogue

The Lutheran-Anglican dialogue in the US (1980) also diagnosed "different emphases" between Lutherans and Anglicans: "Among Lutherans, salvation has commonly been synonymous with the forgiveness of sins; among Episcopalians, salvation has commonly included not only the forgiveness of sins but also the call to and promise of sanctification. As we continue to listen to each other, may God grant that justification by grace and the new life in the Spirit abound."[59]

The Anglican-Lutheran European Commission attempted, without ascertaining any differences of accent, to describe the relation between justification and sanctification or forensic and effective justification: "We are accounted righteous and are made righteous before God only by grace through faith because of the merits of our Lord and Saviour Jesus Christ".[60]

2.4.4. The Anglican-Catholic Dialogue

The Anglican-Catholic dialogue confirmed and made clear what Anglicans had already said to their Lutheran partners: A primarily forensic-imputative understanding of justification was a concern of "Reformation theologians," not of Anglicans. It is stated that: "Anglican theologians of the 16th and 17th century saw imputed and imparted righteousness as distinct to the mind, but indissoluble in worship and life."[61] Thus the problem "forensic-effective justification is essentially a Protestant-Catholic and not an Anglican-Catholic problem. Catholics and Anglicans—so the dialogue seems to wish to say—have here fundamentally always been of the same opinion. In a rather unique "neither-nor" formulation, it is said: "Roman Catholic interpreters of Trent and Anglican theologians alike have insisted that justification and sanctification are neither wholly distinct from nor unrelated to one another"[62] The text then describes the contents of this belonging-together of being declared and being made righteous, of justification and sanctification.[63]

2.4.5. The Lutheran-Methodist Dialogue

The Lutheran-Methodist dialogue, from which one could expect that it would find its focus in the question "justification/sanctification", led in West Germany to a genuine consensus statement, extensively identical with that in the Leuenberg Agreement. It stands under the heading "Justification by Grace Alone." Like the Leuenberg Agreement, it integrates the aspect of renewal "in faith, hope, and love."[64] In the following section, the question of the relation between justification and sanctification was furthered explored. The shared understanding of sanctification as "the appropriation of the holiness of Christ (gift) and also the effect of justification, which is to find expression in the life of the believer (task)" does not eliminate the difference between Lutherans and Methodists in the understanding and interrelation of justification and sanctification: "while Lutherans stress sanctification as a gift of God in the event of justification, Methodists in their understanding of sanctification place particular weight on the life-changing experience of the grace of God and on growth in love." In any case, these differences are seen as a matter of "different emphases," which can contribute to "mutual enrichment" if the danger of "one-sidedness" is avoided.[65]

The international Lutheran-Methodist dialogue formulated no consensus

statement along the lines of the West German dialogue, even though the
individual elements of this consensus are almost without exception found
there.[66] A stronger reference is made to a series of differences in which the
Methodist insistence on the "effective," renewing aspect of the event of
salvation is made clear: the righteousness of Christ is not only "imputed" but
also "imparted; justification as the initiation of a life of personal appropriation
and progressive sanctification; emphasis on the new birth and the effectiveness
of divine grace, to which Methodists "dare set no limit...in this present life"
(perhaps through a *simul justus et peccator*); the possibility of the realization
of "perfect love."[67] Nevertheless, the total Report must be so understood that
also in the question of justification "sufficient agreement" was reached for the
recommendation to both churches "to declare and establish full fellowship of
Word and Sacrament."[68] One of the Lutheran participants, however, was not
able to agree to this recommendation.

2.4.6. The Catholic-Methodist Dialogue

The closeness of Methodist concerns to those of Catholics becomes
especially clear when Methodists and Catholics discuss justification. This
occurred in the international Catholic-Methodist dialogue and
characteristically stands under the heading: "The Holy Spirit at Work in
Justification and Regeneration." First, the graciousness of salvation is assured
("prevenient grace" as key concept). Then "it is the Spirit's special office to
maintain the divine initiative that precedes all human action and reaction."[69] It
is primarily a matter of the work of the Holy Spirit, which is the recreation of
the person, placing the believer in a process of sanctification that "leads to
perfect love," to a "life, lived out in faith, hope, and love."[70] "Forensic"
categories are in fact also used: justification as the restoration of "a right
relationship" of the sinner to God; as being "regarded and treated as
righteous."[71] Such use, however, is always immediately complemented by
"effective" categories, which finally dominate; for "justification is not an
isolated forensic episode, but is part of a process which finds its consummation
in regeneration and sanctification, the participation of human life in the
divine."[72]

Synopsis

This overview shows three things above all:

1) It shows that all dialogues about justification have discussed the
question "forensic (external)" - "effective (internal)" justification. This
question has taken a central place and in some dialogues has been simply the
question.

2) It shows thereby to what degree a conception of justification which emphasizes the "forensic" aspect is a *specificum* which differentiates the Lutheran understanding of justification from that of other churches and confessions.

3) It shows finally how all the dialogues have come to a materially identical result, viz., that there does not exist here a divisive opposition in content, but a difference in viewpoint, accent, or concern, in so far as the non-Lutheran side neither overlooks nor denies, but definitely recognizes and affirms, the concern about the "forensic" and thereby the continuing graciousness of justification and salvation, and in so far as the Lutheran side neither overlooks nor denies, but definitely recognizes and affirms, the concern about the "effective" and thereby the life-renewing power of grace and of the saving divine act.

2.5. The "Dialogue-definitive" Status and Differentiated Structure of Consensus

The broad front upon which the totality of dialogues have discussed justification, the diversity of the partners, the difference of the approaches, the variety of the questions—and nevertheless the material congruence of the results makes it appear that in relation to the churches of the West it is time to speak without reserve or hesitation of an ecumenical consensus in the understanding of justification as such. This consensus should "be ascribed a 'dialogue-definitive' status, which should not be repeatedly called into question by ever more subtle argumentative strategies."[73]

This result presupposes that we have been liberated from an "abstract" conception of consensus. Disregarding the nature of Christian communion, such an abstract conception only accepts unanimity and uniformity of statements and convictions. We should rather understand ecumenical consensus as that agreement in the confession of the faith which is oriented to the nature of Christian communion, a communion which lives in the multiformity of its members.

In accord with its nature and structure, this consensus on the doctrine of justification is such that in it two understandings of justification stamped by different concerns meet one another, which in view of the theological analysis and the biblical findings a) demonstrate themselves to be legitimate, b) do not in their difference block or exclude each other, but rather c) are open to each other, even d) need each other, in so far as they are mutually reinforcing and e) rest on the common confession of salvation in Christ alone, solely given by grace and received in faith.

3. THE "CRITERIOLOGICAL" DISCUSSION OF JUSTIFICATION

T hat the doctrine of justification holds a central position, determining all the church's preaching and doctrine, has belonged inextricably to the Lutheran understanding of justification. Consequently, most dialogues have taken into account that a discussion of justification in a dialogue would be incomplete so long as this aspect is not considered, even if this aspect has then been treated in varying details.

3.1. The Dialogue with Reformed and Methodists

The *Lutheran-Reformed dialogue* in the US (1966) referred to the relative importance of the doctrine of justification as it confirmed, along with a commonality, also a real, contextually understood difference between Lutherans and Reformed. It stated: "We are agreed that the doctrine of justification by faith is fundamental in both traditions. We recognize, however, that for Lutherans this doctrine has played a more formative role in the articulation of theology. This difference is due in part to the historical situations in which Luther and Calvin did their theological work.[74]

The Leuenberg Agreement is stronger in its expression of commonality, but also more differentiated. Only after the doctrine of justification—including its renewing, transforming ("effective") aspects—has been described as the "true understanding" of the gospel is it said: "In this understanding, we... reaffirm the common conviction of the Reformation confessions, that the unique mediation of Jesus Christ in salvation is the heart of the Scriptures, and that the message of justification as the message of God's free grace is the measure of all the church's preaching."[75]

It is here important to note that the doctrine of justification as it was earlier formulaically defined is not itself declared to be the "heart" or "measure." It is rather the "concern" or "subject matter" of the of the doctrine of justification which counts as "heart" and "measure": "*the unique mediation of Jesus Christ in salvation*" and "the message of justification *as the message of God's free grace*."

The approach of the German *Lutheran-Methodist* dialogue was quite similar. The apparent dependence of this dialogue on the Leuenberg Agreement, at least in its formulations about justification, has already been noted. Here also "*the message of the free grace of God*, as it found expression in the Pauline-Reformation doctrine of justification"—thus again not the doctrine of justification in its doctrinal form, but rather its "subject matter"— is described as recognized by both churches as the "key to the understanding of the action of God and as measure of all preaching."[76]

3.2. The Catholic-Lutheran Dialogue

The relative importance of the doctrine of justification has been discussed with special attention and thoroughness in the Catholic-Lutheran dialogue.

Not however in the Ecumenical Study Group! In view of their specific mandate—testing the doctrinal condemnations of the sixteenth century—this is fully understandable. It is all the more striking that in the study's summary one encounters a strong affirmation of the central theological place and comprehensive critical function of the doctrine of justification. Not only does it state the following: "For that reason, the doctrine of justification—and above all, its biblical foundation—will always retain a special function in the church. That function is continually to remind Christians that we sinners live solely from the forgiving love of God, which we merely allow to be bestowed on us, but which we in no way—in however modified a form—'earn' or are able to tie down to any preconditions or postconditions." It then continues and with these words concludes: "The doctrine of justification therefore becomes the touchstone for testing at all times whether a particular interpretation of our relationship to God can claim the name of 'Christian.' At the same time, it becomes the touchstone for the church, for testing at all times whether its proclamation and its praxis correspond to what has been given to it by its Lord."[77]

Earlier sections of the document had indirectly prepared for and grounded this statement. Nevertheless, it requires supplemental references to the Malta Report and especially to the US dialogue text, in which the question of the relative theological importance of the doctrine of justification was discussed in greater detail.

3.2.1. The Malta Report

Already in the report of the first meeting of the international dialogue commission (1967) it was stated (and this passage was taken over by the Malta Report with only small changes[78]): "Although it appeared that considerable agreement could possibly be reached in the understanding of the doctrine of justification itself, questions arose as to what position or degree of importance it has in theology and whether the resultant consequences for the life and teaching of the church are judged in the same way on each side."[79]

This statement has not seldom been understood as if it did not go beyond the *question* of the relative importance of the doctrine of justification. Accordingly, the Malta Report is then interpreted as if it presented a far reaching consensus on the doctrine of justification itself, but lest the question of its relative theological importance open.

Such a reading misses the mark. The cited passage includes a closely coupled, but clearly differentiated double question, which we encounter again in a very similar form in the US Catholic-Lutheran dialogue: on the one hand, the question of the relative theological importance of the doctrine of justification and, on the other hand, the question about the "resultant consequences for the life and teaching of the church."

The first question was discussed and answered in the dialogue commission. The question of the relative theological importance of the doctrine of justification, i.e., of the doctrine of justification as "center" and "measure," content and criterion of the doctrine and life of the church, is addressed in the previous paragraph of the Malta Report.[80] There it is stated with reference to the previously described "far reaching consensus" on the understanding of justification: "In this sense justification can be understood as expressing *the totality of the event of salvation;*" the message of justification "must be articulated ever anew as an important *interpretation of the center of the gospel.*"

Thereby a clear—and also Catholic—Yes is given to justification as the "center" or content of the gospel, even if with two closely interrelated conditions: That justification is a "total expression" of the saving event, an interpretation of "the center of the gospel," holds especially in certain situations, as in Paul's "concrete dispute with Jewish legalism" or generally when "legalistic conditions for the reception of salvation" are imposed. Thus, in situations of a different sort, "the event of salvation...can also be expressed comprehensively in other representations derived from the New Testament."[81]

What holds for the doctrine of justification as "center" or content of the event of salvation holds also for it as "measure" or criterion. When it is jointly said that the message of justification as "interpretation of the center of the gospel ... must be articulated ever anew" for the sake of "the foundation of Christian freedom in opposition to legalistic conditions for the reception of salvation," it implies a recognition in principle of the continuing critical function of the doctrine of justification, at least in view of situations in which the commonly affirmed unconditionality of the saving gift of God[82] appears threatened.

3.2.2. The US Dialogue

The most detailed discussion of the question of the relative theological importance of the doctrine of justification took place in the *US Catholic-Lutheran dialogue*:

First, the Lutheran conception of the article on justification as "the article by which the church stands and falls" is presented in the context of a presentation of the Reformation doctrine of justification and by means of statements in the Smalcald Articles. The Christological orientation (*solus*

Christus) is thus emphasized.[83]

Second, at the end of the treatment of the individual controversial questions related to the doctrine of justification as such, a description of the problematic is given. On the one side, it is shown why and in what sense the Lutheran Reformers thought that the doctrine of justification by faith— "understood as the correlative of the sole mediatorship of Christ"[84] —must be emphasized as comprehensive critical principle and why this is still valid for Lutherans today, even if the possibility of a questionable use of this principle is not overlooked. On the other side, it is shown why Catholics "are wary of using any one doctrine as the absolute principle" by which the doctrine and life of the church is to be measured, although they acknowledge that at all times "the church stands under the gospel and is to be judged by it."[85]

Third, the biblical investigations[86] show that "a faith-centered and forensically conceived picture of justification is of major importance for Paul and, in a sense, for the Bible as a whole, although it is by no means the only biblical or Pauline way of representing God's saving work."[87]

Fourth, the final section of the text ("Growing Convergences") includes a sub-section on "Use of the Criterion."[88] As introduction it is said that for the first time in the document that Catholics recognize the comprehensive critical function of that which Lutherans view as "the heart of the gospel" and describe with the help of the doctrine of justification[89] This agreement on the definition of the criterion does not mean, as is then shown, that agreement always exists on the application of the criterion to certain "beliefs, practices, and structures."

Fifth and finally, this last section closes with a common formulation of a "fundamental affirmation,"[90] which is not fully equivalent with the Reformation understanding of justification, but which includes its central concern, without excluding the Catholic concern. It is equally valid for Catholics and Lutherans as criterion for "all church practices, structures, and traditions," for "all Christian teachings, practices, and offices."[91] This fundamental affirmation, already referred to at the beginning of the document,[92] makes possible a common "Declaration" in the style of a confession. This Declaration presents itself as a "fundamental consensus on the gospel" and with it the document ends.[93]

To what degree has this discussion of the relative theological importance of the doctrine of justification led to an agreement?

The Catholic recognition of the Lutheran conception of the special relative importance of the article on justification is clearly expressed when the description of the Reformation-Lutheran position[94] is taken up into a common statement:[95]

The *former* description states that the Reformers saw in "justification by faith...the heart of the gospel because the gospel message in its specific sense is *the proclamation of God's free and merciful promises in Christ Jesus which can be rightly received only through faith.*" Therefore they view justification by faith "as a criterion or corrective for all church practices, structures, and theology."

The *latter* reproduces this: "Catholics as well as Lutherans acknowledge the need to test the practices, structures, and theologies of the church by the extent to which they help or hinder 'the proclamation of God's free and merciful promises in Christ Jesus which can be rightly received only through faith' (para. 28)."

This is rightly described as an "accord."[96] This commonly defined criterion is then given the formulation of a "fundamental affirmation":[97]

"Our entire hope of justification and salvation rests on Christ Jesus and on the gospel whereby the good news of God's merciful action in Christ is made known: we do not place our ultimate trust in anything other than God's promise and saving work in Christ."

This common affirmation, it is emphasized, "is not fully equivalent to the Reformation teaching on justification according to which God accepts sinners as righteous for Christ's sake on the basis of faith alone."[98] Therefore it "does not necessarily involve full agreement...on justification by faith."[99] In fact, this affirmation, also in its position within the text, does not claim the function of a consensus formulation on justification as this exists in other dialogues. The consensus in the understanding of justification as such, which the US dialogue has definitely achieved, does not possess the character and structure (see above) needed for a formulaic statement.

Rather, it is a matter of an affirmation that belongs to, or better, is involved in a consensus on justification, an affirmation which expresses "a central concern" of the Reformation doctrine of justification.[100]

As such, i.e., as the expression of this "central concern" and not as the formulaic reproduction of the Reformation doctrine of justification or of the Catholic-Lutheran consensus on justification, "this affirmation, like the Reformation doctrine of justification by faith alone, serves as a criterion for judging all Church practices, structures, and traditions."[101] Precisely and only because it does not reproduce the specific Reformation doctrine of justification, but rather concentrates on its "central concern," can it form a common fundamental affirmation and a common criterion, recognized also by Catholics. The "central concern" of the Reformation doctrine of justification is not bound to the specific "forensic"/"proclamatory" shape of this doctrine. As it is formulated in the Affirmation, it requires no "particular concepts and images"[102] and can be stated "also in a transformationist view which emphasizes the change wrought in sinners by infused grace"—and thus in the specific conceptuality of the Catholic doctrine of justification.[103]

By formulating the "central concern" of the Reformation-Lutheran doctrine of justification, preserved and included in the previously worked out consensus on justification as such, as a "fundamental affirmation," the North American dialogue succeeded in the common definition of the criterion for all church preaching and doctrine, practice and structure, and answered the question about the relative theological importance of the doctrine of justification.

In that this dialogue—like the Malta Report—differentiated between the "criterion" or its definition, on the one hand, and the "application of the criterion" on the other, it also pointed to the nature and location of the further tasks of Catholic-Lutheran dialogue. The important and in part divisive differences no longer lie in the understanding of justification as such. Nor do they lie in the question of the relative theological importance of the doctrine of justification or in the question of its function as criterion of the church's preaching, doctrine, and life. They seem to lie rather in the area of the application of the commonly defined and recognized criterion.

3.3. Summary

It is important and, in my opinion, extremely helpful for the correct valuation of this Catholic-Lutheran agreement to again cast a comparative glance at the dialogues discussed at the beginning of this essay, especially the Lutheran-Reformed dialogue. The situation there is very similar, as with the Lutheran-Methodist dialogue. We saw that the Leuenberg Agreement affirmed the centrality and criteriological character of the message of justification by referring not to the Reformation doctrine of justification in its doctrinal form, but rather to the material concern lying in and behind this form. The emphasis fell on "the unique mediation of Jesus Christ in salvation" as "the heart of the Scriptures" and on "the message of God's free grace" as "the measure of all the church's preaching."[104] The US dialogue conforms to this pattern in both form and content. Here also the question of the doctrine of justification as center and measure is jointly answered by means of a reference to the Reformation doctrine's "central concern" rather than to its doctrinal form.[105] This material concern is defined in words almost identical to those of the Leuenberg Agreement: on the one side, more strongly Christological, as "the sole mediatorship of Christ," *solus Christus*,[106] or *solus Deus in Christus*;[107] on the other side, more strongly soteriological, as "God's free and merciful promises in Jesus Christ."[108]

In the agreement on the relative theological importance of the doctrine of justification, the Catholic-Lutheran dialogue is remarkably close to the

Lutheran-Reformed dialogue and through it to other dialogues. Also here there are grounds for recognizing the "dialogue definitive" status of the agreement.[109]

This result is highly significant, not just for the relation of the Lutheran churches to other churches, but also for the total ecumenical movement, and its deserves as such to be emphasized. It signifies that the central concern of the Reformation of the sixteenth century, which was from the beginning oriented ecumenically and not denominationally, has in the process of the ecumenical dialogues of our day increasingly found a hearing and reception throughout the whole church.

At the same time the remaining problematic, which must under no circumstances be trivialized, has become more precisely identified. It lies in the *consequences* which flow from this agreement, in other words, in the concrete *application of the jointly affirmed criterion of the material concern of the doctrine of justification to the preaching and doctrine, life and form of our churches.*

The Catholic-Lutheran dialogue of the last two decades was certainly conscious of this problematic. It attempted to maintain and to test the consensus on justification in the treatment of other questions, e.g., about the Eucharist, ordained ministry, marriage, etc. The results claim success in relation to important questions, but also show that this enterprise has by no means been brought to a close. From case to case it encounters significant difficulties and can even prove unsuccessful.[110]

It is of decisive important that these kinds of difficulties and even the continued lack of success are not allowed either to rebound back upon the consensus on justification which has been reached or to call it into question. That would be a theological frivolousness to be avoided. To preserve and to test in the life and teaching of the church the common confession of "the unique mediation of Jesus Christ in salvation" and of "God's free and gracious promise in Jesus Christ" is by its nature an unceasing task, never concluded or capable of being concluded. It is a question asked of each person and of the entire church, the question of loyalty to the gospel, from which it lives and which it serves.

Notes

1.   In the following essay, references will repeatedly be made to dialogue documents. Some of these are scattered and hard to locate. These texts, including the section of *The Condemnations of the Reformation Era* on "The Justification of the Sinner," are included in the volume *Rechtfertigung im Ökumenischen Dialog: Dokumente und Einführung* (Ökumenische Perspektiven, 12; Frankfurt

a.M.: Verlag Lembeck, 1987) and I have there discussed and compared them in an extended introduction.

2. Para. 4; reprinted in *An Invitation to Action: A Study of Ministry, Sacraments, and Recognition*, The Lutheran-Reformed Dialogue Series III, 1981-1983, edited by James E. Andrews & Joseph A. Burgess (Philadelphia: Fortress Press, 1984), pp. 61-73.

3. *Marburg Revisited: A Reexamination of Lutheran and Reformed Traditions*, edited by Paul C. Empie & James I. McCord (Minneapolis: Augsburg Publishing House, 1966), p. 152.

4. Paras. 6-12 (see nt. 2).

5. *Invitation to Action* (see nt. 2), paras. 1-36, esp. 9-13.

6. *Lutheran-Episcopal Dialogue: A Progress Report* (Cincinnati: Forward Movement Publications, [1973]), p. 22.

7. *Anglican-Lutheran Dialogue*: The Report of the Anglican-Lutheran European Regional Commission. Helsinki, August-September 1982 (London: SPCK, 1983): para. 62.

8. Ibid., paragraphs 17-21 [91f].

9. Weinhauer, William G. & Robert L.Wietelmann, eds., *The Report of the Lutheran-Episcopal Dialogue: Second Series 1976-1980* (Cincinnati: Forward Movement Publications, 1981), pp. 22-24.

10. Ibid., 24f.

11. Paras. 26, 28, in *Growth in Agreement: Reports and Agreed Statements of Ecumenical Conversations on a World Level*, edited by Harding Meyer & Lukas Vischer (New York: Paulist Press; Geneva: World Council of Churches, 1984), p. 174f.

12. "Unpublished report of a Catholic-Lutheran Planning Meeting on "Future Work of the Joint Roman Catholic-Lutheran Commission" (Rome, March 19-20, 1995). [Translator's note: The report of this phase of the dialogue has now appeared, *Church and Justification: Understanding the Church in the Light of the Doctrine of Justification* (Geneva: Lutheran World Federation, 1994).]

13. *Justification by Faith,* Lutherans and Catholics in Dialogue, vol. 7, edited by H. George Anderson, T. Austin Murphy, & Joseph Burgess (Minneapolis: Augsburg Publishing House, 1985), p. 8 (Preface).

14. *Justification by Faith*, p. 15 (para. 2).

15. George A. Lindbeck, "Justification by Faith: An Analysis of the 1983 Report of the US Lutheran-Roman Catholic Dialogue" *LCA Partners* (December 1984/January 1985): 7.

16.   *Justification by Faith*, para. 2.

17.   Ibid., p. 16 (para. 3).

18.   *The Condemnations of the Reformation Era: Do They Still Divide?*, edited by Karl Lehmann & Wolfhart Pannenberg, translated by Margaret Kohl (Minneapolis: Fortress Press, 1989): 179.

19.   Ibid, 178f.

20.   Ibid., 186f.

21.   [Translators' note: This dialogue has since published its report: Baptist-Lutheran Joint Commission, *Baptists and Lutherans in Conversation: A Message to our Churches* (Geneva: Lutheran World Federation, 1990). It dealt with justification only in passing.]

22.   In *Texte aus der VELKD* 17 (1981), p. 5.

23.   Lutheran-Baptist Dialogue, *Three Common Statements*, in *Growing Consensus: Church Dialogues in the United States, 1962-1991*, Ecumenical Documents, Vol. 5, edited by Joseph Burgess & Jeffrey Gros (New York: Paulist Press, 1995): pp. 102ff.

24.   In *Rechtfertigung im Ökumenischen Dialog* (see nt. 1), p. 250.

25.   *Tradition und Glaubensgerechtigkeit: Das Arnoldshainer Gespräch zwischen Vertretern der Evangelischen Kirche Deutschlands und der Russischen Orthodoxen Kirche* (Witten, 1961), esp. p. 11.

26.   Das Heil in Jesus Christ und die Heiligung der Welt," in *Informationen aus der orthodoxen Kirche* 15 (1986): 3f.

27.   In *Dialogue Between Neighbours*: The Theological Conversations between the Evangelical-Lutheran Church of Finland and the Russian Orthodox Church 1970-1986, Communiques and Theses, Publications of the Luther—Agricola Society B17, edited by Hannu T. Kamppuri (Helsinki: Luther—Agricola Society, 1986): 73-76. [Translators' note: More recent Lutheran-Orthodox dialogue texts dealing with justification are the 1980 ("Faith and Love as Elements of Salvation") and 1986 ("Holiness, Sanctification and the Saints") statements from the Finnish Lutheran-Russian Orthodox dialogue (in *Dialogue between Neighbors*, pp. 86-88, 110-112); the 1988 statement of the EKD-Romanian Orthodox dialogue, *Rechtfertigung und Verherrlichung [Theosis] des Menschen durch Jesus Christus*, edited by Klaus Schwarz (Hermannsburg: Missionshandlung Hermannsburg, 1995); and the 1992 North American Lutheran-Orthodox statement *Salvation in Christ* (Minneapolis: Augsburg, 1992). The conclusion in the previous paragraph on the non-continuation of early beginnings would thus today need to be revised.]

28.   I explore this third mode of discussing the doctrine of justification in more detail in *Rechtfertigung im Ökumenischen Dialog* (see nt. 1), pp. 72-82.

29.   For example, the Leuenberg Agreement, paras. 7f; US Lutheran-Episcopal

dialogue (1980, see nt. 9), para. A; Joint Statement on Justification, para. A; the Lutheran-Catholic Malta Report in its movement from paras. 14f ("The Question of the Gospel") through 24ff ("The Center of the Gospel...") to 26ff ("The Problem of the Doctrine of Justification").

30. Such consensus formulas on justification are to be found in documents from dialogues by Lutherans with Reformed, Anglicans, Methodists, Catholics, and Old Catholics. They are brought together and briefly analyzed in *Rechtfertigung im Ökumenischen Dialog* (see nt. 1), pp. 33-39.

31. SD III,25.

32. *Justification by Faith* (see nt. 13), paras. 4, 157; cp. 161.

33. Ibid., para. 158.

34. Ibid., paras. 157, 158, 160.

35. Ibid., para. 164.

36. Ibid., para. 159.

37. 1. Forensic Justification (paras. 98-101); 2. Sinfulness of the Justified (paras. 102-104); 3. Sufficiency of Faith (paras. 105-107); 4. Merit (paras. 108-112); 5. Satisfaction (paras. 113-116).

38. *Condemnations* (see nt. 18), pp. 48f, 45f.

39. "Salvation and the Church," *Origins* 16 (1987): 611-616. Under the heading "Salvation and Faith" (paras. 9-11; cp. 4) it deals primarily with certainty of salvation and the relation between faith and love; under the heading "Salvation and Justification" (paras. 12-18, cp. 5) it deals with forensic and effective justification and the relation between justification and sanctification; and under the heading "Salvation and Good Works" (paras. 19-24, cp. 6) it deals again with faith and love, justification and sanctification, and in relation to these with the *simul justus et peccator* and the concepts of merit and reward.

40. Ibid., paras. 25-31; cp. 7.

41. In *Rechtfertigung im Ökumenischen Dialog* (see nt. 1), pp. 39-54, I have attempted to describe and briefly summarize in eight points the discussions of the individual problem areas and their results.

42. Malta Report (see nt. 13), para. 26.

43. *Condemnations* (see nt. 18), pp. 33, 47f; *Justification by Faith* (see nt. 13), para. 98.

44. *Justification by Faith* (see nt. 13), para. 98.

45. Ibid., para. 100.

46. *Condemnations* (see nt. 18), pp. 33, 47f.

47. *Justification by Faith* (see nt. 13), para. 101.

48. *Condemnations* (see nt. 18), p. 49.

49. *Justification by Faith* (see nt. 13), para. 101.

50. *Condemnations* (see nt. 18), p. 47; cp. *Justification by Faith* (see nt. 13), para. 101.

51. Ibid., 47f; cp. *Justification by Faith* (see nt. 13), paras. 131f, 137f.

52. "Transformational" or "transformationist" characterizes the concern of the Catholic understanding of justification, shaped by Augustine's doctrine of grace (paras. 6f, 10, 20, et al.), in so far as it is a matter of "the transformation of the individual" which "takes place by grace" (para. 7). The Reformation understanding of justification is characterized as "proclamatory" (paras. 90f) in so far it maintains that "justification in unconditional in the sense that the justifying word effects its own reception" (para. 89). "The central point is that the proclamation of God's grace in word and sacrament is itself the saving event...God's word does what it proclaims" (para. 88).

53. Cp. para. 90 and also Lindbeck (see nt. 15), pp. 9f.

54. paras. 120, 20.

55. It states: "*No one can condemn and accuse of departing from the Christian faith those who—experiencing the misery of their sins, their resistance against God, and their lack of love for God and their neighbor—in faith put their whole trust in the saving God, are sure of his mercy, and try in their lives to match up to this faith*—even though Christians and theologians who (following the Reformers) think in this way must always be asked whether, because of their profound sense of sin, they do not think too little of God's regenerative power. *Nor, on the other hand, can anyone condemn and accuse of departing from the Christian faith those who, deeply penetrated by the limitless power of God, stress above all, in the event of justification also, God's glory and the victory of his gracious acts on behalf of men and women, holding human failure and halfheartedness toward these gracious acts to be, in the strict sense, of secondary importance*—even if Christians and theologians who (following the Council of Trent) think in this way must always be asked whether they take the misery of sin sufficiently seriously." *Condemnations* (see nt. 18), p. 40.

56. *Marburg Revisited* (see nt. 3), p. 152.

57. para. 10 (see nt. 2).

58. Marc Lienhard, *Lutherisch-reformierte Kirchengemeinschaft heute* (Frankfurt a.M.: Lembeck, 1973): pp. 73f

59. Lutheran-Episcopal Dialogue (1980, see nt. 9), para. D.

60. para. 20 (see nt. 7).

61. para. 5 (see nt. 39).

62. Ibid., para. 14.

63. Ibid., paras. 15-18.

64. *Vom Dialog zur Kanzel- und Abendmahlsgemeinschaft*: Eine Dokumentation der Lehrgespräche und der Beschlüsse der kirchenleitenden Gremien, Edited by the Lutherisches Kirchenamt and the Kirchenkanzlei der Evangelisch-methodistischen Kirche (Hanover: Lutherisches Verlagshaus; Stuttgart: Christliches Verlagshaus, 1987): section 2.2, p. 15.

65. Ibid., sections 3.1 and 3.2, p. 15.

66. Lutheran-Methodist Joint Commission, *The Church: Community of Grace* (Geneva: Lutheran World Federation; Lake Junaluska: World Methodist Council, 1984), esp. para. 23.

67. Ibid., paras. 23-26.

68. Ibid., paras. 90f.

69. para. 14, in *Growth in Agreement* (see nt. 13), p. 370.

70. Ibid., para. 18.

71. Ibid., para. 15.

72. para. 13.

73. Hans Jorissen, Ökumenische Erschliesung Martin Luthers," in *Martin Luther im Spiegel heutiger Wissenschaft*, edited by Knut Schäferdiek, Studium Universale 4 (Bonn: Grundmann, 1985): p. 222. Jorissen cites Gerhard Sauter as the source of the concept "dialogue-definitive."

74. *Marburg Revisited* (see nt. 3), p. 152.

75. para. 12 (see nt. 2).

76. section, 2.1; p. 15 (see nt. 64).

77. *Condemnations*, p. 69 (see nt. 18).

78. para. 28 (see nt. 13).

79. "The Joint Lutheran-Roman Catholic Study Commission on 'The Gospel and the Church'," *Lutheran World* 16 (1969): 364.

80. para. 27 (see nt. 11).

81. Ibid.

82. Ibid., para. 26.

83. *Justification by Faith* (see nt. 13), para. 27f.

84. Ibid., para. 117.

85. Ibid., para. 118.

86. Ibid., paras. 122-149.

87. Ibid., para. 146; cp. 123, 132, 149.

88. Ibid., paras. 153f.

89. Ibid., para. 28.

90. Ibid., para. 157.

91. Ibid., para. 160.

92. Ibid., para. 4.

93. para. 164.

94. Ibid., para. 28.

95. Ibid., para. 153.

96. Ibid., para. 153. The "incomplete convergence" (para. 152) which the document then discusses in detail (paras. 153f) no longer exists on the level of the *definition* of the criterion but on the level of its "use" (para. 152) or its "application."

97. Ibid., para. 157.

98. Ibid., para. 157.

99. Ibid., para. 4.

100. Ibid., para. 157.

101. Ibid., para. 160.

102. Reference should here by made to the statement of the Malta Report that "the event of salvation to which the gospel testifies can...be expressed comprehensively" not only in the terminology and images of justification, but also "in other representations derived from the New Testament, such as reconciliation, freedom, redemption, new life, and new creation" (para. 27, see nt. 13). It is interesting that a similar statement can be found already in the first North American dialogue between Lutherans and Reformed (1966): "The churches of the Reformation confessed this gospel [of the saving act of God in Jesus Christ] by means of the biblical concept of justification by grace through faith alone. The scriptures also present the same gospel in other concepts, such as reconciliation, regeneration, and redemption. An evangelical confession accordingly may be, and has been, framed in terms of one or more of these" *Marburg Revisited* (see nt. 3), p. 37.

103. *Justification by Faith* (see nt. 13), para. 158.

104. para. 12 (see nt. 2).

105. *Justification by Faith* (see nt. 13), para. 157.

106. Ibid., paras. 117, 160.

107. Ibid., para. 4.

108. Ibid., paras. 153, 28.

109. See nt. 73.

110. I refer again to my analysis of the "criteriological-applicative discussion of justification" in the Catholic-Lutheran dialogue in *Rechtfertigung in Ökumenischen Dialog* (see nt. 1), pp. 72-82.

Chapter Six

Damnamus?

The Condemnations in the Confessions of the Lutheran Church as a Problem for the Ecumenical Dialogue between the Lutheran and Roman Catholic Churches[1]

Gunther Wenz

1. THE CONFESSIONAL WRITINGS AND THE NORMATIVE CONFESSION

1.1. The Book of Concord

THE CONFESSIONAL WRITINGS of the Lutheran church which will be discussed here are "normed in relation to their content by the Book of Concord (BC) of 1580" (BSLK, vii), whose origin was most closely related to the creation of the Formula of Concord (FC) of 1577. The FC was the result of numerous attempts in the face of internal doctrinal controversies to establish and protect the doctrinal unity of the territorial churches that had come out of the Lutheran Reformation.[2] Thus it primarily attempts to remove the doctrinal differences that appeared after Luther's death within the Lutheran camp (particularly between the "Philipist" followers of Melanchthon and the Gnesio-Lutherans led by Flacius). Its primary relation is thus not to other communions.[3] "The background of the attempts at unity, both requiring and limiting them, was the conflict with the Catholic powers both over a religious settlement through a council and over a general Protestant political alliance that

would provide greater security than that offered by the Peace of Augsburg"
(BSLK, xxxii).

As the title page of the BC already shows, the intention behind its
composition corresponded to that behind the FC also:[4] the creation a binding
confessional basis for the unity of Lutheranism.[5] According to the Preface to
the FC, which in the printed edition of 1580 was placed at the beginning of the
BC (cp. BSLK, 739-766, 3-17), the BC contains the following texts: The three
symbols of the ancient church, that is, the Apostles Creed, the Nicene-
Constantinopolitan Creed, and the so-called Athanasian creed; the Augsburg
Confession (CA) of 1530, together with Melanchthon's Apology (Apol) which
was published in the following year in response to the Confutatio; the Smalcald
Articles (SA) formulated in 1537 as Luther's theological testament in response
to the Council called by Pope Paul III for Mantua; and finally the Small and
Large Catechisms of Luther (cf. BSLK, 768f). Attached to the SA is
Melanchthon's "Treatise on the Primacy and Power of the Pope" (Tr), which
was dealt with and accepted by the assembly at Smalcald, but which was not
conceived as an appendix to the SA but as a supplement and completion of the
CA. To these are added the FC itself in both its condensed Epitome (Epit) and
detailed Solid Declaration (SD) and a long debated Catalogue of Testimonies,
which was to provide evidence from the Fathers for the legitimacy of the
Christology of the FC. Luther's Little Book for Marriage and Baptism is also
sometimes included.

1.2. Corpora doctrinae

The impression must not be given that "the conception of the Book of
Concord was only taken up after the completion of the Formula of Concord."[6]
Since the middle of the 16th century, various "corpora doctrinae" had been
constructed, in many cases closely connected to territorial or city church
orders. These collections of individual doctrinal texts were to norm the
teaching of the gospel and preserve it from distortion.[7] Since it is "relatively the
most widely" accepted,[8] the BC can be called the most important Corpus
Doctrinae of Lutheranism. Nevertheless, due to the only partial reception of the
FC, the BC was and is not recognized in its full extent by all Lutheran
churches.[9] One cannot thus say without qualification that the BC as such is the
confession of the Lutheran church. "Rather it contains all the symbolic books
acknowledged by the individual Lutheran churches."[10] The binding character
of these books varies, as can be shown in the differing ordination vows.

For a hermeneutic of the Lutheran confessions, this state of affairs raises a
series of highly incendiary questions inseparably connected with the theory of
church constitutions.[11] One of the most difficult yet important tasks of a

contemporary theology of the Lutheran confessions would be to go beyond a mere recording of the external facts and reflect in a systematic and theological way upon the complicated historical process of consensus formation during the century of the Reformation, which in the FC and BC led to an impressive yet still only partial agreement.[12]

1.3. The Normativity of the Formula of Concord

In relation to the acceptance of the FC by the totality of Lutheranism, one should remember the old rule which said that church fellowship is possible without the FC but not against it. While this rule may have been superseded as a legal norm, it remains worth considering in its intention.[13] It grasped the self-understanding of the FC as an (authentic) interpretation of the CA.[14] The historical necessity of this interpretation cannot be fundamentally denied from the Lutheran side. Thus one cannot simply say that the FC has "no immediate significance" for ecumenical dialogue.[15] In the end, "even in the local and territorial churches which have not received the entire BC, the Confessio Augustana is not to be viewed in isolation. The entire history of the formation of a distinctive confessional church is in fact present, together with the demarcations that go with it, even if they are not thus explicitly stated in the Augsburg Confession."[16] This historical reality cannot theologically be suppressed; one cannot in ecumenical dialogue with the Roman Catholic church avoid dealing with the severe condemnations that are present in the FC as well as the SA. "Nevertheless, the sharp clarifications that later became necessary must be measured by the positive statements of Augsburg and the Small Catechism, and not vice-versa."[17] Here is already a methodological guideline which should be taken into account in the ecumenical and theological discussion that follows.

That the central place in the confession of the Lutheran churches is given to the CA alongside the Small Catechism agrees completely with the self-understanding of the Fathers of the Concord, as has been said. Even the ordering of the FC's articles is oriented to the CA, whose structure could not be strictly maintained only because the necessary relation to the controversies addressed in the FC determined not only the selection but also the ordering of the doctrinal issues. Like the FC, the BC also had no other task than to represent "the correct Christian interpretation of the Augsburg Confession" [Preface to the FC and BC; BC,8].

The special position of the CA in the framework of the Lutheran confession results not just from its legal significance in the Holy Roman Empire, which became definitive in 1555,[18] nor just from its becoming the actual norm for liturgy and for the doctrinal commitments of office holders in the confessionally united territorial churches. Its normative claim lay primarily in the binding character of its content, in the fact that the CA convincingly brought to bear the original faith of the church renewed through Luther. Only so could the CA become "the origin of the theological and literary genus 'Confession' and...prototype for the binding character of confession in the Lutheran church."[19]

1.4. The Ancient Creeds

The CA is not, however, to be understood as an isolated doctrinal norm. It is connected to the confession of the ancient church by its subordination in the BC to the three ecumenical creeds. Thus, the unbroken connection to the faith of the Fathers and the continuous agreement with the one, holy, universal and apostolic church is expressed. The Lutheran confession explicitly joins the ancient church's consensus about the one faith as it is "briefly summarized in the approved ancient symbols" [Preface to the FC and BC; BC,3].

The CA corresponds to this self-understanding by presenting its doctrinal articles formally and materially as an interpretation of the faith of the ancient church.[20] "That one holy church is to continue forever" is, according to CA 7, beyond doubt. "And from this may be deduced its manifestation in the preaching of the gospel and the administration of the sacraments in accord with the gospel."[21] CA 1 thus presupposes the continuum of Christian doctrine when, with a reference to the Nicene Creed, it states programmatically: "Our churches teach with great unanimity...." "Placed before all other matters is the doctrinal consensus which agrees with the conciliar decision of the ancient church."[22] This placement has more than merely the formal ground of a desire explicitly to stand on the basis of the law of the Empire: "the continuity with the one ancient church is shown materially in the text of the CA itself at the decisive points."[23] It was not just diplomatic wisdom, but well-founded theological conviction that led the former Electoral Saxon Chancellor Brück in the Preface to the CA, with a verbatim reference to the imperial summons, to appeal to the unity in Christ as the common presupposition of the contending parties and the basis for the settlement of the conflict (BC, 24.2-25.4) "The 'specifically Reformation' confession intends no new content over against that of the ancient church. The well known thesis that the Reformation created no new church can be true...only if the Reformation confession is also a repetition of that of the ancient church,"[24] whereby repetition here is not a mere repristination, but is to be understood in the unity of continuity and contemporaneity. The FC also "has in no way abandoned the idea of a common Christendom which encompasses the contending religious parties. This idea was still important even for the Lutherans of the 17th century."[25]

1.5. Scripture and Confession

The connection with the one Christian faith, which was constitutive for their own confession, was seen as theologically grounded in the common witness to the one gospel of Jesus Christ as normatively found in the Bible.[26] The complex question of the relation between Bible and confession thus acquires a decisive significance for the hermeneutic of the confessions. It is then striking that the CA has no article on the Bible and its authority. The Preface does already emphasize that the confession of faith is submitted "on the basis of the Holy Scriptures" (BC,25,8). The closing words of Part 1 stress anew the commitment to "the pure Word of God" and the Holy Bible as the one basis of all doctrine (BC,47,1). The "Conclusion" to the entire text ends with the corresponding statement: "If anyone should consider that it [the CA] is lacking in some respect, we are ready to present further information, on the basis of the divine Holy Scripture" (BC,96,7). There can be no doubt that the witness of the Bible is declared to be the criterion of the Confession.[27] Nonetheless, the authority of Scripture does not become a distinct doctrinal theme. This absence has its theological basis; for the CA, the issue "is precisely not a matter of a formalized scripture principle, but of the truth of the gospel through the ages, even if one is indebted to Holy Scripture for this gospel in its fundamental and authoritative form."[28] The category "gospel" is of central significance for the Confession.[29] "The way in which the doctrinal articles are related to the gospel in the CA makes it clear that the Reformation was not concerned with the restoration in church and doctrine of an original state of 'conformity to Scripture', much less with the establishment of a new church.... No new (or 'original') church of Scripture is postulated, but rather the given, existing church is critically reinterpreted in the light of the gospel."[30]

A kerygmatic actualism with little content is not being proposed. But the *viva vox evangelii* in the sense of the CA is also not a deposit of doctrinal propositions to be attached to theological quotations. It is "rather the event which takes place in proclamation and in the administration of the sacraments, the event in which God's justification in Jesus Christ is truly given to a person through the Holy Spirit (cf, the interrelation of CA 4, 5, and 13)."[31] All doctrines and forms of the church, and thus also its confession, must serve this event.

In reaction to Trent's "Decree on Sacred Books and on Traditions to Be Received" (Dz 1501-1505), the formalization of the Reformation *sola scriptura*[32] which will be characteristic for Protestant Orthodoxy already begins to take shape in the FC.[33] Alone among the Lutheran Confessions, the FC prefaces its articles with a "comprehensive summary, rule, and norm according to which all doctrines should be judged and the errors which intruded should be explained and decided in a Christian way" (BC,464). Here it is stated that "the prophetic and apostolic writings of the Old and New Testaments are the only rule and norm.... Other writings of ancient and modern teachers, whatever their names, should not be put on a par with Holy Scripture. Every single one of them should be subordinated to the Scriptures and should be received in no other way and no further than as witnesses to the fashion in which the doctrine of the prophets and apostles was preserved in post apostolic times" (BC,646,1-647,2).[34] It is significant, though, that unlike Trent no definition of the canon is given and no doctrine of scripture in presented in the sense of an epistemological principle for theology. Even if the Protestant orthodox dogmatics did in its prolegomena define scripture as the principle of knowledge [*principium congnoscendi*] in theology, it demonstrated in its repeated discussions of the doctrine of the means of salvation a remaining soteriological understanding of scripture.[35] A literalistic biblicism cannot grasp the content of scripture, but only justifying faith which depends on the promise of salvation.

1.6. The Self-Understanding of the Lutheran Confession

In its so-called "Comprehensive Summary," the FC also expresses itself on the self-understanding of the Lutheran confessions.[36] After listing the individual confessions, the "distinction between the Holy Scripture of the Old and New Testaments and all other writings" is stressed. It is again emphasized that Holy Scripture alone is and remains "the only judge, rule, and norm,...the only touchstone" of all doctrine (BC,465,7). "Other symbols and other writings are not judges like Holy Scripture, but merely witnesses and expositions of the faith, setting forth how at various times the holy Scriptures were understood by contemporaries in the church of God with reference to controverted articles, and how contrary teachings were rejected and condemned" (BC,465,8). Determinative for the self-understanding of the Lutheran confession is the decided self-differentiation from its ground. Witness and object of witness are not immediately identical, but constitute a differentiated relation. Confession is witness; not an independent word, but, like the church which it is to serve, *creatura verbi*.[37] The church can and should through its confession "distinguish the gospel from human teachings, but it should not claim that only through its own judgment about truth does the gospel come into effect."[38] It then follows that the Lutheran confession neither can and nor wishes to be an immediate object of faith or a doctrinal law.[39]

In summary one can say: "In service to the clarity of preaching and the unity of the church, the confession receives its binding character only by being bound to the Gospel as witnessed to in Holy Scripture. It understands itself as a hermeneutical aid to the right understanding of scripture and to the differentiation between pure and false preaching and doctrine."[40] This conclusion leads, however, to "the creation of an highly tension-filled circle: the interpretation of scripture takes place in light of the church's confession; the church's confession has its binding character only through its relation to Holy Scripture."[41] The precise determination of this relation raises a series of very difficult theological problems, which are also the real problems of present ecumenical dialogue in relation to this question. As is explicitly documented in the 1972 consensus document "The Gospel and the Church" (para. 21), the Roman Catholic and Lutheran churches are in fundamental agreement "that the authority of the church can be only in service to the Word and can never be master of the Word of the Lord." Controversial is "not the primacy of Scriptural authority, but how this authority makes itself present."[42]

The open questions within a contemporary ecumenical doctrine of Scripture are concentrated around the problem of a binding interpretation of Scripture. Within the ecumenical dialogues, the much discussed theme of scripture and tradition has also tended to reduce to this problem.[43] It is not contested from the Lutheran side that the Bible cannot be placed simply over against tradition. Contemporary Roman Catholic theology agrees to a large extent that the church's teaching about tradition is not concerned with supplements or completions of Holy Scripture, but with a binding interpretation of Scripture (see Malta Report, esp. paras. 17ff).[44]

This theme, which will be a constant concern in connection with the theology of ministry, has been problematic also within a confessionally bound Lutheranism. This can be seen in the discussion going back to the early period of pietism[45] over whether the confessions claim their recognition and binding validity because (*quia*) or in so far as (*quatenus*) they are the true interpretation of scripture. Problems arise here which modern Lutheran theology certainly has not solved. If one is going to avoid abstract alternatives in addressing these questions, one always must keep in view the undoubted self-understanding of all Lutheran confession: it does not refer immediately to itself, but places itself within a network of historical references directed toward the self-demonstration and self-confession of Jesus Christ and thus toward the self-revelation of God. Lutheran confession stands and falls with trust in the self-demonstration of divine truth. (The theorem of the self-interpretation of Scripture and the doctrine of the attributes of Scripture is to be interpreted in this context.)

1.7. The Confessional Subscription of the Lutheran Churches

All that has been said needs to be kept in mind when we take up the condemnations in the Lutheran confessions. They are not to be understood simply in themselves. Rather they can be rightly judged only on the presupposition that theological clarity exists about the confessional commitment of the Lutheran church. This can be quickly summarized: The Lutheran churches around the world possess "their confessional unity by 1) recognizing the Holy Scripture as the highest rule and norm of all the church's teaching and life, 2) expressing their unity and agreement with the faith of the true catholic and apostolic church through the recognition of the ancient creeds, and 3) assigning the character of binding doctrinal norm to the CA as the fundamental confession of the Lutheran Reformation. The remaining writings in the Book of Concord are not authoritative in all Lutheran churches. The Lutheran World Federation has taken the differences in the confessional commitments of its member churches into account in speaking in its doctrinal basis of the 'confessions of the Lutheran church,' but giving special emphasis to the CA and the Catechism."[46]

2. THE GOSPEL OF THE JUSTIFICATION OF THE SINNER AS THE CENTER AND LIMIT OF THE LUTHERAN CONFESSION

2.1. The Theological Place of the Doctrine of Justification

The self-demonstration of God in Jesus Christ, from which all confession comes, which all confession is to serve, and in which all confession is fulfilled, is manifest according to the Book of Concord in the gospel of the justification of the sinner by grace alone "for Christ's sake, through faith" (CA 4). The doctrine of justification is seen as "the main doctrine of Christianity" (Apol 4:2; cp. BSLK 239,14ff), as the formal center and safeguarding summary of the new recognition and preaching of Christ that forms the Reformation's answer to its central question about the true church."[47]

Nevertheless, it is not easy to determine exactly the theological relative importance of the doctrine of justification. It is definitely misunderstood when it is made one doctrine among others. Thus Ernst Wolf raised the question whether the Council of Trent's doctrine of justification already on formal grounds is fundamentally different from that of the Reformation.[48] It is likewise misunderstood in its basic character when the doctrine itself is made an object of faith, when salvation is made directly dependent on the acceptance of a particular doctrine. Equally mistaken is the attempt to make the doctrine an axiomatic principle from which the total truth of faith can be deductively unfolded. Rather, the doctrine is always oriented toward the concrete activity of the promise of the gospel of Jesus Christ through Word and sacrament. To ensure pure preaching and right administration of the sacraments, so that they are media of the unreserved grace of God—this is the theological function of the doctrine of justification in which it corresponds to its content, nothing more and nothing less.

It is thus not without reason that in the Confessions that come from Luther, "no formula for the doctrine of justification" is provided.[49] "In his Confession of 1528 as well as in the Small and Large Catechisms and the Smalcald Articles, justification is derived through biblical concepts directly from the power of the work of Christ."[50] Thus it is said in SA: "The first and chief article is this, that Jesus Christ, our God and Lord, 'was put to death for our trespasses and raised again for our justification.'... Inasmuch as this must be believed and cannot be obtained or apprehended by any work, law, or merit, it is clear and certain that such faith alone justifies us.... Nothing in this article can be given up or compromised, even if heaven and earth and things temporal should be destroyed" (SA II,1,1,4-5). The manner in which Christ and faith come together in the event of justification determines the theological understanding of God and of humanity, and thus also of the totality of Christian doctrine. To know the doctrine of Christ is nothing other than "to believe in Christ without any works" (WA 29,481,17). Faith is what it is, a *fides apprehensiva*, because it expects nothing from its own powers but all from the possibilities of God in Jesus Christ. *Fiducia* as the fulfilled form of faith is thus in itself that self-abandonment which seeks its own not in itself, but only in the *extra nos* of Jesus Christ. Oriented to itself and its own power and capacity, faith becomes in itself false and by that very act becomes unfaith and sinks into self-assertion. In pregnant formulas (*simul iustus et peccator*;[51] *iniustus in me, iustus in spe*) Luther impressively contrasted this eccentric nature of faith with the self-occupied non-being of unfaith.[52]

Just as the content of Christian truth opens itself in faith, so false doctrine always is present "where the gospel is not effective as a word to faith, but is made into a law, an instruction how one can oneself provide the fundamental Yes. "Not having true faith makes heretics" [WA 6,294,30; AE 39:67][53] Doctrine and false doctrine are not thereby subjectivistically watered down. Faith cannot speak to itself the Word from which it lives. Rather, it requires a promise, an external Word, whose specific content and mediating character cannot be "set aside in favor of a hierarchically privileged or ecstatically grasped immediacy."[54]

Even if justification is already treated in CA 4 as a particular doctrinal article, its place in the structure and organization of the CA[55] shows that with the content of this article is also posited the theme of theology in itself and in all its individual articles. Under this presupposition (even if only under it) is it true: "if I deny God in one article, I have denied God in all" (WA 40II, 48,6).[56] Clearly, one can also say in the sense of Luther: "if I believe in God in one article, I believe in God in them all." Two essential, mutually complementary consequences can be drawn for the general understanding of Reformation theology, which are fundamental for the following presentation. First: to perceive the inner unity of Reformation theology one must discover within it that organizing structure which founds its unity and from which its particular content becomes transparent to its functional significance. Second: the material value of the doctrine of justification must not stand and fall with the power to convince of its historically conditioned form of expression, which was tightly bound to the medieval tradition of penance. What is presented in the doctrine of justification can be compared to a regulative idea which is present in all moments of the truth of faith in a determinative way. Luther can thus easily develop his central reformation insight in connection with the theme of freedom.[57] In this and only in this sense is the doctrine of justification the center[58] and limit of reformation theology: "*center*—which means that everything in Reformation theology relates to it...*limit*—which means that whatever is not determined and summed up in this center is *error et venenum* in theology."[59]

2.2. The Condemnations in the Book of Concord

We now have the basis for understanding and judging the condemnations in the BC. They concern us here only insofar as they relate to the actual or alleged doctrines of the Roman Catholic Church.

Nine of the 21 doctrinal articles of the CA have attached condemnations; twelve are without.[60] Article 1 rejects all heresies which contradict the right doctrine of God and the Trinity. It names the Manichees, Arians, and other false teachers of the patristic church, in addition to the "Mohammedans." Article 2 condemns the Pelagians; Article 8 the Donatists; Article 12 the Novatians. Articles 5, 9, 12, and 17 contain condemnations of the Anabaptists. "Disapproval" [*improbant*] is expressed in Article 10 of the enemies of the Lutheran doctrine of the Lord's Supper. Of particular interest for our study are two condemnations in the context of the doctrines of penance and original sin. In addition to the Pelagians, Article 2 condemns those "who deny that the vice of origin is sin and who obscure the glory of Christ's merit and benefits by contending that man can be justified before God by his own strength and reason" (BC,29). Article 12 rejects those "who do not teach that remission of sins comes through faith but command us to merit grace through satisfactions of our own" (BC,35).

On the whole, it is striking that, apart from the Anabaptists, "no contemporary opponents are named, neither individuals nor groups." Rather, all explicit condemnations are directed "against old heresies, long condemned by all of Christianity."[61] Contemporary references are given only sparingly and indirectly. "Zwinglians are the *secus docentes* (those who teach otherwise; CA 10), the teachers of works-righteousness remain anonymous (CA 12.10), as do the ethical perfectionists in monasticism (CA 16,4) and elsewhere (CA 12.8). Obviously the Confession does not intend to brand contemporary false teachers with a public condemnation. It prefers to choose guarded expressions in referring to them: *reicere*, "reject" (CA 12.10), is the strongest, and *admonere*, "admonish" (Ger.: "unterrichten...lehren," CA 15.2-3), the weakest. Words like *improbare*, "disapprove" (CA 10.2), or "dem Glauben an Christ (dem Evangelium) entgegen sein", "are contrary to the Gospel and... faith in Christ" (CA 15.3), lie more or less in the middle."[62]

As far as the relation to Rome is concerned, one cannot deny that the condemnations in CA 2 (see BSLK 53, nt 2) and CA 12 (see BSLK 67, nt 4)[63] among others are directed against theologoumena of the medieval church.[64] They are not, however, more precisely identified, much less presented as teachings of the whole church. The same holds, as has been said, for the rejection of ethical perfectionism.[65] Finally, there is no mention in the CA of the Pope as Antichrist, as is to be found in Luther's Confession of 1528. This assertion is "never officially repeated" until the SA.[66] Thus the first part of the CA can conclude with the assurance that the confession is "grounded clearly on the Holy Scriptures and is not contrary or opposed to that of the universal Christian church, or even of the Roman church (in so far as the latter's teaching is reflected in the writings of the Fathers)."[67] The listing of the names of the old heresies is to confirm and strengthen this assurance. "But that is still not all. If evangelical doctrine corresponds to the teaching of the ancient church and repeats its condemnations, then the dialogue partners of the old religion are not only obliged to recognize the evangelical truth but must also ask themselves whether they take this truth seriously. Every repetition of ancient anathemas contains within itself a critique of the contemporary Roman church. The church is called to account whether its original basis has been abandoned and the faith of the fathers damaged by abuses that have crept in over time."[68]

This conscious connection to the tradition of the ancient church is also manifested in the self-differentiation from "other factions and sects" which ends the FC.[69] The situation had significantly changed between 1530 and 1577. The FC had in no way fundamentally given up the idea of the unity of the entire church. Nevertheless, one can already find there the tendency towards "confession" in the sense of a religious party. This had consequences for the intra-Protestant controversies that had led to the FC and for the relation to the papal church, whose Roman character had already been understood separatistically. The methodical procedure of the FC already leads one to suspect that the idea of an integral church unity has retreated before an idea of unity governed decisively by oppositions. The state of the controversy (*alternativa*) is first established, then the positive assertions (*affirmativa*) decided, and finally the rejected statements (*negativa*) spelled out. No fundamental "distinctions are made between the Roman or Calvinist errors" in the degree of condemnation. "The words are sometimes varied, but that which is only "rejected" (*verworfen*) in the Epitome, is "condemned" (*verdammt*) in the Solid Declaration."[70]

The anathemas formally directed against Rome concern above all the following doctrines: original sin (Art. 1) and free will (Art. 2), the righteousness of faith before God (Art. 3) and good works (Art. 4), and finally the Lord's Supper (Art. 7) and the group of questions related to church usages (Art. 10). Rome is not always explicitly named in the corresponding judgments, but the FC makes no effort to hide the shaping of its outlook by an opposition to "the false worship, idolatry, and superstition of the papacy" (BC,465,4; cp. BC,504,5), even if the total structure is stamped by the intra-Protestant doctrinal controversies in such a way that many individual points of controversy with Roman theology are not explicitly discussed.

We will continue to follow the method already developed (see I,3) and begin with the rejections in the FC, in order then to place them in the total structure of the FC and to measure them by the positive teachings especially of the CA. The precise theological status of the condemnations will be dealt with below.

2.3. The Doctrine of Original Sin

On original sin, the FC attempts to distinguish pure doctrine both from a Manichean understanding of sin as a substance (Flacius) and from the manifold gradations of Pelagianism. It sees as necessary an explanation of the controversial concepts of the nature and substance of humanity (see Epit: BC,466-467; SD: BC,508-510). One can appreciate the complicated distinctions made in this regard only if it is clear that FC interprets the doctrine of original sin from two points of view: "Viewed by God, original sin and human nature are distinguishable; seen by humanity, they are not."[71] The distinction between corrupted human nature (*natura hominis corrupta*) and the substance of human corruption (*substantia corrupti hominis*) is made theologically, but it lies beyond human capacity. It is inferred from the divine act of salvation. In justifying the distinction, SD I, 34-47 refers to "all important articles of faith of the bible and summarizes these in four statements. First, human nature is even after the Fall a creature of God.... Second, the Son of God has taken on a human, yet sinless nature in order to become our Brother.... Third, the sinner is cleansed and liberated from sin in baptism and sanctification. It is impossible to say that original sin is itself baptized or saved. Fourth, the substance of our body and soul will some day rise and at that time be finally liberated from sin. These four statements are clearly related to the transitions between the four traditional states of the human person [see BSLK 870 A.1]. A common presupposition of all of them is that the transformations of human nature, however deep, occur to the same nature—because God's transforming effectiveness is also presupposed."[72] It should be noted: the identity of human nature in the process of its transformation, or better, its renewal, cannot be immediately derived from this nature itself. A continuing human self-identity exists here only and exclusively thanks to the gracious activity of the love of God, despite and against the sinful human self-constitution. A person's human existence fails when it seeks to identify and ground itself on the basis of itself. The primal sin is precisely the desire to be one's own presupposition and self-identical ground. What Luther classically formulated in relation to Romans 3 in his "Disputation Concerning Man" of 1536 remains true: "the definition of man is that man is justified by faith" [WA 39,I,176; AE 34, 139, translation altered].

On this basis are developed in FC the condemnations of Pelagianism and semi-Pelagianism in connection with the doctrine of original sin (Epit: BC,467ff; SD: BC,512ff). The formulations make clear that Rome is intended, even if not explicitly named. The condemnations follow from the conviction "that original sin is not a mere *defectus* or *carentia*, and thus a sort of privation, but rather a real corruption, a *congenita prava vis, interna immunditia cordis, pravae concupiscientiae et inclinationes*, thus a positive orientation against God."[73] This conviction is in no way explicitly contradicted by the Council of Trent in its Decree on Original Sin (see Dz 1510-1516). On the question whether concupiscence is sin or an evil effect of sin, a question related to the doctrine of baptism, the Council did contradict the Lutheran teaching (Trent, V,5; Dz 1515; cp. esp. SD: BC,511,18). Lutheran misgivings about the Roman Catholic understanding of original sin thus continued to exist, especially since they seemed to be confirmed by contemporary Catholic theology[74] and by the assertion in Trent's canons on justification (cp. esp. Dz 1554-1557) of an efficacious continued existence of free will after the Fall.[75]

One must keep the basic relations always in mind and make precise differentiations within this controversial question if one wants to see more clearly the point of difference. In relation to the confessionally different understandings of concupiscence, H.-G. Pöhlmann[76] has argued that finally a mere "verbal misunderstanding" exists here, a prime example that polemical theological controversies often "arise out of different contents being given to the same concept or different concepts being used for the same content, and that this situation was too little noted."[77] He is right that the dispute over the concept "concupiscence" had little importance in itself. It can be for the most part reduced to the general problem of the understanding of original sin and the particular question of whether and how far original sin remains in the baptized. As is well known, in relation to CA 2 the Confutatio warned "that to speak of concupiscence as sin can be understood to mean that original sin remains also in the baptized. This notion is rejected by referring to the papacy's previous condemnation of two statements of Luther about sin remaining after Baptism."[78] Correspondingly, Canon 5 of Trent's "Decree on Original Sin" (Dz 1515) states: "If anyone says that the guilt of original sin is not remitted through the grace of our lord Jesus Christ which is given in baptism, or even asserts that all which pertains to the true essence of sin is not removed, but declares it is only erased and not attributed: let him be anathema." Determinative here is the intention consistently to prevent any devaluation of baptismal grace, the validity and efficacy of which one believed understated by a "non-attribution" of sin.

Melanchthon in the Apology (Apol 2:35-45) firmly indicated that Luther "has always written that holy baptism removes and erases the total guilt and hereditary debt of original sin, although the material element (as they [the opponents] call it) of sin, namely the evil inclination and desire, remains" (BSLK 154, German of Apol. Cp. BC, 105:35). That the guilt of original sin is forgiven through baptism was not controversial. Nevertheless, the Reformation side insisted that the evil inclination and desire remaining in the baptized, i.e., concupiscence, is not only "a burden and imposed penalty" (*poena*) [BSLK 154, German of Apol. Cp. BC, 105:38) but also "damnable [*verdammliche*] sin" (BSLK 155, German of Apol. Cp. BC, 105:38). To this extent, original sin remains in the baptized. Like Luther, the Apology here cites Augustine: "Sin is forgiven in Baptism, not that it no longer is, but it is not imputed" (BC,105,36; cp. Augustine, *On Marriage and Concupiscence*, I, 25: PL 44, 430; CSEL 42, 240 17; English in NPNF, series 1, vol. 5, p. 274).

In no way, however, did one thus wish to devalue the effective validity of baptismal grace, but rather to sharpen the *abiding* dependence of the baptized upon it. Baptism did not grant a habitual possession such "that now, viewed in isolation, the person is a different and better human being. Rather, baptism initiates a new relationship with God so that, insofar as the person clings to Christ, that person partakes in his righteousness."[79] In their judgment upon themselves and their properties, the baptized also remain—in contradiction to their baptism—sinners before God. If they depend not upon themselves and their supposed possessions, but rather, in correspondence to the *sacramentum* of baptism (*mortificatio/vivificatio*), upon the prevenient grace of God in Jesus Christ, then they are righteous and free of all sins. One must here think theologically of the *simul*, central for all Lutheran doctrine (cp. II,1), in order not to lose oneself in terminological squabbles. Thus the Apology concludes its discussion of the problem-complex "baptism and original sin" with a critique of the idea of merit "through which the knowledge of Christ and the gospel was totally suppressed. For this reason Dr. Luther wanted to declare and teach on the basis of Scripture how original sin is great and mortal sin before God and how we are born in great misery and that the remnant of original sin which remains after baptism is not in itself something neutral but stands in need of the mediator Christ in order not to be ascribed to us by God and in need of the constant illumination and working of the Holy Spirit, through which it is swept out and slain" (BSLK 156, German of Apology, cp. BC, 106:45).

"To insist on the abiding weakness of the baptized person's own powers was the consequence of the fundamental evaluation of the possibilities for attaining one's own salvation."[80] From this vantage point, the Lutheran doctrine of original sin in general opens itself up, which cannot be discussed here in greater detail. Especially significant for controversial theology are the different confessional determinations of original righteousness and of the image of God in humanity (the meaning of the traditional distinction between *imago* and *similitudo*).[81] Since the Lutheran Reformation equated the image of God in humanity with original righteousness, the loss of original righteousness in the Fall had to signify also the loss of the image of God. In this theological state of affairs, it was not a matter of a simple deduction from one to the other, but of each reciprocally providing a basis for the other. The insight into the radicality of original sin as the root of all actual sins definitively excluded any thought of an undistorted remainder.[82] "While the privative and positive aspects in the scholastic doctrine of original sin mutually limited each other, they were henceforth interpreted in a sharpened way against each other."[83]

In all this discussion it is important to note that the Lutheran confession of a radical, abject depth of sin stands in a negative correspondence—if one may say so—to the witness to the unmerited, unmeritable, and thus unconditioned justifying grace of God in Jesus Christ. Only on this basis does it wish to be understood and can it be understood.[84]

2.4. The Doctrine of Free Will

The doctrine of the free or unfree will, closely connected to the doctrine of original sin, is treated analogously. FC 2 explicitly rejects "the error of the papists and scholastics... that by his natural powers man can start out toward that which is good and toward his own conversion, and that thereupon, since man is too weak to complete it, the Holy Spirit comes to the aid of the good work which man began by his natural powers" (SD 2:76). This error was more subtle than that of "the coarse Pelagians" (SD 2:75), but it still led away from the prevenient power of God. It ascribed freedom in spiritual things to the natural person and so referred such persons to themselves and their own alleged possibilities, which necessarily leads into sin (cp. Trent, Session VI, 1-5; Dz 1551-1555). In this connection belongs also the further rejection of the "teachings of the papists and the monks" that those born again can be righteous before God and merit eternal life by a complete fulfillment of the law in this life (cp. Trent VI, 32; Dz 1582; also see Dz 1902, 1913). As with the preceding, so also here the anathema is related to the doctrine of justification in that it seeks to prevent any impulse toward an attempt at human self-justification.[85] In this sense, FC[86] shares with CA 18 the conviction that persons possess a certain freedom in the external things of the world. Without the grace, help, and activity "given through the Word of God," however, the sinner is not capable "of making himself acceptable to God, of fearing God and believing in God with his whole heart, or of expelling inborn evil lusts from his heart" (CA 18).

A voluntary cooperation in salvation is also not conceded to worldly freedom, as Apol 18 makes unmistakably clear. Worldly freedom is explicitly described as external; "internally to grasp heart, mind, and outlook, that the Holy Spirit alone can work" (BSLK 312; German of Apol. 18:9).

This "inequality of inner and outer",[87] which is characteristic for the merely worldly human freedom in all its forms, is canceled only through the activity of the freedom of God in the person. It converts the self-misguided interiority of the sinner. The sinner is thus freed to true freedom and out of the existing unfreedom, an unfreedom only confirmed anew in self-referential acts which concentrate on the self's own powers. The gift of this foundation does not mean one can now derive one's freedom from oneself. Rather this foundation is withdrawn from the immediate grasp of the self-realizing act, which is foundationless precisely in its self-concern and declines into the abyss of sin. This self-reference is itself the deformity and driving power of sin.[88] For Lutheran doctrine, human freedom can be described only as liberation by God without any human contribution. A general denial is implied of a human capacity to apply the self to grace [*facultas applicandi se ad gratiam*] and of any action or cooperation toward salvation by a free will understood as a capacity of human freedom.

The divine liberation in no way, however, addresses the "subject of conversion" as a lever does a block. The liberating address of the Holy Spirit claims persons as the free rational creatures they have failed to be in sinful self-disorder. The basis of human freedom given by God thus cannot be defined as a mere given and then be played off against its practical realization. Through the divine liberation persons are freed to themselves.

2.5. The Doctrine of the Righteousness of Faith before God

The anathemas of FC discussed so far group themselves together in the condemnations within the text's teaching on justification.[89] This teaching is directed against a particular understanding of the doctrine of Osiander[90] and against the Roman doctrine. Anathematized is any synergism, any analytic understanding of justification, any reversal of the relation between justification and sanctification, faith and love, etc (cp. Epit III; SD III). "If one asks about the function of the detailed presentation of the common doctrine of justification, it is initially striking that this article seemed to be intended as a criterion for other points in the work of unification. It real task, however, was to meet the common interest of all Lutheran parties in an agreed basis for the struggle with the now self-reforming church of the old faith."[91]

Martin Chemnitz, who took no small part in the creation of the Concord, had already in his Examination of the Council of Trent[92] devoted particularly concentrated attention to the Lutheran understanding of justification[93] "in its characteristics and in its difference from that of the papal church, again stabilized by Trent."[94] Chemnitz clearly saw and explicitly acknowledged that Trent taught no self-salvation of the sinner through works. Controversial theological problems arose in connection to the question "what that is on account of which God receives sinful man into grace;... whether it is the satisfaction, obedience, and merit of the Son of God, the Mediator, or, indeed, the renewal which has been begun in us, the love, and other virtues in us."[95] This alternative may at first seem abstract; for Chemnitz, the paths divide here between nothing less than the true and the false understanding of the gospel. If the divine judgment of justification finally relates to the constitution and works of the person, then the total theological perspective is falsified, despite all earlier emphasis that the new quality of the person comes not from the self but is the work of God. In what is decisive, one is finally made to stand on oneself and one's own righteousness. For Chemnitz, self-righteous and thus unbelieving existence exists not only where human righteousness is presented as more or less self-produced, but also "where grace is seen as indwelling the person and, joined with the person's own capacities, is made the basis of divine judgment."[96] Chemnitz sees here again the transformation of the eccentricity of fides justificans into self-centeredness.[97]

Chemnitz believes that the Tridentine anathemas condemn all the prophets and the teaching of the apostles.[98] Against this he again places the basic confession of the Reformation: "a man is justified, that is, received into grace and accepted to life eternal, solely by the imputation of the righteousness of Christ, or solely through the remission of sins, faith laying hold of the mercy of God, which remits sins for Christ's sake."[99] One must not isolate individual terms and view each in isolation. Chemnitz sees the common sense of these formulas in the basic event that justifying faith is withdrawn from all self-concerned self-relation and exists and lives solely from its relation to Christ. An understanding of being, however, "which can only grasp the reality of things and persons as in themselves stable substances"[100] cannot understand this relation; it rather blocks such understanding. On this basis alone can the repeated basic alternative be understood which according to Chemnitz constitutes the real issue at stake in the post-Tridentine period: "whether we are absolved before the tribunal of God, have an appeased and gracious God, are adopted as children, and are received to life eternal on account of the merit, obedience, or righteousness of Christ or on account of our newness, which follows and is begun."[100] This alternative is also decisive for the condemnations within the FC, whether the object of rejection is the statement "that faith saves because by faith there is begun in us the renewal which consists in love toward God and our fellow man" (Epit III,19), or "that faith indeed has the most prominent role in justification, but that also renewal and love belong to our righteousness, but that nevertheless our righteousness before God is incomplete and imperfect without such love and renewal" (Epit III, 20), or "that believers are justified before God and saved both by the righteousness of Christ reckoned to them and by the incipient new obedience, or in part by the reckoning to them of Christ's righteousness and in part by our incipient new obedience" (Epit III.21; see further esp. SD III:45ff.)

The bluntness of these statements has not seldom been the object of criticism and complaint, even from Lutheran theologians: here "the understanding of justification in the sense of regeneration"[102] is said to be in fact given up, in contrast to the early Reformation. It is said that the FC's one-sided understanding of justification as forensic imputation creates the impression that the righteousness of Christ is ascribed to faith only externally, without becoming effective in and through it. The FC does in fact understand justification as forensic imputation and explicitly condemns the assertion "that when the prophets and the apostles speak of the righteousness of faith, the words 'to justify' and 'to be justified' do not mean 'to absolve from sins' and 'to receive forgiveness of sins,' but to be made really and truly righteous on account of the love and virtues which are poured into them by the Holy Spirit and the consequent good works" (FC SD III:62). Nevertheless, it would be a fundamental misunderstanding if one discovered behind such language only an external legal formalism which did not touch the inner, ethical life-thematic of the person. It cannot be easily denied that this misunderstanding found adherents in the dogmatics of Protestant scholastic orthodoxy and formed the background for the criticism carried out by early Enlightenment and Enlightenment theology in the name of the moral self-understanding of the person. It is to be granted that the turn to an increasingly forensic form of presentation in reaction to enthusiastic confusions did not offer an adequate terminology to state unmistakably the basic idea of the Reformation understanding of justification: faith's communion with Christ. Nevertheless, it would be simply false to say that the Fathers of the Concord were no longer conscious of this idea, or, even more, that they had not applied their full conceptual powers precisely to this one idea. For them also the insight undoubtedly remained fundamental for all individual points: the external righteousness of Jesus Christ is *really and effectively* present in faith precisely when faith eccentrically rests solely on the righteousness of Christ promised it by the Gospel, and in no way rests on it own *empirical* and *actual* righteousness. Over against this one Reformation fundamental idea, all terminological questions have only a serving function.

This thesis could, in my opinion, be confirmed in all the Lutheran Confessions, although that cannot be done here in detail. In relation to Article 4 of the CA and Apol,[103] G. Müller and V. Pfnür have convincingly shown by means of a detailed analysis of concepts and context[104] that the question whether the Reformation taught a forensic or an effective justification is abstract and obscures rather than illumines the inner structure of the foundations of the Reformation teaching. While it is beyond argument that between 1530 and 1577 a series of conceptual shifts occurred, extensively situationally conditioned, it is equally beyond argument that a structural unity of Lutheran doctrinal formation can be identified which stamps each conceptual moment. It consistently aims at that relation to God in which persons, removed from all willful self-power, depend totally on the righteousness of God in Jesus Christ, in order in him to come truly to themselves and their right determination.

Ecumenical dialogue will need to concentrate on this nexus, especially in comparing the Tridentine[105] and Reformation understandings of justification. Significant preparatory work along this line has already been done.[106] How far they justify the judgment that "a far-reaching consensus is developing in the interpretation of justification"[107] would need to be tested in detail and documented in an agreed text. A beginning in this direction is offered by the so-called Malta Report. It is there made clear that, on the Catholic side, "God's gift of salvation for the believer is unconditional as far as human accomplishments are concerned." On the Lutheran side it is emphasized that "the event of justification is not limited to individual forgiveness of sins" and is not to be seen as "a purely external declaration of the justification of the sinner. Rather the righteousness of God actualized in the Christ event is conveyed to the sinner through the message of justification as an encompassing reality basic to the new life of the believer" (para. 26).

2.6. The Doctrine of Good Works

The Lutheran Confessions are unanimous that in every aspect of doctrine all forms of self-justification active in works, however subtle, are to be rejected without reservation for the sake of a right understanding of faith as *fides apprehensiva*. An example can be found in the doctrine of penance (see Article 12 in the CA [also 11] and Apol [esp. 12:17ff, where a long series of false doctrines "of the scholastics and canonists" on penance are criticized], SA III,3, and the remarks in SD III:31).[108] Works-righteousness and forms of doctrine corresponding to it are already explicitly condemned in the Apol (IV:204). No corners can or may be cut in the teaching about good works. FC thus explicitly agrees with Luther's oft-repeated condemnation (see BSLK 946, nt 2) of papist trust in one's own good works (SD IV:26) in order then on its own part to reject the "decree of the Council of Trent... that our good works preserve salvation, or that our works either entirely or in part sustain and preserve either the righteousness of faith that we have received or even faith itself" (SD IV:35; cp. Council of Trent, Session 6, canons 24, 32; Dz 1574, 1582).

It seems even more radical when it is rejected and condemned "that it is taught and written that good works are necessary to salvation; or that no one has ever been saved without good works; or that it is impossible to be saved without good works" (Epit IV:16). The obligation to good works is in no way here being denied. One cannot then say that "good works are detrimental to salvation," a misunderstanding FC explicitly condemns (Epit IV:17). Rather, it is made clear that the basis of Christian being and action is removed from any basis or maintenance by self-active human works in that God's work in Jesus Christ precedes and has preceded all we do. Meaningful human practice is not made impossible by this divine prevenient action, but rather is all the more empowered. Because faith can rest in total trust in God, it is free from all care about the self and, at the same time and for the first time, is free for thankful care and meaningful acts of love. If persons nevertheless seek to effect their own salvation in their own activity, then they are inevitably turned back on themselves. In all their alleged good works they are only self-related; concerned with their own self-constitution.[109] The Reformation identified such self-circling with the piling up of pointless pious obligations. Thus, everything finally depended on the right ordering of law and gospel (cp. FC V[110]) so that the gospel is not again made into a teaching of law "as happened in the papacy (SD V:27).

A corresponding grounding of Christian practice is given in Articles 6 and 20 of CA and their explication in the Apol as well as in the other Confessions. That the subject matter here is foundational for the entire Reformation ethic is impressively confirmed in the Heidelberg Catechism, when it entitles its third Part, which deals with questions of Christian action, "Thankfulness." It is thus implied that Christian action has its origin and preservation not in itself but in the prevenience of a divine act. It is carried out as thankfulness, which presupposes a reception. This thankfulness cannot be understood as a repayment which wishes to erase the debt, refusing to receive anything as gift. True thankfulness must finally say that it owes its thanks to the one it thanks. Thankfulness, however, is not in opposition to action on one's own part. Meaningful action rather develops out of thankfulness. In distinction to a self-grounding, self-justifying, and thus totally self-concerned action, thankfulness knows itself as a giving which has itself been given. As thankfulness related to the priority of the action of God, Christian action is liberated from care for self and thus free for active care of the other. In the sphere of thankfulness, dependence/freedom and activity/passivity do not appear as alternatives, but are perceived in a relation of reciprocal openness.

Notes

1. For the sake of documentation, the following study is published in the form in which it was presented to the participants in the 43rd Working Session of the Ecumenical Study Group of Evangelical and Catholic Theologians at Schloß Friedewald in 1982. More recent relevant literature is taken into consideration only to the extent that it was mentioned in the discussion within the Study Group. On some themes (esp. I,5; II,7), I have since then more precisely defined my understanding.

2. On the history of the FC and the other confessional texts in the BC, see BSLK, xi-xliv, as well as the literature there cited.

3. An overview of the controverted issues can be derived from the corresponding accounts in the twelve articles of the FC. They deal with (1) the controversy between Flacius and Strigel over whether original sin is substance or accident; (2) the synergistic controversy concerning the problem of free will; (3) the Osiandrian controversy over the doctrine of justification; (4) the debate among

Andreae, Major, and Musculus over the question whether good works are useful or harmful to salvation; and (5, 6) the so-called antinomian controversy. A further article (7) deals with the controverted understanding of the Lord's Supper. The 8th addresses the closely related problematic of the doctrine of the person of Christ. The central issue here was the relation between the two natures within the unity of Christ's person (communicatio naturarum and communicatio idiomatum). Articles 9 addresses Aepinus' doctrine of Jesus' descent into Hell and Article 11 the theme of predestination. The 10th article is dedicated to the so-called adiaphoristic controversy which had arisen out of the Augsburg and Leipzig Interims (May and December 1548, following the defeat of the Protestants in the Smalcaldic War) and concerned the permissibility of concessions to one's opponents in matters of church order and usages in a time of the persecution of doctrine. The FC concludes (12) with a self-differentiation from "factions and sects which never accepted the Augsburg Confession."

4.   E. Koch, *Der Weg zur Konkordienformel, in Vom Dissensus zum Konsensus: Die Formula Concordiae von 1577*, Fuldaer Hefte 24 (Hamburg, 1980): 10-46.

5.   B. Lohse, "Das Konkordienwerk von 1580," in *Kirche und Bekenntnis: Historische und theologische Aspekte zur Frage der gegenseitgen Anerkennung der lutherischen and der katholische Kriche auf der Grundlage der Confessio Augustana*, edited by P. Meinhold (Wiesbaden: 1980), 94-122.

6.   W.-D. Hauschild, "Corpus Doctrinae und Bekenntnisschriften: Zur Vorgeschicthe des Konkordienbuches," in *Bekenntnis und Einheit der Kirche: Studien zum Konkordienbuch im Auftrag der Sektion Kirchengeschichte der Wissenschaftlichen Gesellschaft für Theologie*, edited by M. Brecht & R. Schwarz (Stuttgart: 1980): 235.

7.   E. Wolf, "Bekenntnisschriften," in RGG (3rd ed.), I:esp. 1012-1014. On the pre-history of the BC, see esp. H. Heppe, *Die Entstehung und Fortbildung des Luthertums und die kirchlichen Bekenntnisschriften derselben von 1549-1576* (Kassel: 1863); H. Heppe/G. Kawerau, "Corpus doctrinae," in RE (3rd ed.), vol IV:293-298; as well as the relevant articles in the already cited *Bekenntnis und Einheit der Kirche* (nt. 6).

8.   E. Wolf, "Konkordienbuch," in RGG (3rd ed) III:1776f, here 1776.

9.   See I. Mager, "Aufnahme und Ablehnung des Konkordienbuches in Nord-, Mittel- und Ostdeutschland" and W.-U. Deetjen, "Concordia Concors— Concordia Discors: Zum Ringen um das Kondordienwerk in Süden und mittleren Westen Deutschlands," both in *Bekenntnis und Einheit der Kirche* (see nt. 6), pp. 271-302 and 303-349.

10.   H. Weissgerber, "Die geltenden Bekenntnisschriften: Ein Überblick über die Verfassungen der lutherischen Kirchen," in *Das Bekenntnis im Leben der Kirche: Studien zur Lehrgrundlage und Bekenntnisbindung in den lutherischen Kirchen*, edited by V. Vajta and H. Weissgerber (Berlin/Hamburg: 1963), 21-53, here 23.

11.   See in this regard the differing conceptions of a "theology of the confessions." E. Schlink (*Theology of the Lutheran Confessions* [Philadelphia: Fortress Press, 1961]) and F. Brünstad (*Theologie des lutherischen Bekenntnisschriften*

[Gütersloh: 1951]) understand the BC as "a single whole, as a doctrinal totality" (Brünstad, p. 16). H. Fagerberg (*A New Look at the Lutheran Confessions* (1529-1537) [St. Louis: Concordia, 1972]), on the basis of tensions within the BC which Schlink also explicitly notes (op cit, p. 17), decides upon a more historically oriented presentation and limits himself "materially to the earlier confessions written by Luther and Melanchthon (op cit, p. 12). "Behind this decision lies an historical concern to be able to illumine the theology of the Reformation as it came to be during its years of consolidation, i.e., the 1530s" (ibid.).

12. The difficulty of defining the doctrinal unity of the church under evangelical premises is shown by this laborious process, which was only partially a success and cannot be considered closed. One must ask whether the conscious perception of this difficulty would reveal only a weakness in the formation of the Lutheran confessions.

13. G. Kretschmar, "Die Bedeutung der Confessio augustana als verbindliche Bekenntnisschrift der Evangelisch-Lutherischen Kirche," in *Confessio Augustana: Hindernis oder Hilfe?* (Regensburg:1979) 31-77, here 76, nt 61.

14. Cp. the preface of the SD (BSLK, 829-832) or the demarcation "from all heretics and sectarians" (BSLK, 1091-1100).

15. Against W. Maurer, "Die Geltung des lutherischen Bekenntnisses im ökumenischen Zeitalter," in *Publica doctrina heute*, Fuldaer Hefte 19 (Berlin/Hamburg: 1969) 94-112, here 103.

16. Kretschmar, op cit, 63.

17. Ibid.

18. Cp. M. Heckel, "Die reichsrechtliche Bedeutung des Bekenntnisses," in *Bekenntnis und Einheit der Kirche* (nt. 6), 57-88.

19. Kretschmar (nt 13), 62.

20. See in this connection also P. Fraenkel, *Testimonia patrum: The Function of the Patristic Argument in the Theology of Philip Melanchthon* (Geneva: 1961).

21. U. Asendorf, "Die Funktion der publica doctrina nach den lutherischen Bekenntnisschriften in den gegenwärtigen Kirchenordnungen und in der kirchlichen Praxis (Kirchenrechtliche und kirchkundliche Fragen)," in *Publica doctrina heute* (Berlin/Hamburg:1969), 28-53, here 38f.

22. Ibid, 39.

23. Ibid.

24. V. Vajta, "Das Bekenntnis der Kirche als ökumenisches Anliegen," in Vajta and Weissgerber (see note 10): 243-276; here 260.

25. F. W. Kantzenbach, "Der argumentative Schriftgebrauch in der reformatorischen Theologie des Heils," in *Lebendiger Umgang mit Schrift und Bekenntnis:*

Theologische Beiträge zur Bezeihung von Schrift und Bekenntnis und zu ihrer Bedeutung für das Leben der Kirche, edited by J. Track (Stuttgart: 1980), 85-125. On the problem "biblical theology and ecclesial confession," see the article by G. Hausmann with the same title in the same volume, pp. 41-61. See further H.-J. Kühne, *Schriftautorität und Kirche: eine kontroverstheologische Studie zur Begründung der Schriftautorität in der neueren katholischen Theologie*, Kirche und Konfession: Konfessionskundlisches Institut des Evangelischen Bundes, vol. 22 (Göttingen: 1980); N. Appel, *Kanon und Kirche: Die Kanonskrise im heutigen Protestantismus als kontrovers-theologisches Problem*, Konfessionskundliche und Kontroverstheologische Studien, J.-A. Möhler Institute, vol. 9 (Paderborn: 1964); Die Berbindlichkeit des Kanons (articles by H. Braun, W. Andersen, W. Maurer), Fuldaer Hefte 12.

26.   F. W. Kantzenbach, "Der argumentative Schriftgebrauch in der reformatorischen Theologie des Heils," in *Lebendiger Umgang mit Schrift und Bekenntnis. Theologische Beiträge zur Beziehung von Schrift und Bekenntnis und zu ihrer Bedeutung für das Leben der Kirche*, edited by J. Track (Stuttgart: 1980): 85-125. On the problem "biblical theology and ecclesial confession," see in the same volume G. Hausmann, "Biblische Theologie und kirchliches Bekenntnis," pp. 41-61. See further H.-J. Kühne, *Schriftautorität und Kirche: Eine kontroverstheologische Studie zur Begründung der Schriftautorität in der neueren kotholischen Theologie* (Göttingen: 1980); N. Appel, *Kanon und Kirche: Die Kanonskrise im heitigen Protestantismus als kontroverstheologisches Problem* (Paderborn: 1964); and Die Verbindlichkeit des Kanons (with essays by H. Braun, W. Andersen, and W. Maurer), Fuldaer Hefte, 12.

27.   Cp. SA II,2: "This means that the Word of God shall establish articles of faith and no one else, not even an angel" (BC,295,15).

28.   Wenzel Lohff, "The Significance of the Augsburg Confession for the Lutheran Church and its Relationship to the Roman Catholic Church," in *Confessing One Faith: A Joint Commentary on the Augsburg Confession by Lutheran and Catholic Theologians*, edited by George Wolfgang Forell and James F. McCue (Minneapolis: Augsburg, 1982), 25.

29.   See in this connection "The Gospel and the Church: Report of the Lutheran/Roman Catholic Study Commission" (commonly called the Malta Report).

30.   Ibid., 24.

31.   Ibid.

32.   See on this theme in general, *Sola Scriptura*: Ringvorlesung der theologischen Fakultät der Philipps-Universität Marburg, edited by C.-H. Ratschow (Marburg 1977).

33.   "Common to both positions—the Counter-Reformation and the anti-Counter-Reformation, is the falling apart of authority (the formal) and message (the substantive), the double structure of the normative which followed (*et-et/partim-partim* and *norma normans-norma normata*), and then the confessionalization of scriptural interpretation." I. Lønning, *Kanon im Kanon* (Oslo/Munich, 1972): 213.

34. Cp. H. Günther, "Das Schriftverständnis der Konkordienformel," in *Bekenntnis zur Wahrheit: Aufsätze über die Kondordienformel*, edited by J. Schöne (Erlangen: 1978):25-33.

35. Cf. Heinrich Schmid, *The Doctrinal Theology of the Evangelical Lutheran Church* (Philadelphia: 1899, rpt. 1961), 38ff, 500ff; C. H. Ratschow, *Lutherisch Dogmatik zwischen Reformation und Aufklärung*, Part 1 (Gütersloh: 1964), 71ff.

36. Cp. also the essay by P. Fraenkel, *"Satis Est?* Schrift, Tradition, Bekenntnis" as well as the response by S. Wiedenhofer and the following discussion in *Confessio Augustana und Confutatio: Der Augsburger Reichstag 1530 und die Einheit der Kirche*, Reformationsgeschichtliche Studien und Texte, 118, edited by Erwin Iserloh (Münster: Aschendorff, 1980): 286-324.

37. "The Lutheran confession binds the congregations, their shepherds, and their teachers exclusively to the apostolic gospel. Thus the Lutheran confession contains no self-subsistent truths. Everything within it which speaks the truth receives its validity only from the apostolic gospel. It belongs to the inalienable foundations of Luther's Reformation that the Church can from itself define no article of faith" (Peter Brunner, "The Present Significance of the Lutheran Confession," in *The Unity of the Church*: A Symposium (Rock Island: Augustana Press, 1957), 89 [translation altered].

38. K. G. Steck, *Kirche des Wortes oder Kirche des Lehramts?* (Zürich, 1962), 21; see also his *Das römische Lehramt und die Heilige Schrift* (Munich, 1963). Whether Steck's essays do justice to the present state of ecumenical dialogue remains an open question.

39. "It is thus an unevangelical understanding which wishes to view the confession from its written deposit, its external dimension. The written formulation has rather the sense of enabling the act of preaching by, on the one hand, referring the church to its own center in the proclamation of the word and, on the other, reminding the church of its obligation to make secure the external proclamation by the strength of divine law" (Asendorf, [see note 21], p. 37.) That the text is fixed in writing must not mean that "the obedience of faith becomes a faith of pure obedience" (W. Kasper, "The Catholic View of Confessions and Confessional Community," in *Confessing One Faith*, p. 53). Rather, "in confession is grasped, both literally and figuratively, that faith is not a matter of a relation of an independent subject to a separate, supernatural, or even only historical object but the present process in which subjects wasting away in their self-identity are taken into the historically mediated event of God's self-opening for communication" (J. Baur, "Kirchliches Bekenntnis und modernes Bewußtsein," in his *Einsicht und Glaube* [Göttingen, 1978] 284).

40. "Verbindliches Zeugnis der Kirche als ökumenische Aufgabe: Arbeitsbericht einer Studiengruppe des Deutschen Ökumenischen Studienausschusses," in *Beiheft to Ökumenische Rundschau*, 33 (1978), p. 17.

41. Ibid.

42. Lønning [see nt. 33], p. 192, nt. 742.

43. P. Lengfeld, *Überlieferung, Tradition und Schrift in der evangelischen und katholischen Theologie der Gegenwart* (Paderborn: 1958).

44. On this point, W. Kasper (see nt. 39, p. 49) has said in relation to Dz 1507: "The decisive point for the Council of Trent was not an addition to the content of Scripture, but the interpretation of Scripture by the church, or, said in another manner, the indissoluble connection of the Scriptures with the church and with the sense of the Scriptures which both originated in the church and has continually been maintained by it."

45. Cf. W. Caspari, *Die geschichtliche Grundlage des gegenwärtigen evangelischen Gemeindelebens* (Leipzig, 1908), 261f.

46. Weissgerber (see nt. 10), p. 26.

47. E. Wolf, "Die Rechtfertigungslehre als Mitte und Grenze reformatorischer Theologie," in his *Peregrinatio: Studies zur reformatorischen Theologie* (Munich, 1965), 11. See also Schlink (nt. 11), p. 14: "Every individual doctrine is to be understood only in relation to the center of the confessions, that is, from the article of justification."

48. Wolf (nt. 47), 13.

49. The Malta Report (D24) is thus to be unconditionally affirmed when it states that the center and limit of the gospel cannot be reduced to a theological formula. Rather, they are "constituted by the eschatological saving act of God in Jesus' cross and resurrection. It is this act which all proclamation seeks to explicate."

50. Maurer (nt 15), 109.

51. "Theologically to think this 'simul' " in fact belongs "to the continuing, fundamental problems of the doctrine of justification" (J. Werbick, "Rechtfertigung des Sünders—Rechtfertigung Gottes. Thesen zur ökumenischen Diskussion um die Rechtfertigugnslehre," *Kerygma und Dogma* 27 (1981): 47.

52. "Whatever is in me and all my powers, except grace, is sin and damned" (WA 28,12,17f).

53. J. Baur, "Lehre, Irlehre, Lehrzucht," in his *Einsicht und Glaube* (Göttingen, 1978), 234.

54. Ibid.

55. Cp. G. Müller and V. Pfnür, "Justification—Faith—Works," in *Confessing One Faith* (see nt 39), pp. 119-121. Cp. also A. Kimme, "Die ökumenische Bedeutung der Augsburgischen Konfession," in *Die Aktualität des Bekenntnisses*, Fuldaer Hefte 21 (Hamburg, 1971), p. 14: "In the doctrinal outline of CA 1-17, a clear caesura occurs between articles 4 and 5. The opening words of CA 5 ("In order that we may obtain this faith,") refer to the preceding Article 4 on justification. This fourth article is itself the conclusion of the first three fundamental articles on the Trinity, fallen humanity, and Christ. This justifying faith, based on the doctrine of God, humanity, and Christ, is elaborated in Articles 5-17 from the perspectives

of ordained ministry, the means of grace, ethical fruits, the church, the individual sacraments, church order, civil life, and final judgment." On the outline of the first part of the CA, see further W. Pannenberg, "Die ökumenische Bedeutung der Confessio Augustana." Sitzungsberichte der Bayrischen Akademie der Wissenschaften, Phil.-hist. Klasse, 1981. Heft 6, 12-15.

56. On this basis one can understand why Luther at the end of the first part of SA, initially wrote that over the "sublime articles of the divine majesty" (BC, 291), there was no dispute or contention, "for both parties (believe and) confess them" (BC, 292), but then eliminated the two words in parentheses: "the formal agreement to the ancient creeds did not suffice if saving faith is not present" (W. Maurer, "Die Geltung" [see nt. 15] p. 109).

57. See "On the Freedom of the Christian"; cp. E. Jüngel, *The Freedom of a Christian: Luther's Significance for Contemporary Theology* (Minneapolis: 1988).

58. One must test the assertion (Malta Report D25) that the "idea of the hierarchy of truths" is in fact "very close to the idea of the center of the gospel." The following, however, is certainly correct (Malta Report D27): "As the message of justification is the foundation of Christian freedom in opposition to legalistic conditions for the reception of salvation, it must be articulated ever anew as an important interpretation of the center of the gospel. But it was also pointed out that the event of salvation to which the gospel testified can also be expressed comprehensively in other representations derived from the New Testament, such as reconciliation, freedom, redemption, new life and new creation."

59. Wolf (see nt 47), 14. Cp the foundational sentences of Melanchthon at the beginning of Apol 4.

60. On the prehistory of the condemnations, see W. Maurer, *Historical Commentary on the Augsburg Confession* (Philadelphia: Fortress, 1986), 48-57; Hans-Werner Gensichen, *We Condemn: How Lutheran and 16th-Century Lutheranism Condemned False Doctrine* (St. Louis: Concordia, 1967), 83ff.

61. Maurer, "Die Geltung," (see nt. 15), 110.

62. Maurer, *Historical Commentary* (see note 60), 50.

63. On the history of these texts, see Maurer, *Historical Commentary*, pp. 277-280, and 409-413.

64. Cp the version of the condemnation in CA 12 in Na (the German translation of a preliminary text of CA sent on June 3, 1530, to Nuremberg).

65. On the textual history of CA 16 and CA 18.1-2, see Maurer, *Historical Commentary*, 98-101.

66. Maurer, *Historical Commentary*, 48.

67. BSLK 83; BC, 47.

68. Maurer, *Historical Commentary*, 54.

69. On FC, see in general, F. H. R. Frank, *Die Theologie der Concordienformel historisch-dogmatisch entwickelt und beleuchtet* (Erlangen, 1858ff), Vol. 4, 345-391.

70. K.-H. Kandler, "Bedingungen der Eintracht: *Beobachtungen zur Struktur der Konkordienformel*," in Schöne (see nt 34), p. 181f.

71. W. Sparn, "Begründung und Verwirklichung. Zur anthropologischen Thematik der lutherischen Bekenntnisse," in *Bekenntnis und Einheit der Kirche* (see nt 6), p. 143.

72. Ibid. [Translator's note: The four traditional states referred to are: before the law, under the law, under grace, and in glory.]

73. Frank (see note 69), I, 54.

74. Cp. SA III (esp BC,302f) as well as Apol II (BSLK 149f; BC,102,14ff), where the "scholastics" are "criticized" who make "too much of free will and our works" [In German of Apol, not translated in BC].

75. Frank (see nt. 69), I, 54.

76. "Das Kondupiszenzverständnis der CA, der Confutatio, der Apologie und des Konzils von Trient," in Iserloh (see nt 36)389-395.

77. Ibid. 389.

78. Leif Grane, *The Augsburg Confession: A Commentary*, trans. John H. Rasmussen (Minneapolis: Augsburg, 1987), 44. The reference is to the following sentences cited in the bull of Leo X against Luther of June 15, 1520, *Exsurge Domine*: 2. "To deny that sin remains in a child after baptism is to disregard both Paul and Christ alike. 3. The seed of sin (*fomes peccati*) hinders a soul departing from the body from entering into heaven, even though there is no actual sin." (Dz 1452f; ND 554.)

79. Ibid, p. 46. Translation altered.

80. Wilhelm Breuning and Bengt Hägglund, "Sin and Original Sin," in *Confessing One Faith*, p. 105.

81. See W. Pannenberg, *Gottebenbildlichkeit als Bestimmung des Menschen in der neueren Theologiegeschichte*, Sitzungsbericht der Bayerischen Akademie der Wissenschaften, Phil.-hist. Klasse, 1979, Heft 8.

82. See SA III.

83. Sparn (see nt. 71), 132.

84. So also Pöhlmann (see nt. 76), 395 and passim.

85. Cp Frank (see nt 69) I, 113ff.

86. Cp. A. Kimme, "Reformatorische Anthropologie. Das Bild des Menschen nach der Konkordienformel," in Schöne (see nt. 34), 35-48.

87. Sparn (see nt 71): 134; emphasized by Sparn.

88. Cp Art 19 of CA, which is deliberately attached to the article on free will. "Its purpose is to prevent any possibility of blaming the reformers for making God the cause of sin" (Grane [see nt 78], 191). Sin is itself to blame.

89. See F. Jacob, "Von Christi Tat und unserem Tun. Zur Interpretation von Article III and IV der Konkordienformel," in Schöne (see nt 34), 49-63.

90. See M. Stupperich, "Zur Vorgeschichte des Rechtfertigungsartikels in der Konkordienformel," in *Bekenntnis und Einheit der Kirche* (see nt 6): 175-194.

91. Ibid., p. 191.

92. 1565-1573. Critical edition of Latin: Darmstadt, 1972. English translation: St. Louis: Concordia, 1971-1986.

93. Chemnitz (see nt 92): I, 461ff.

94. J. Baur, "Martin Chemnitz," in his *Einsicht und Glaube* (Göttingen, 1978): 155.

95. Chemnitz (see nt. 92), I, 468.

96. Baur (see nt. 93): 169.

97. "Therefore they bring back into the church that Scholastic figment that Christ merited only the first grace for us, with the help of which, while our own free will concurs, we can afterwards merit with out own good works that we become more pleasing to God, and are received to life eternal on account of our own good work." Chemnitz (see nt. 92): I, 541.

98. Ibid., I, 461ff, 469ff, etc.

99. Ibid., I, 462.

100. Baur, (see nt. 93): 167.

101. Chemnitz (see nt. 92): I, 166.

102. H. Fagerberg, "Die Rechtfertigungslehre in CA and Apologie," in Iserloh (see nt. 36), 337f.

103. On the criticism of the theological distinction between a congruous and a condign merit, see Apol. IV:20ff.

104. Cp. also Fagerberg (see nt. 102).

105. Adolf von Harnack's statement (that "it may be doubted whether the Reformation would have developed itself if this Decree [i.e., Trent on justification] had been issued at the Lateran Council at the beginning of the century, and had really passed into the flesh and blood of the Church" [*History of Dogma*, Vol. 7, translated by Neil Buchanan, {Boston:Little, Brown, 1900}, p. 57]) should not make us forget that the Fathers of the Concord, for theological reasons which they thought were truly Lutheran and which have not canceled themselves out, were of the opinion that the basic insight of the Reformation had been broadly misperceived in Trent's decree.

106. G.Maron, *Kirche und Rechtfertigung: Eine kontroverstheologische Untersuchung, ausgehend von den Texten des Zweiten Vatikanischen Konzils* [Göttingen, 1969]; V. Pfnür, *Einig in der Rechtgertigungslehre? Die Rechtfertigungslehre der Confessio Augustana (1530) und die Stellungnahme der katholischen Kontroverstheologie zwischen 1530 and 1535* [Wiesbaden, 1970]; H. G. Pöhlmann, *Rechtfertigung. Die gegenwärtige kontroverstheologische Problematik der Refertigungslehre zwischen der evangelisch-lutherischen und der römisch-katholischen Kirche* [Güterloh, 1971], as well as, on the whole, H. Rückert, *Die Rechtfertigungslehre auf dem Tridentischen Konzil* [Bonn, 1925].

107. Malta Report, 26.

108. It suffices here to cite H. Jorissen's excellent investigations on this theme: "Steht die Bußlehre der Confessio Augustana einer Anerkennung durch die Katholische Kirche im Wege?," in *Katholische Anerkennung des Augsburgischen Bekenntnisses*, Ök. Persp. 9 (Frankfurt a.M., 1977), 132-150; "Die Sakramenta: Taufe und Buße," in Iserloh (see nt. 36), 524-544, and with H. Fagerberg, "Penance and Confession," in *Confessing One Faith* (see nt. 39), 234-261. The question whether CA's doctrine of penance stands in the way of its recognition by the Catholic Church gains importance in relation to the explicit reference to the definition of penance in CA 12 by Trent. Canon 4 of Trent on penance (Dz 1704) states: "If anyone denies that, for the full and complete forgiveness of sins, three acts are required in the penitent to form as it were the matter of the sacrament of penance: namely, contrition, confession and satisfaction, which are called the three parts of penance; or says there are only two parts of penance, namely, terrors afflicting the conscience once sin is acknowledged, and faith arising from the gospel or from the absolution, with which a person believes that his sins have been forgiven through Christ: let him be anathema." In relation to this, Jorissen and Fagerberg have shown with convincing arguments: "Exactly what Melanchthon opposed is not condemned in that form by Trent, and what Trent anathematized was not meant in that way by Melanchthon" (ibid., p. 253).

109. Note here the well-known image of the tree and its fruits: "And as a good tree bears good fruits, while the fruits do not make the tree good, so must good works follow the new birth, although they do not make the person pleasing before God" (Apol IV:253, German version; BSLK 209f; not in BC).

110. See in detail Frank (see nt. 69), vol. 2, pp. 243-341.

Chapter Seven

The Condemnations on Justification in the Confessio Augustana, the Apology, and the Smalcald Articles

Vinzenz Pfnür

PRELIMINARY REMARKS

F OR THE SPECIFICATION of the goal of the present contribution, we should first recall the dilemma of our present ecumenical situation. On the one side, the confession of faith necessarily requires demarcations if we do not wish the faith to evaporate into a contentless introspection. On the other side, the maintenance of the traditional reciprocal doctrinal condemnations, denying or at least calling into question each other's salvation and Christian existence, endangers the credibility of the Christian proclamation, and indeed all the more so—as paradoxical as it sounds—as more Lutheran and Catholic Christians and congregations recognize and confess a deeper mutuality in faith.

The way out of this dilemma does not lie in a fundamental relativization of the truth, but on the contrary in taking the truth more seriously in a double sense: first in a more differentiated view of one's own position, and then in a more differentiated view of the other side.

Here two points of view are of importance: on the one hand, the readiness to distinguish between the position of a theological school or viewpoint and the position of the common confession of the Christian communities, and on the other, the readiness to distinguish between the sense and point of a condemnation as the reverse side of the confession and the application of that condemnation to a concrete counterposition. If these distinctions are not made, then the limits of the respective theological schools become the border between the confessions, and also the corresponding contrast and reverse image (which in liberal theology, e.g., turns out somewhat differently than in dialectical theology) is projected onto the confessional counterposition without taking the other confession seriously in its self-understanding.

Thus the goal of the present investigation is not to represent the confessional oppositions as they appear from the viewpoint of the theological schools of the nineteenth and twentieth century, as important a task as that might be. Rather, the goal here is to investigate the condemnations within the confessional writings (extending into the viewpoints of the theological schools). It is to be observed that in the confessional writings themselves, the condemnations are qualified in different ways. The present contribution concentrates on the formal damnations pronounced by the communities and directed to persons who represent specific teachings (*ecclesiae damnant eos, qui docent*). It includes the rejections in the broader sense (*reprehendimus doctrinam adversariorum*, etc.) for the illumination of these strict damnations.

The chief goal is then to determine the exact target and direction of these damnations and to place them in relation to the responsible catholic-ecclesiastical doctrinal position.

A further problem is one of fundamental and technical demarcation. In principle, one should avoid both an over-systemization (for instance, by deriving the entire content of the Christian faith from the doctrine of justification) as well as an isolation of the doctrine of justification. The solution attempted here is first to work through the damnations aimed at the Catholic side in relation to their terminological and objective reference to the doctrine of justification. In this process, several groups of issues arise: condemnations in relation to the understanding of sin, free will, penance, effect of the sacraments, the mass, monasticism, veneration of the saints, the papacy.

For technical reasons (corresponding to the distribution of the study groups), questions about "justification and sacraments" and "justification and ecclesiastical office" are either completely set aside or only briefly addressed.

1. THE CONDEMNATIONS IN RELATION TO THE UNDERSTANDING OF SIN, GRACE, AND FREE WILL

In reference to the questions of sin, grace, and free will, the two condemnatory sentences quoted below from CA 2 and CA 18 (Ed. pr.)[1] are the only formal damnations from the confessional writings handled here.

Confessio Augustana, Art. 2:[2]

Damnant Pelagianos et alios, qui vitium originis negant esse peccatum et, ut extenuent gloriam meriti et beneficiorum Christi, disputant hominem propriis viribus rationis coram Deo iustificari posse.

Hieneben werden verworfen die Pelagianer und andere, so die Erbsund nicht fur Sund halten, damit sie die Natur fromm machen durch naturlich Kräft, zu Schmach dem Leiben und Verdienst Christi.

They condemn the Pelagians and others who deny the vice of origin is sin and who obscure the glory of Christ's merit and benefits, they contend that a human being can be justified before God by his/her own strength and reason.

Rejected in this connection are the Pelagians and others who deny that original sin is sin, for they hold that nature is pious through natural power, to the disgrace to the suffering and merit of Christ.

Confessio Augustana (Ed. pr.), Art. 18:[3]

Damnant Pelagianos et alios, qui docent, quod sine spiritu sancto solis naturae viribus possimus Deum super omnia diligere, item praecepta Dei facere quoad substantiam actuum.

Hie werden diejenige verworfen, so lehren, dass wir Gottes Gepot ohn Gnad und heiligen Geist halten können.

They condemn the Pelagians and others who teach that without the Holy Spirit,by the powers of nature alone we are able to love God above all things, and so can do the commandments of God is far as the substance of the acts is concerned.

In accord with the study's mandate, the first question to be raised is: Against whom are these concrete doctrinal condemnations directed?[4] Is the Catholic doctrinal position generally condemned, or is it a question of a fictitious counterposition?

In the light of the historical context of CA, the rejection in CA 2 is first directed clearly against Zwingli[5] and the Anabaptists.[6]

But the damnations of CA 2 and especially of CA 18 (Ed. pr.) also have in view specific scholastic theological positions of the Catholic side:

According to Apol 2,7f, it is the *scholastici doctores* "who weaken original sin" and "accord to human nature undamaged powers to love God above everything and to fulfill the commandments according to the substance of the act".[7] According to Apol 4,9, it is the "scholastics who follow the philosophers... and invent this dream that human reason without the Holy Spirit can love God above everything."[8] In Luther's Smalcald Articles (SA) seven doctrinal formulations of the "scholastic theologians" (*scholasticorum doctorum dogmata*) are listed and rejected as "error" and "truly pagan teaching, which we cannot tolerate":[9:]

Post Adae lapsum hominis naturales vires mansisse integars et incorruptas et hominem naturaliter habere rationem rectam et bonam voluntatem, sicut philo-sophi docent.

1. Nämlich, dass nach dem Erbfall Adae des Menschen naturlichen Kräfte sind ganz und unverderbt blieben.Und der Mensch habe von Natur eine rechte Vernunft und guten Willen, wie die Philosophi solchs lehren.

1. That after the fall of Adam the natural powers of a person have remained whole and uncorrupted, and that a person by nature possesses a right understanding and a good will, as the philosophers teach.

Et hominem habere liberum arbitrium faciendi bonum et omittendi malum et econtra omittendi bonum et faciendi malum.

2. Item dass der Mensch habe einen freien Willen, Guts zu tun und Boses zu lassen und wiederumb Guts zu lassen und Boses zu tun.

2. Again, that a person has a free will, either to do good and refrain from evil or to refrain from good and do evil.

Item hominem posse naturalibus viribus omina mandata Dei servare et facere.

3. Item dass der Mensch muge aus naturlischen Kräften alle Gebot Gottes tun und halten.

3. Again, that a person is able by natural powers to observe and to keep all the commandments of God.

Et posse naturalibus viribus Deum super omina dilgere et proximum sicut seipsum.

4. Item er muge aus naturlichen Kräften Gott lieben uber alles und seinen Nächsten als sich selbs.

4. Again, that a person is able by natural powers to love God above all things and the neighbor as itself.

Item si faciat homo, quantum in se est, Deum largiri ei certo suam gratiam.

5. Item wenn ein Mensch utu, soviel an ihm ist, so gibt ihm Gott gewisslich seine Gnade.

5. Again, if persons do what they can, God is certain to grant them grace.

Et si accedere velit homo ad eucharistiam, non opus esse bono proposito recte faciendi, sed sufficere, si non adsit malum propositum peccandi: tam bonam scilicet esse naturam et tantam esse vim sacramenti.

6. Item wenn er zum Sakrament will gehen, ist nicht von ein guter Fursatz, Guts zu tun, sondern sei gnug, dass er nicht einen bosen Fursatz, Sunde zu tun, habe, so gar gut ist die Natur und das Sakrament so kräftif.

6. Again, when a person goes to the sacrament there is no need of a good intention to do what ought to be done, but it is enough that there is not an evil intention to commit sin, for such is the goodness of human nature and such is the power of the sacrament.

Item non posse ex scriptura probari ad bonum opus necessario requiri spiritum sanctum et ejus gratiam.

7. Es sei nicht in der Schrift gegrundet, dass zum guten Werk vonnoten sei der heilig Geist mit seiner Gnaden.

7. That it cannot be proven from the Scriptures that the Holy Spirit and his gifts are necessary for the performance of a good work.

The more precise identification of the rejected counterposition must first be limited negatively.

The rejections are not directed at Augustine or the teaching of the fathers, not even at the position of Thomas Aquinas, Bonaventure, and William of Paris. Rather these are contrasted with the disputed opponents as witnesses for the correct teaching on original sin and on justification.[10]

The CA certifies to its contemporary dialogue partners that its teaching is "more tolerable than the earlier teaching."[11] Nevertheless, in the draft of the Apol it is stated: "Formerly, when they spoke of the forgiveness of sins justification, then they never thought about faith.... Now several theologians have im-proved and confessed... that one has conceded too much to human powers."[12] Only after the breakdown of the negotiations for an agreement did the Apol cease to differentiate between the position it rejects and the teaching of its opponents.

Even if the outlined disputed doctrinal positions are assigned exclusively to the *scholastici*, the rejections specified above are directed at the "more recent" (*recentiores*) theologians of late scholasticism,[13] especially Gabriel Biel. He is explicitly mentioned four times in the Apol and his theological position often lies in the background.[14]

The position condemned in CA (Ed.pr.) 18 is illuminated in detail by a look at the beginnings of the argument of Luther[15] with Gabriel Biel,[16] as the following comparison shows:

Gabriel Biel:	Martin Luther:
Collectorium circa quatuor libros Sententiarum lib. III dist. 27 qu. un. art. 3 dub. 2 lit. Q-U: Secundo dubitatur, utrum voluntas humana viatoris possit Deum ex suis naturalibus diligere super omina et ita implere praeceptum dilectionis... Propter illas duas rationes quidam dixerunt quod natura hominis non sufficit dilgere Deum super omnia sine habitu infuso, quia non plus quam seipsum. Sed illae rationes nihil probant.* Arguunt enim de appetitu naturali. Dubium quaerit de appetitu ut libero, qui... potest in utrumque oppositorum et in diversa obiecta etiam non opposita...	Disputatio contra scholasticam theologiam 1517. * = Luther's marginal comments to the Sentence commentary of Gabriel Biel
	* optime probant...
	5. Falsitas est, quod appetitus liber potest in utrunque oppositorum, immo nec liber sed captivus est.
Prima: Viatoris voluntas humana ex suis naturalibus potest diligere Deum super omina. Probatio: Omni dictamini rationis rectae voluntas ex suis naturalibus se potest conformare;* sed dilgere Deum super omnia est dictamen rationis rectae; ergo illi se potest voluntas ex suis naturalibus conformare et per	* hoc est falsum 6. Falsitas est, quod voluntas possit se conformare dictamini recto naturaliter.

consequens Deum super omnia diligere.* ...
Maior probatur: Quia circa quodlibet dictamen
practicum intellectus, quo sibi ostenditur
objectum ut circa ipsum aliquid volendum vel
nolendum, voluntas ex suis naturalibus potest
habere actum, et non necessario malum, se
deformando dictamini; alioquin esset
naturaliter mala*; ergo potest habere actum
bonum, se conformando dictamini recto.

Item: si sic, voluntas non esset naturaliter libera
ad tendendum in quodlibet secundum rationem
sibi ostensam*. Non enim esset in sua potestate
quodlibet ostensum velle vel nolle; quod est
contra Augustinum iij De libero arbitrio: "Nihil
est magis in potestate voluntatis quam ipsa
voluntas"*. Quod non est intelligendum de
voluntate quoad essentiam, sed quoad actum
elicitum.
Praeterea: "Homo errans potest diligere
creaturam super omnia et frui ea puris
naturalibus; ergo pari rationi potest" diligere
Deum ex suis naturalibus super omnia et frui
eo.* Mirum enim esset, quod voluntas posset se
conformare dictamini erroneo et non recto.*

Item: " Homo potest ex puris naturalibus velle
Deum esse Deum et nihil aliud a Deo esse
Deum; sed talis vult Deo maximum bonum,
nulli alteri vult tantum bonum"; igitur sic
seipsum et quodcumque aliud.
Addit Scotus rationem de forti politico, quam
ponderat, quia fortis politicus magis diligit rem
publicam quam seipsum.* Nam secundum
rectam rationem exponit se pro re publica et
vult non esse, ut bene sit rei publicae. Vult
enim magis mori quam turpiter vivere...

Secunda propositio. Actus amoris Dei
amicitiae super omnia non potest stare in
viatore de potentia dei ordinata sine gratiaet
charitate infusa. Probatur: Quia secundum

* Et per consequens non est infirma nec eget
gratia Dei. Omnia ista ex stulto fundamento
procedunt liberi arbitrii, quasi li. arb. possit ex
se ipso in utrunque oppositorum, cum solum ad
malum sit pronum: Aut si contra pronitatem se
erigit, manet saltem invita...

7. Sed necessario elicit actum difformem et
malum sine gratia dei;
*quod et verum est. quia vitiatae naturae
8. Nec ideo sequitur, quod sit naturaliter mala,
id est natura mali secundum Manicheos;
* et hoc est verum ut patet li 1 retract. 9
[Augustini]

10. Conceditur, quod voluntas non est libera ad
tendendum in quodlibet secundum rationem
sibi ostensum;
11. Nec est in potestate eius velle et nolle
quodlibet ostensum:
12. Nec sic dicere est contra B. Augustinum
dicentem: Nihil est ita in potesta voluntatis
sicut ipsa voluntas.
* Vide quam absurde alleget.
13. Absurdissima est consequentia: Homo
errans potest diligere creaturam super omnia,
ergo et Deum
* negatur consequentia et insuslse arguit,
sanam voluntatem praesupponens.
14. Nec est mirum quod potest se conformare
dictamini erroneo et non recto.
* Immo Mirum quod haec dicis, et tantum
pelagio consentis quasi non sit ad malum prona
natura.

17. Non potest homo naturaliter velle Deum
esse Deum, Immo vellet se esse deum et deum
non esse deum;

19. Nec valet ratio Scoti de forti politico
rempublicam plusquam seipsum diligente. *
Sed nil probat. Quia talis fortis quaeret quae
sua sunt. Quin adhuc semper propter creatum
bonum id facit.

56. Nec per Dei absolutam potenciam fieri
potest, ut actus amiciciae sit et gratia Dei
praesens non sit.

legem ordinatam cuilibet facienti quod in se est et per hoc sufficienter dispositio ad gratiae susceptionem Deus infundit gratiam secundum illud Prophetae: "Convertimini ad me, et ergo convertar ad vos" Zach. 1 et illud Jac. 4: "Appropinquate Deo, et appropinquabit vobis", scilicet per gratiam, et illud Luc. 11: "Quaerite, et invenietis: pulsate, et aperietur vobis", et Jer. 29: "Cum quaesieritis me in toto corde vestro, inveniar a vobis" et in Ps. 21 ...*

28. Illae authoritates "Convertimini ad me, et convertar ad vos", Item: "Appropinquate Deo, et appropinquabit vobis", Item: "Quaerite, et invenietis", Item "Si quaesieritis me, inveniar a vobis" et iis similes...
* Quasi illa dicta id velint, quod nostrae virtutis sit seclusa gratia quaerere, converti, cum dicat ps. 13 [,2] Non est intelligens, non est requirens deum etc. Omnia ergo ista non sunt ad propositum.

Sed perfectissimsu modus faciendi quod in se est, quaerendi Deum, appropinquandi Deo et convertendi ad Deum est per actum amoris amicitiae, nec alia dispositio perfectior ad gratiam est homini possibilis. Nam nullo actu magis appropinquare Deo possumus quam diligendo Deum super omnia. Hic enim actus perfectissimus est omnium actuum respectu Dei viatori ex naturalibus haberi possibilium; ergo est immediata et ultima dispositio ad gratiam infusionem...

26. Actus amiciciae non est perfectissimus modus faciendi quod est in se: Nec est dispositio perfectissima ad gratiam Dei aut modus convertendi et appropinquandi ad Deum;

20. Actus amicitiae non est naturae, sed gratiae praevenientis;

Ex quo sequitur quod actus diligendi Deum super omnia amore amicitiae non est prior tempore gratia, licet sit prior natura, sicut dispositio prior est ad formam, ad quam disponit.

27. Sed est actus iam perfectae conversionis, tempore et natura posterior gratia

Tertia propositio: Quamvis dilectio Deiex naturalibus, quae dicta est, sit prior natura charitate et gratia infusis in esse naturae, charitas tamen prior est in meriti ratione.
...Ad actum enim meritorium non sufficit coexistencia gratiae... sed requiritur quod gratia concurrat effective...

54. Ad actum meritorium satis est coexistentia gratiae aut coexistencia nihil est;
55. Gratia dei nunquam sic coexistit ut ociosa, Sed est vivus, mobilis et operosus spiritus;

Quinta propositio post dominum Petrum de Alliaco: Stante lege, nullus homo per pura naturalia potest implere praeceptum de dilectione Dei super omnia.

Probatur: Quia lex iubet, quod actus cadens sub praecepto fiat in gratia, quae est habitus supernaturalis, ergo licet existens extra gratiam per sola naturalia posset Deum diligere super omnia, non tamen implet praeceptum ad intentionem praecipientis, nisi sit in gratia. Et

58. Periculosa est haec oratio: lex praecipit, quod actus praecipti fiat in gratia dei;
59. Sequitur ex ea, quod gratiam deihabere sit iam nova ultra legem exactio;
60. Ex eadem sequitur quod actus praecepti possit fieri sine gratia dei;
61. Item sequitur, quod odiosior fiat gratia dei

hoc est, quod multi doctores dicunt, quod homo potest implere praeceptum quantum ad substantiam facti cadentis sub praecepto, non tamen quantum ad facti circumstqntiam et intentionem pracipientis...*

[Dubium 4] Per hoc ad rationes: Ad primam negetur consequentia, quod superflueret habitus charitatis; quia habitus non solum ponitur, ut dirigat voluntatem in actu, ne erret a regula rationis rectae, sed etiam, ut frequentius actum eliciat, ut etiam facilius eliciat...**

quam fuit lex ipsa.
69. Impossibile est itaque, legem impleri sine gratia dei ullo modo.

**... praecepta Dei facere quoad substantiam actuum (cf. footnote 19)
93. Insolubile est argumentum, superfluam esse charitatam, si homo naturaliter potest in actum amicitiae.
91. Gratia dei datur ad dirigendum voluntatem, ne erret etiam in amando deum.
92. Nec datur, ut frequentius et facilius eliciatur, Sed quia sine ea non elicitur actus amoris.
**... habitum... ut facilius diligamus Deum... ut idem faciat libentius (cf. footnote 27)

This comparison shows that Luther in the theses cited from the "Disputation against Scholastic Theology" opposed Gabriel Biel, even if in the title he speaks generally of "Scholastic Theology".

Luther has already summarized the substantive issue around which the argument revolves[17] in the Lectures on Romans:[18]

> For this reason it is plain insanity to say that man of his own power can love God above all things and can perform the works of the Law according to the substance of the act, even if it is not according to the intentions of Him who gave the commandment because he is not in a state of grace. O fools, O pig-theologians! By your line of reasoning grace is not necessary except because of some new demand from above and beyond the Law. For if the Law can be fulfilled by our powers, as they state, then grace is not necessary for the fulfillment of the Law, but only for the fulfillment of some new exaction imposed by God above the Law. Who can bear these sacrilegious views?

A comparison of the Latin text of the quoted passages with the formulations of the condemnation in CA (Ed. pr.) 18 shows the essential and almost verbatim agreement.[19]

Quocirca mera deliria sunt, que dicuntur, quod homo ex viribus suis possit Deum diligere super omnia Et facere opera praecepti secundum substantiam facti, Sed non ad Intentionem praecipientis, quia non in gratia.

Damnant Pelagianos et alios, qui docent, quod sine spiritu sancto solis naturae viribus possimus Deum super omnia diligere, item praecepta Dei facere quoad substantiam actuum.

They condemn the Pelagians and others, who teach that without the Holy Spirit, by natural powers alone, we are able to love God above all things and can do the commandments of God in so far as the substance of the acts is concerned.

The textual comparison establishes:

The condemned position (namely, that persons, out of their own natural powers and without grace, can love God above all things and thus can fulfill the commandments of God according to the substance of the act, even if not according to the intention of the one who commands) is not a freely invented, fictive counterposition. The Catholic doctrinal position, however, is not thereby condemned in general. What stands in the background is rather a controversy—beginning in Luther's Lectures on Romans and running through to Melanchthon's later Loci[20]—with the position of a highly specific theological school, represented by Gabriel Biel.

Attending to this background has important consequences for the interpretation of the controversies over free will,[21] sin,[22] and grace.

The Reformation rejection of the importance of love for justification itself rests on the presupposition that "love" is understood as "love from one's own power without grace." Therefore *fides caritate formata* is rejected.[23] Through the equation "grace" = *habitus* = *caritas infusa*, the concept of grace has become corrupted for the Apol: "They interpret grace as the habitus through which we love God, just as if the fathers wished to say that we should place our trust in our love."[24] In order to come to a more open terminology in the doctrine of justification and grace,[25] it should be noted that the Reformation way of speaking is understandable and justifiable on the basis of these presuppositions. Yet it also should be noted that on the basis of a different concept of love, itself also warranted by the New Testament, talk of "justification through love" need not contradict Reformation statements about "justification through grace", if love means the love poured into our heart by God through the Holy Spirit.[26]

The criticism of the *habitus-doctrine* in the Apol is not that grace is made a graspable thing, as the criticism might appear when read from the perspective of a theological school shaped by existentialism. It is directed against a "Too little": "They do not allot much to this *habitus*, since they say that the act of will before and after this *habitus* is of the same sort." The *habitus* brings only an inclination, so that reason can better and more easily do that which it could do already.[27] The Apol "does not struggle against the doctrine of habitual grace in general, but against a particular version of the doctrine of *habitus* for which the *gratia habitualis* itself has become meaningless."[28]

In the negotiations at the Diet of Augsburg in 1530, agreement on this question came precisely through attending to different terminology and by relating what the Reformation side meant by justification through faith to what the scholastic mode of expression meant by *gratia gratum faciens*.[29]

This is also confirmed by the Apology:

Formula of Agreement (Augsburg 1530):

Das auch Verzeihung der sundt geschehe durch gnad, die gott angenehm machet und den glauben formlich unnd durch das Wortt und sacramenta als ein Instrument oder werckhzeug

Quod remissio peccatorum fit per gratiam gratum facientem et fidem formaliter et per verbum et sacramenta instrumentaliter

Apol 4, 116:

Et quia haec fides accipt remissionem peccatorum et reddit nos acceptos deo et affert spiritum anctum; rectius vocari, gratia gratum faciens poterat, quam effectus sequens, videlicet dilectio.

And because this faith alone receives the forgiveness of sins, makes us acceptable to God and brings the Holy Spirit, it should better be called gratia faciens rather than what is the effect resulting from it, namely love.

Substantively, both aspects of a correctly understood scholastic doctrine of *habitus* (viz. 1. The new beginning established by God, and, 2. the valid state of being accepted by God, extending beyond the moment) appear in the Apol through the concepts *iustum offici* and *iustum reputari*. Thereby *ex iniusto iustum effici*—that which occurs with the acquisition of the forgiveness of sins and rebirth in baptism and absolution through the Holy Spirit—refers to the new beginning, while *iustum reputari* (similar to *peccata non imputari*) expresses the ongoing validity. "The Apology clearly teaches a continuing state of grace, a state of justification, of reconciliation and rebirth, which of course is lost through a fleshly life of 'mortal sin'[30] and is endangered through a weakening of love.[31]

2. THE CONDEMNATIONS IN RELATION TO JUSTIFICATION THROUGH THE SACRAMENTS *EX OPERE OPERATO*

Confessio Augustana (Ed. pr.), Art. 13:

Damnant igitur illos, qui docent, quod sacramenta ex opere operato iustificent, nec docent fidem requiri in usu sacramentorum, quae credat remitti peccata.

Darumb werden diejenigen verworfen, so lehren, die Sakrament machen gerecht ex opere operato ohne Glauben dazu getan soll werden, dass da Vergebung der Sünde angeboten werd, welche durch Glauben, nicht durchs Werk erlangt wird.

They therefore condemn those who teach that the sacraments justify ex opere operato and who do not teach that faith which believes sins are forgiven is required in the use of the sacraments.

Apology, Art. 13, 18:

Hic damnamus totum populum scholasticorum doctorum, qui docent, quod sacramenta non ponenti obicem conferant gratiam ex opere operato sine motu utentis.	Da müssen wir frei verdammen den ganzen Haufen der scholasticorum und ihren Irrtum strafen, dass sie lehren, dass diejenigen, so die Sakrament schlecht gebrauchen, wenn sie nicht obicem setzen, ex opere operato Gottes Gnad erlangen, wenn schon das Herz alsdenn kein guten Gedanken hat.	Here we must certainly condemn the whole crowd of scholastic doctors who teach that unless there is some impediment the sacraments confer grace ex opere operato without a good disposition in the one using them.

In the condemnation in of CA (Ed. pr.) 13,[32] justification *ex opere operato* is equated with justification "without faith." Correspondingly in the Apol *ex opere operato* is typically linked with *sine bono motu untentes, sine bono motu accipientis, sine bono motus cordi, hoc est sine fide*—"if the heart has no prior good disposition," "if the heart were not even a factor."[33] Thereby Duns Scotus is intended, whom Luther in his Assertio expressly designates as the author of the opinion "that the sacraments of the New Testament give grace to those who offer no impediment." "To place no impediment"[34] is interpreted to imply "it suffices if the recipient of the sacrament ceases to sin or forms an intention to cease to sin, even if no good intention is formed." As evidence, Luther continues: "Some of them say, that a good impulse of the heart is not necessary."[35] Luther take over here Gabriel Biel's interpretation of the Scotist position, as stated in the "Theological Dictionary" of Johannes Altenstaig:

> And a fruit of the sacrament is that we obtain through it grace, not only *ex opere operantis* but also *ex opere operato* (as Gabriel [Biel] writes in the first sermon for the festival of the Circumcision of the Lord)... They impart the grace *ex opere operato*, because, according to [Duns] Scotus, to obtain grace through them one does not need a good impulse *de congruo* adequate for the infusion of grace, but it is sufficient that the recipient of the sacrament places no impediment of unbelief through which the opposite is desired or consent is given to a mortal sin committed or to be committed.[36]

The condemnation in CA (Ed. pr.) 13 is aimed at an understanding of the sacramental teaching of Scotus mediated through Gabriel Biel. Even if this was often so represented,[37] the Catholic position is not thereby actually touched.[38]

In retrospect, it turns out that:

If in CA 2 and CA (Ed. pr.) 18 a justification through love from one's own power was condemned, it was a matter of the rejection of an opposed position, viz., of a justification through external works without a good impulse in the recipient. The rejections are directed at "the two forms of justification" which, according to the Apol, the opponents teach[39] and which have a certain analogy in the theological positions of Gabriel Biel and Duns Scotus.

The background of these two stances plays a role in the debate over the understanding of penance.

3. THE CONDEMNATIONS IN THE CONTEXT OF THE UNDERSTANDING OF PENANCE

Confessio Augustana, Art. 12:[40]

Reiiciuntur et isti, qui non docent remissionem peccatorum per fidem contingere, sed iubent nos mereri gratiam per satisfactiones nostras.

Auch werden die verworfen, so nicht lehren, dass man durch Glauben Vergebung der Sünde, sondern durch unser Genugtun.

Rejected also are those who do not teach that remission of sins comes through faith but command us to merit grace through satisfactions of our own.

Rejected also are those who teach that forgiveness of sin is not obtained through faith but through the satisfactions made by man.

While the German text is differentiated, the Latin text is formulated somewhat more cautiously with *reiiciuntur* instead of *damnant ecclesiae*.

According to the Apol, the doctrine of penance was, prior to Luther's appearance, "sheer darkness," "confused," and suppressed by "many harmful, loathsome errors."[41] Duns Scotus and Gabriel Biel are named as the primary authorities for the opposed position.[42] In summary, a list is presented of eleven "obviously false teachings, deviating not only from the Holy Scripture but also from the fathers."[43]

Penance is treated in the third part of the Smalcald Articles and thus among the articles about which one could speak with learned and reasonable people.[44] "The false penance of the papists" for Luther follows from their false teaching about original sin. They "say the natural powers of the person are whole and remain uncorrupted; reason can correctly teach, and the will can do correctly according to it; so much is in a person, according to her or his free will." Altogether, one has referred people to their own works.[45]

The condemnation in CA 12 concerns the third of the three traditional parts of penance: satisfaction (*satisfactio*).

In the Apol the background is explained: "We have spoken for this reason especially about satisfactions (*satisfactionibus*), so that no one would understand satisfaction in a way that suppresses the teaching of faith, as if we could through our works merit the forgiveness of sins. For the dangerous error of satisfactions is spread and confirmed by some clumsy teachings, for the adversaries write that satisfaction is such a work that through it divine anger and displeasure are atoned."[46] Here is clearly reflected Duns Scotus' definition of satisfaction, as is repeated in Gabriel Biel and in Altenstaig's "Theological Dictionary":[47]

Gabriel Biel:	Apol 12, 117:
Et sic eam describit Scotus. Satisfactio est operatio exterior laboriosa seu penalis voluntarie assumpta ad puniendum peccatum commissum a se et ad placandam divinam offensam.	quod in definitione satisfactionis ponunt: fieri eam ad placandam divinam offensam.

Duns Scotus is also alluded to when the Apol further states: "They say that these satisfactions are powerful, even when they are performed by those who have again fallen into mortal sin, as if those who are in mortal sin could atone for the divine displeasure."[48]

In distinction from Alexander of Hales, Thomas Aquinas, Bonaventure, and Richard of Mediavilla, for Duns Scotus the satisfaction performed while in mortal sin is valid for the release from punishment. Duns Scotus rejects, however, the consequence to be drawn from this, that the mortal sinner could atone for the displeasure of God.

In this context can be seen a further element in the background of the Reformation rejection of *opus operatum*:

"Certain fasts", "some prayers, certain alms" have been appointed so that these "are a divine service, which makes atonement to God *ex opere operato* and releases from eternal punishment. For they say and teach that such work *ex opere operato*, that is, through the accomplished work, makes satisfaction for sin, and they teach that such a satisfaction is valid, although the person lives in mortal sins."[49] Also the Apol, referring to Gabriel Biel, sees the mass as such a work, "which justifies *ex opere operato* and releases those from guilt and punishment for whom it is done. Thus writes Gabriel."[50]

The condemnation in CA 12 does not contain a fundamental rejection of a third part of penance which goes beyond *contritio* and *fides*: "If anyone says, Christ means the fruits of penance or the whole new life, we have here no disagreement."[51] The rejection here is aimed at a specific understanding of satisfaction, ascribed to Duns Scotus or spread among the people.[52]

If this background, viz. the theological positions of Duns Scotus and Gabriel Biel, is attended to, then the view of the controversies over the certainty of salvation and the meaning of absolution are also affected.

In the list of eleven false teachings mentioned above, this sentence is quoted:[53]

V. Quod potestas clavium valeat ad remissionem peccatorum non Deo, sed coram ecclesia.2	V. Dass die Gewalt der Schlüssel verleihe Vergebung der Sunde nicht für Gott, sondern für der Kirchen oder den Leuten.	The power of the keys avails for the forgiveness of sins not before God, but before the church.

For the Apol. this sentence is "a fatal error. For if the power of the keys does not comfort us before God, what then should make the conscience restful?"[54] In the background here stands the conception of Gabriel Biel, cited by Altensteig in his "Theological Dictionary": "The power of the keys extends to the remission of sins, not before God, but before the church, for it does not forgive sin but presupposes forgiveness by God."[55]

Over against Biel, for whom absolution has a merely declarative function, CA, the Apol, and Luther, stress the power of absolution,[56] similar to Duns Scotus: "Because God truly quickens through the Word, the keys truly forgive sins before God, according to that saying: He who hears you, hears me. Therefore the voice of the one who absolves must be believed, not other than the voice which sounds from heaven. And absolution can properly be named the sacrament of penance, as even the learned scholastics declare."[57]

In relation to the controversy over the certainty of salvation, a closer attention to the disputed counterposition has a significant meaning. For Luther the certainty of salvation is endangered by the concept of the "false key," the concept that the power of the keys could objectively err and miss the mark. Thus for Biel the key errs, on the one hand, from the side of the priest if he neglects to ask necessary questions, e.g., whether the one confessing does or does not have full repentance, or, on the other hand, from the side of the ones confessing, if they imagine they have full repentance when they do not.[58] For Luther this position means that the key "may in itself err" and thus the power of the keys becomes a "inconstant key," "which does not point us to God's word but to our repentance."[59] In view of this background, a clarification of the question of the certainty of salvation is thoroughly possible.[60]

Conclusion

1. In the doctrine of justification, the CA, the Apol and the SA do not condemn the officially represented doctrinal position of the Catholic church. Nevertheless the condemnations in the doctrine of justification are not drawn from thin air. Rather they are directed toward positions of late scholasticism, as they were represented by Duns Scotus, William of Ockham, and Gabriel Biel and they have in this regard a basis in reality. This does not mean that at all

points of the doctrine and concern of these theologians have been appropriately addressed.

2. The precise consideration of the intended counterposition is an unconditional presupposition for a clarification of the controversial questions.

3. A resolution of the question of these Reformation rejections means: The Reformation condemnations in this question are justified and must also be regarded as continuing warning signs. Nevertheless they aim at an extreme position and do not touch the ecclesiastically responsible and representative Catholic position, neither at that time nor today. The attempts in the Apol and in the SA to ascribe the rejected counterpositions in general to the *adversarii* or the "Papists" should be corrected.

Notes

1. The consideration of the "editio princeps" of the CA is of special importance in the framework of our question since this edition was taken over into the Book of Concord.

2. CA 2,3

3. CA 18 (Ed. pr.): BSLK 74, additions to the Latin at line 12 and to the German at line 16.

4. Cf. *Condemnations*, 8.

5. Cf. Melanchthon, "Report to the Elector's Heir Johann Friedrich of Saxony about the Marburg Conversation" (perhaps October 17, 1529): "Das Zwinglius geschriben, das kein Erbsundt sey ... das wir von natur got nit furchten, nicht glauben, sey nicht sundt" (MSA VII/2, 113, 7-114, 12).

6. Melanchthon, "Adversus anabaptistas iudicium" (1528): "... qui vetus dogma de peccato originis irident" (MSA I, 286, 13 ff.). Further documentation in V. Pfnür, *Einig in der Rechtfertigungslehre?* (Wiesbaden: 1970) 90.

7. "... tribuunt interim humanae naturae integras vires ad diligendum Deum super omnia, ad facienda praecepta Dei, quoad substantiam actuum."

8. Apol 4,9 f.: "Hic scholastici secuti philosophos tantum docent iustitiam rationis, videlicet civilia opera et affingunt, quod ratio sine spiritu sancto possit diligere Deum super omnia"; cf. Apol 4,17.

9. SA III,1,3-10: cf. SA III,3,10.

10. Cf. CA 20,13; Apol 2,27 ff; Apol 18,10. "This distinction is not our invention [between external, human righteousness and the spiritual righteousness, which has validity before God] for Augustine discusses it and more recently William of Paris has treated it very well. But is has been criminally suppressed by those who invent that human beings can obey the law of God without the Holy Spirit and that

the Holy Spirit is given to them without regard for the merit of this obedience."
Cf. Pfnür (see footnote 6), 29-34.

11. CA 20,7.

12. *Urkundenbuch zu der Geschichte des Reichstages zu Augsburg im Jahre 1530*, edited by K.E. Förstemann, II (Halle 1835), 488f (Latin trans.)/534f (German trans.).

13. Cf. Apol. 21,40: "Ipsi audivimus excellentes theologos desiderare modum in scholstica doctrina, quae multo plus habet rixarum philosophicarum, quam pietatis. Et tamen in his veteres fere propriores sunt scripturae, quam recentiores. Ita magis magisque degeneravit istorum theologia. Nec alia causa fuit meltis bonis viris, qui initio amare Lutherum coeperunt, quam quod videbant eum explicare animos hominum ex illis labyrinthis confusissimarum et infinitarum disputationum, quae sunt apud scholasticos theologos et canoistas, et res utiles ad pietatem docere."

14. Apol,4,210,; 12,68; 21,23; 22,9. Cf. Pfnür (see footnote 6), 34f.

15. In the following Luther's marginal comments to the sentence commentary of Gabriel Biel are indicated with * (cf. H. Degering, *Luthers Randbemerkungen zu Gabriel Biels Collectorium in quattuor libros sententiarum und zu dessen Sacri Canonis missae expositio 1514* (Weimar: 1933), esp. 14-17; H. Volz, "Luthers Randbemerkungen zu zwei Schriften Gabriel Biels," in: *ZKG* 81 [1970] 207-219, esp. 213). The numerals refer to the theses of Luther "Disputation gegen die scholastische Theologie" (Cl 5, 320-326).

16. Luther used the edition "Collectorium in quattuor libros sententiarum" which appeared in 1514 in Lyon and is cited here. Cf. the critical edition of W. Werbeck and U. Hofmann, III (Tübingen 1979) 503-511.

17. Cf. for these detailed question: Pfnür (see footnote 6), 67-77.

18. Luther's marginal comments to lib. III dist. 27 qu. un. of the Sentence commentary of Gabriel Biel are to be dated to this time.

19. Luther, Lectures on Romans 4:7 (WA 56, 274, 11-18; cf. WA 56, 279, 3-21); American ed. 25:4-524; CA 18, Ed. pr. (BSLK 74).

20. Cf. WA 56,274,11ff; 279,5f; 337,16ff; 355,7ff; 359,14; 503,1 ff; Cl5, 320-326; American ed. 25, 4-524; WA 57; Gal 80,6 ff.; American ed. 29, 109-241; WA 1,373,6ff.; 468,35ff; 469,37ff; American ed. 31, 39-252; WA 2,401,22-28; 516,10-21; 521,3f; American ed. 27, 153-410; WA 8,54,3ff; 467,1-6; 550,30-551,4; 596,13ff; American ed. 32, 137-260 and 36, 133-230; WA 23,505,3-9; II, MSA II,31,18f; MSA I,150,4-9; CCath I,61,20ff; WA 30,II,672,25-29; WA 40,I,226,20-228,26; MSA V,14,7-12; 37,13-16; 93,1-7; WA 38,160,1-15; American ed. 35, 209-223; WA 39,I,419,19ff; 420,24 ff; American ed. 34, 109-144; CR XXI, 281; WA Br9,462,75-88; MSA II,262,30ff.
    Ockham is intended in SA (III,1,7) when it is formulated: "It is not established in Scripture that for a good work the Holy Spirit is necessary with his grace." Cf. WA 38,160; 39,I,420.

21. *Condemnations*, 42f.

22. *Condemnations*, 44f.

23. Cf. Luther, *Lectures on Romans*: "Maledictum vocabulum illud 'formatum' quod cogit intelligere animam esse velut eandem post et ante charitatem ac velut accedente forma in actu operari, cum sit necesse ipsam totam mortificari et aliam fieri, antequam charitatem induat et operetur" (WA 56,337,16f); American ed. 25, 4-524.

24. Apol, 4,380f.

25. Cf. Malta, para. 27.

26. Cf. Romans 5:5; *Condemnations*, 48.

27. Apol 4,17; cf. Biel, Coll. lib. I dist. 17 qu. 1 art. 2 concl. 1 lit. C; ebd. lib. IV dist. 27 qu. un. art. 3 dub. 4 (see Luther, Disputatio contra scholasticam theologiam, Thesis 92).

28. Pfnür (see footnote 6), 75ff, 197.

29. Cf. V. Pfnür, "Die Einigung in der Rechtfertigungslehre bei den Religionsverhandlungen auf dem Reichstag zu Augsburg 1530," in E. Iserloh (edit.), *Confessio Augustana und Confutatio. Der Augsburger Reichstag 1530 und die Einheit der Kirche* (Münster: 1980), 366f; *Condemnations*, 50f.

30. P. Brunner, "Rechtfertigung. Wiedergeburt und neuer Gehorsam in Melanchthons Apologie," in: *Informationsblatt für die Gemeinden in den niederdeutschen lutherischen Landeskirchen* 7 (1958), 302.

31. Cf. Apol 4, 219: "Si quis dilectionem abiecerit etiamsi habet magnam fidem, tamen non retinet eam." Pfnür (see footnote 6), 185 ff.

32. CA 13 (Ed. pr.): BSLK 68 App. to 11. Cf. also CA 24, 29: "Iam si missa delet peccta vivorum et mortuorum ex opere operato, contingit iusticatio ex opere missae, non ex fide, quod scriptura non patitur."

33. Cf. Lutheran/Roman Catholic Joint Commission, *The Eucharist* (Geneva: 1980), Excursus 3, p. 74, nt 29

34. Luther, Assertio: "Quare haeretica sententia est ... At talis eorum qui dicunt, sacramenta novae legis dare gratiam iis, qui non ponunt obicem, quorum autor Scotus est" (WA 7,102,16-19); cf. Luther, Asterisci: "Eckius vero obelisticus Theologus ex illo Scotico procedit somnio, quod sacramenta efficiunt sine opere hominis accipientis, modo non ponat obicem" (WA 1,286,20ff).

35. Luther, Assertio: "Obicem autem vocant peccatum mortale vel propositum eiusdem, quale est homicidium, libido et similia, adeo, ut satis sit suscepturo sacramentum, si desinat peccare et propositum deponat, etiam si nullum bonum propositum format. Quidam enim ex eis dicunt nec motum bonum cordis requiri (WA 7,102,21-25); cf. also WA 57,III,170,4ff; American ed. 29,109-241; WA

1,544,35ff; American ed. 31,83-252; WA 2,13-16; 2,751,36ff; 5,124,20ff; 6,85,11ff;91ff; American ed. 31,259-292 and 35,29-73; cf. also W. Schwab, Entwicklung und Gestalt der Sakramententheologie bei Martin Luther (Frankfurt a. M./Bern 1977).

36. *Vocabularius Theologiae complectens vocabulorum descriptiones/ diffinitiones et significatus ad theologiam utulium* (Hagenau: 1517—further editions appeared among others 1576 in Antwerp and 1619 in Cologne), Capiton: Opus operatum: "Et fructus sacramentorum est, ut per ea consequamur gratiam, non solum ex opere operatis, sed ex opere operato (ut scribit Gabriel sermone I de Circumcisione Domini) ... Sic autem conferunt gratiam ex opere operato, quia ad consequendem gratiam per ea *non requiritur secundum Scotum motus bonus interior* de congruo sufficiens ad gratiae infusionem, sed sufficit quod suscipiens ea non ponat obicem infedelitatis contrariae voluntatis aut consensus in mortale peccatum commissum vel committendum."

37. Cf. O.H. Pesch, "Das katholische Sakramentenverständnis im Urteil gegenwärtiger evangelischer Theologie," in *Festschrift für Gerhard Ebeling zum 70. Geburtstag,* ed. by E. Jüngel/J. Wallmann/W. Werbeck (Tübingen: 1982), 317-340, esp. 321.

38. For an extensive discussion of this problem, reference should be made to the essays in *Lehrverurteilungen—kirchentrennend?,* III, Materialien zur Lehre von den Sakramenten und vom kirchlichen Amt, ed. by Wolfhart Pannenberg (Freiburg i. Br.: 1990).

39. Apol 4, 287ff. Cf. Pfnür (see footnote 6), 38.

40. CA 12,10.

41. Apol 12,3-5.

42. Apol 12, 68: "Sed habent magni nominis auctores, Scotum, Gabrielem et similes, dicta patrum, quae in decretis truncata citantur."

43. Apol 12, 16-17. For proof of verbatim agreement with Gabriel Biel cf. Pfnür (see footnote 6), 80 f.

44. Cf. SA,III,Introduction.

45. SA III,3.

46. Apol 12,116f. Cf. Apol 12,24: "VIII. Quod canonicae satisfactiones necessariae sint ad poenam purgatorii redimendam, aut prosint tanquam compensatio ad delendam culpam. Sic enim imperiti intelligent."

47. Gabriel Biel, Collectorium lib. IV dist. 16 qu. 2 art. 1 not. 1 lit. C; J. Altenstaig, *Vocabularius theologiae,* Capiton: Satisfactio. Cf. Pfnür (see footnote 6), 40-45.

48. Apol 12,118. Cf. Apol 12,132; Apol 12,140; Apol 12,144.

49. Apol 12,143f. Cf. Apol 12,162: "... per illa opera satisfactionum canonicarum,

hoc est per illa opera traditionum humanarum, quae ipsi sic valere dicunt ex opere operato, ut, etiamsi fiant in peccato mortali, tamen redimant poenas."

50. Apol 4,210.

51. Apol 12,45. Cf. *Condemnations*, 61f.

52. Cf. Apol 12,24: "Denn wiewohl man in der Schule die satisfactiones allein für die Pein abrechnet, so versteht doch männiglich, dass man dadurch Vergebung der Schuld verdiene."

53. Apol 12,21. Cf. Apol 12,7.3

54. Apol 12,7. Cf. Luther, *Von den Schlüsseln*: "Und geben die schlüssel bey ihn nichts mehr denn die gnade des Bapste oder wie sie reden die gnade der kirche, das der sunder mit dem Bapst oder der kirchen versünet wird. Aber Gottes gnaden mus er selbs, on die schlüssel verdienen" (WA 30,II,485,6ff); American ed. 40, 325-377.

55. J. Altenstaig, *Vocabularius theologiae*, Capiton: Clavis. Cf. Biel, Coll. lib. IV dist 18 qu. 1 art. 2 concl. 3 lit I; ibid. lib. IV dist. 14 qu. 2 art. 1 not. 2 lit. F.

56. CA, Melanchthon's Draft of Preface, BSLK 42,29; Art. 25,3; Apol 11,2; WA 30,II,287,27ff; 506,23ff.

57. Apol 12,40-42. Cf. the outcome of the negotiation over agreement to CA 12: "Beicht. Doch soll man hierinn sehen auf die absolution und derselbigen glauben, das uns die sunde umb Christus verdienst vorgeben wirt" (Pfnür [see footnote 29], 367 f.; *Condemnations*, 61).

58. Cf. J. Altenstaig, *Vocabularius theologiae*, Capiton: Clavis: "Error clavis scientiae potest contingere, vel ex parte sacerdotis vel ex parte confitentis. Ex parte sacerdotis, quando omittit investigare necessaria: puta an confitens sit contritus an non ... Potest etiam contingere error ex parte confitentis, quia, scilicet fictus est, et fingit se contritum, cum tamen non sit, et per hoc sacerdos credit, qui non est, et ita errat in suo iudicio." Biel, Coll. lib IV dist. 18 qu 1 art. 3 dub. 2 lit N. Cf. Pfnür (see footnote 6), 217 f.

59. WA 30,II,499,9-25.

60. *Condemnations*, 54f.

Chapter Eight

The Doctrine of Justification in the Formula of Concord

How Far Do its Condemnations Apply to the Roman Catholic Church?

Friedrich Beisser

T HE QUESTION CAN be raised whether the Formula of Concord (FC) needs to be considered in this connection at all. In relation to its reception, this text was recognized by many Lutheran churches, but not by all. In addition, Lutheran theologians in recent years have criticized various aspects of the FC: its doctrine of ubiquity, its (alleged) purely forensic and imputative doctrine of justification, or, more generally, its doctrinaire character and the retreat into separate confessional church it is supposed to represent.

It is true that the FC limited itself to existing *intra-Lutheran* controversies. It did not seek to lay out the total range of Christian faith in a confession. Its goal was to overcome tensions and divisions that had in fact appeared in Lutheranism and thus it concerned itself with the questions discussed in these controversies.

In no way, however, did it constitute the establishment of a merely Lutheran confessional theology. No doubt is permitted that it sought to hold fast to the one truth which is binding and indispensable for the Christian Church (e.g., "our Christian faith," SD, Rule, 1; "the Christian doctrine," SD, Rule, 6; SD, Summary, 1).

Even if the FC differentiates itself primarily from certain teachings represented among Lutherans, its condemnations reach further. They also relate directly or indirectly to Roman and Calvinist positions.

Thus, the FC must be included in the framework of our concern, viz., whether and to what degree the condemnations of the Reformation era are to be maintained today. In relation to justification, Articles 1-6 and 11 are to be investigated, with an emphasis on Articles 1-4.

It must specifically be examined in what sense FC speaks of condemnation or rejection. A few short comments: The Christian Church requires for its existence the true teaching of the gospel from which it lives. Therefore and for this purpose, the true teaching must be established and the false rejected. Persons are not judged. Even if the opinions of an individual theologian are being considered, the total structure of thought involved is not weighed nor is an evaluation given of particular assertions in their systematic relation. Rather certain pointed statements or positions are set forth to be critically tested and, if necessary, rejected.

It is exceedingly important to note the method of the FC. Many misinterpretations of the FC would be avoided if one only paid closer attention to the way it proceeds. Usually the state of the question is first presented, i.e., the controversy is presented, usually be stating two opposed positions. These positions are of course not those of the FC. Afterwards the FC states its decision, setting forth "the true Christian teaching in this controversy." Then follow as a consequence the condemnations or rejections.

At times this structure is obscured by additions and excurses which came to seem necessary in the negotiations over the text.

In the following reflections, I cannot offer a more precise historical investigation of individual questions. Rather, I will take up the most significant doctrinal theses. On this basis, how far the individual condemnations apply to the teaching of the Roman Catholic Church can be assessed. I will limit myself to the theme of justification.

The "Summary Formulation" (BC,503ff) deals with the *foundations* of doctrine: e.g., questions of the relation between Scripture and confession, scripture and tradition, etc. These statements are indirectly connected to the theme of justification. The unique position of the word of God in relation to doctrine corresponds to the sole efficacy of God's grace in justification. This side of the matter will not, however, be here further investigated.

Article 1, "Original Sin," describes the *issue to be decided* so: One party (Flacius et al.; see BSLK, 844, nt. 1) stated that original sin had become the *essence of the human person* (SD,I,1), so that no distinction could now be drawn between sin and the essence of the human person. The opposing party

(Chemnitz et al.; SD,I,2) insisted that original sin and the essence of the human person must be distinguished.

The *decision* of the FC states: A *distinction* must be drawn, even now, after the Fall, between God's good creation and the work of the devil which corrupts humanity. (Article 2 will take up the extent of this corruption). God is not the creator of sin. Even after the Fall, the human person remains fundamentally God's creature. Described ontologically, sin must not be viewed as *substantia* (essence) but as *accidens* (attribute; SD,I,57).

This conclusion is secured by a great number of arguments. It is evident that in this basic decision a fundamental agreement exists with Roman doctrine.

The *condemnations* are directed, on the one hand, against "Pelagian errors" (SD,I,16-25) and, on the other, against "Manichean errors" (SD,I,26-33). In detail, the following assertions are rejected:

1. That original sin is only a debt, the debt of Adam, which does not corrupt our essence.

2. That the tendency toward the evil is only a natural condition and not really sin.

3. That original sin is not so grave that the person (prior to acceptance through Christ) stands under the wrath of God and his damnation.

4. That the essence of the person even after the fall is not damaged, remains in terms of its relation to God and salvation "good and pure," and could be perfect on its own *(in suis naturalibus)*.

5. That original sin is only a harmless external, which affects only parts of the person or the essence of the person only superficially.

6. That original sin only constitutes an external obstacle, while the moral powers of the person remain themselves good.

7. That the person is in fact weakened by original sin, but has not lost all capacities in relation to "spiritual and divine matters" and remains capable of cooperation toward the good.

Two points are to be underlined here: a) These statements apply neither to the Christian nor to the person as created good by God. They apply rather to the person "after the Fall." b) The boundness of the person here spoken of does not imply a total lack of freedom, but an incapacity for *salvation*, for "*spiritual matters*," for obtaining of divine grace.

If we now test how far these condemnations touch the Roman side, the results, in my judgment, are the following:

1. Does not apply (Dz 1512, 1521).

2. Does not apply (Dz 1511, 1521). The BSLK [and BC] are mistaken (850, nt. 3; 511, nt. 7) when they judge that Trent here is of a different opinion.

The statements of the Council they refer to relate to the baptized Christian (Dz 1515).

3. Does not apply (cp. e.g., Dz 1511, 1513, 1515).

4. Does not apply (cp. e.g., Dz 1521, 1522). Again, the reference in BSLK (850, nt. 5 [Here not in BC]) to Dz 1515 is mistaken because at this point the person *after* baptism is spoken of. On this whole matter, one should compare FC 2 and also CA 18. In my judgment, there exists here not conflict with the official Roman teaching.

5. I believe that the emphasis on the remaining freedom of the will (Dz 1521) cannot and must not be understood as if there were undamaged parts of the person (e.g., reason or morality) which could gain salvation without the grace of God. Such is excluded through Dz 1525, according to which *every* movement of the person towards grace must be incited and supported by God's grace itself. With this presupposed, the condemnation does not apply.

6. Here I would judge that the official teachings of the two churches agree (cp. Dz 1522, etc.).

7. Here arises the decisive controversial point. Since it is addressed in greater detail in Article 2, it will be discussed in connection with that article and at this point passed over.

It is self-evident that the condemnations of "Manichean errors" do not form a point of controversy. The Lutheran churches also clearly differentiate themselves from a total demonization of the "natural" person or from an understanding of sin which would make out of it a counter-world over against God's creation from we could finally dissociate ourselves.

Their concern is rather that in "spiritual matters," in questions of the relation to God and salvation, we are not only capable of nothing on our own, but rather all our efforts remain only sin (SD,I,25).

The first serious conflict appears to arise in Article 2, "Free Will."

The precise question is whether human free will is capable of "spiritual matters" *between the Fall and acceptance through Christ.* The issue is "preparation for grace." For FC, this question means: what can the understanding or will of the still unregenerate person do when God's grace is offered through Word or sacrament (SD,II,2). That persons possess, on their own, a free will (even if perhaps weakened) in *worldly matters* is granted, as is the presence of a freed, good will *in the Christian.*

The FC defines the *issue to be decided* so: On the *one hand* it is said that while natural persons are incapable of faith or of fulfilling the commandments, they can and must pronounce their "yes" to the offered grace. With this opinion are grouped those who say that the Spirit works the preparation for grace immediately, apart from the proclamation of the Word (so, Schwenkfeld and others; SD,II,4).

On the *other hand* it is said that natural persons are incapable of even understanding the Word by which grace is offered to us, not to speak of accepting it. They are enemies of God and are converted by God's grace alone, without their help.

The *decision* of the FC (SD,II,7f) is that natural persons are totally and completely captives of sin, so that no spark or capacity remains which might move them toward grace. Rather, conversion occurs through God's word and sacrament, the means of the Holy Spirit (SD,II,48-52). The Spirit thus effects in us true repentance.

The first position is thus clearly rejected. There is no "yes" of the person which constitutes a supplementary contribution to the work of the Spirit. But a differentiation is also drawn over against the second conception. Persons are capable of an external understanding of the Word of God and of a decision to listen to it (SD,II,53). In conversion, which is the sole work of the Spirit through the Spirit's means, persons participate in a truly personal way. On the basis of the Word and through the Spirit, they feel remorse. They have faith within their hearts (SD,II,50-55,58-60). This is not their own work, since they are sinners, but an act of God, of the Spirit. But through the power of the Spirit, we "can and must cooperate," having been renewed by the Spirit (SD,II,65). Here, however, the FC is speaking of Christians.

The following *condemnations* follow (SD,II,74-90):

1. Against the "stoic-Manichean" teaching that everything occurs under compulsion, so that the person is incapable of resisting even such gross sins as murder.

2. Against the opinion of the "coarse Pelagians" that free will can convert itself to God without the Holy Spirit.

3. Against the opinion of "papists and scholastics" (cp. BSLK, 903, nt. 2; BC, 536, nt. 7) that the person, on the basis of natural powers, can initiate conversion which the Holy Spirit then completes.

4. Against the "synergists" (BSLK, 903, nts. 3, 4; BC, 536, nt. 8) who teach that the natural person is not totally incapable of the good, but is only deeply wounded, that the beginning lies with the Holy Spirit, but we must provide our assent to this offer if grace is to be received.

5. Against the doctrine of "the papists and the monks" that the Christian is able *after* baptism to fulfill the law completely and totally and thereby merit salvation (*de condigno*).

6. Against the opinion that grace is given to persons apart from the means of word and sacrament.

7. Against the opinion that grace creates in us another person, different from our former self.

8. Here FC deals with the misunderstood statement that the human will, before and after conversion, is always directed against God.

The FC states: The Holy Spirit works renewal in us, makes friends out of enemies. Nevertheless, resistance against God *also* remains alive in the *Christian*.

Persons participate in *conversion* (SD,II,86-89), not by a cooperation with grace which effects salvation, but by the Word moving their hearts to true faith.

Talk of the "three causes" of conversion (God's Word, the Holy Spirit, our will) is on these grounds misleading.

This article is clearly to be related to the former. The person is neither to be demonized (Art. 1), nor is it to be doubted that, in relation to salvation, the person is without remainder a captive of sin.

In this connection, teachings of the Roman church are explicitly rejected, and this occurs *after* the Council of Trent has taken a position on these questions. (M. Chemnitz had written his large *Examination of the Council of Trent*).

I will now attempt a assessment of the individual condemnations. No difference exists between the churches in relation to the first and second. The third thesis is also, in my opinion, rejected by Trent (Dz 1525). The teaching rejected in the fifth point is in my judgment not put forward by Trent. The Thomist tradition has always rejected this opinion. The churches are in fundamental agreement concerning the sixth thesis, that grace is not given immediately, but requires sacramental mediation.

The relation of word and sacrament might require further clarification both within the evangelical church and between the churches. In addition, no conflict exists over thesis 7.

The possible difference that exists over thesis 8 points back to the real point of contention, named in thesis 4.

The FC leaves no doubt that in conversion we are not treated like automata, but as personal beings and are involved with our whole hearts. But this involvement is of such a nature—and here can be seen the decisive difference—that we thereby can make no sort of contribution to our own salvation. Even if the Spirit through the Word works in us and calls forth effects in us, this is entirely the Spirit's act and work and in no way also ours.

It might be of significance here that the FC speaks primarily of "conversion," i.e., a moment which forms simply another side to the event of faith. Trent, however, addresses preparation as a distinct phase, prior to baptism.

The question whether this rejection (4) applies to Roman teaching is not easy to decide.

Trent unambiguously emphasizes at the outset the *priority* and the *superiority* of grace over our wills. Grace is *excitans* (inciting) and remains always *adjuvans* (supporting). It is further emphasized that human free will is not extinguished, but is and always must be involved (Dz 1521, 1525). Conversion signifies the human "yes" to the offered grace. It means that the beginnings of faith, hope, and especially love can be found in the person (Dz 1526). All this together forms the "disposition or preparation" (*dispositio seu preparatio*) for the actual reception of grace in baptism (Dz 1528).

Both sides thus agree on the necessity and priority of grace and also agree that in conversion persons remain personal beings who make a decision. The question is about the significance of this free will in gaining salvation. Does it make a contribution? Does it form a *conditio sine qua non*? The FC rejects the teaching that we could make any kind of positive contribution. Trent, in my opinion, takes no clear position. While it emphasizes the *existence* of the free will, it does not declare whether and, if so, in what way this will contributes to attaining salvation. Is this free will only a personal "participation," in which the Holy Spirit is completely effective (as FC states)? Or is it a cooperating and co-producing element, even if impelled and borne by the Spirit, an element which must be clearly specified because it constitutes a condition for the divine gift of grace (baptismal grace)?

In short: is this human participation something which I must be able to demonstrate? Or can I take no account of all this and hold simply to God's grace? Herein lies the spiritual concern of FC: When I look to myself, to what I myself am or ought to bring forward, then I fall into anxiety and anguish. Then both the sole efficacy of the grace of Christ and the degree to which I am lost are misperceived.

If Trent can at this point be interpreted in an acceptable sense, then this condemnation need not stand.

Article 3 deals with "The Righteousness of Faith." Its occasion is the controversy with Osiander (BSLK, 913, nt. 3), but the Article goes further and asks in what sense faith is a power working within us.

The *issue to be decided* is first laid out. The FC differentiates between *Position a1* (The righteousness of the Christian is Jesus Christ, who dwells in his divine nature in Christians, moves them to the good, and so is their righteousness), *Position a2* (Christ is our righteousness according to his human nature [SD,III,3]), and *Position b*, "held unanimously" by "the other teachers of the Augsburg Confession (Christ is our righteousness according to both natures; the righteousness of faith consists in the forgiveness of sins, acceptance by God, which is reckoned to us as justification.

An important point must be made immediately. The just formulated pure imputation doctrine, according to which the righteousness of faith consists (only) *in the divine acquittal*, is not yet the final position of the FC. It is rather one of the opinions it describes and is to judge. Whether this represents its own teaching (as is repeatedly maintained) must now be tested.

FC makes its own *decision* with the help of a *distinction between justification and regeneration or rebirth*. Conscious that the meaning of these concepts in the tradition (e.g., with Luther himself) had been elastic, it gives a clearly outlined explanation of them. *Justification* in the strict sense is the acquittal from sin and damnation for the sake of the righteousness of Christ which is reckoned to faith (SD,III,17). *Regeneration* strictly defined means our vivification, the new life that occurs within us (SC,III,18-20).

The central assertion is that these two must be clearly and unambiguously *distinguished*, for the ground of our justification is *only* the grace of Christ reckoned to us, *not* the renewal which we takes place in us (SD,III,30-31).

Nevertheless, the two must *not be separated*. Faith cannot exist where there is no active repentance (SD,III,26). In addition, love is the necessary consequence of faith. Those who do not love thereby show that they are not justified or have lost their faith (SD,III,27).

One must therefore insist that all of our works are excluded from justification (SD,III,37), that faith alone justifies (SD,III,38), and that our regeneration is in no way a part or cause of our righteousness (SD,III,39). In justification our renewal must be strictly left out of consideration. Justification is exclusively based on the pledge of God's grace and in no way upon that which occurs in or to us. This does not mean that nothing happens to us. On the contrary, all justifying faith is an event within us and leads to acts of new life. But this state of affairs is never in any way a ground or condition of our acceptance and acquittal.

FC summarizes, quoting Luther: "It is faith alone which apprehends the blessing without works. And yet faith is at no time ever alone" (SD,III,41).

The constantly repeated assertion that FC, unlike Luther, puts forward a merely imputational understanding of justification is manifestly untenable. What FC states is the same as that which Luther, Melanchthon, and Calvin held to be indispensable in this regard. *Calvin* makes the same point when he states (*Institutes*, Book III) that faith encompasses two things: justification and repentance. "Repentance" here stands for what FC calls renewal, the rebirth that occurs within our lives. It belongs—as the second part of the matter—necessarily to faith. Without it, there is no faith. But it has no place in justification. Justification is the forgiveness of sins through Christ and that alone.

There thus exist *differing concepts of justification* on the evangelical and Roman Catholic sides. For the Reformation understanding, justification is acceptance before God, which at any moment stands at risk and now becomes an event. For the understanding of the Council of Trent, justification is a process of making righteous, through which a person, in stages, is effectively reshaped into a righteous person.

Different structures of thought are clearly at work here, but the existing differences cannot simply be eliminated by ascribing one view to the category of the "personal" and the other to that of the "ontological."

As a result of this difference, the opposing sides speak past each other as they advocate different concepts. What the Reformers understood by "justification" was, in my judgment, not really attacked by Trent. Here lies a definite opportunity for ecumenical discussion.

The real difference is that one side is convinced that justification can and may be described only as the process of effectively making righteous, while the other is convinced that it can be grasped as the pledge of God's grace here and now. In this latter connection, the situation of the person is simply not considered. Faith holds entirely to the promise of God which grants righteousness.

From this perspective, the condemnations can be tested. The FC objects to the following (SD,III,45-53):

a1: that our *love* or our *works* are totally or partially a cause of our justification;

a2: that persons must prepare themselves through good works in order to receive the merit of Christ;

a3: that our "formal righteousness" (that which is essential to our righteousness or also the fully realized righteousness) consists in the indwelling of love within us;

a4: that our righteousness before God has two parts, the forgiveness of sins *and* rebirth (or sanctification or renewal);

a5: that faith and love are to be ordered along lines suggested by Osiander (BSLK, 931, nt. 5), so that faith is the decisive beginning of righteousness, but renewal then constitutes its full realization;

a6: that justification consists simultaneously in the forgiveness of sins and the renewal beginning within us;

a7: that the promise is grasped by us through faith *and* through the confession of sins or other demonstrations of goodness.

In relation to talk of the "indwelling" of God's righteousness in us, FC rejects the following (SD, III, 60-65):

b1: that Christ is our righteousness before God only through his divine nature;

b2: or only through his human nature;

b3: that in the Bible "justification" does not mean "acquitted of sin" but rather "made righteousness through love" (in the power of the Spirit);

b4: that faith looks primarily to the divine nature of Christ which works and dwells within us, rather than to Christ's sacrifice on the cross;

b5: that true faith can exist without repentance or can exist while simply persisting in sin;

b6: that not God but only God's gifts dwell in the person.

Let me now take up these theses, beginning with series a:

a1: I do not venture to say whether or not the Council of Trent ascribes this significance to love. At any rate, it does state that love must exist in the person prior to baptismal grace (Dz 1526); that baptismal grace itself is effective in the person as love (Dz 1530); and that our justification can only be concluded if the believer preserves the grace received. What is the significance of this love for our acceptance? Is it only the product and effect of grace or is it a condition for the granting of justification to us? In the first case, the condemnation does not apply.

a2: Neither Thomas Aquinas nor the Council of Trent teaches that baptismal grace is communicated on the basis of previously produced works either *de congruo* or *de condigno*. Over against the actual communication of grace the person is simply the God's material cause (Dz 1529). But what is the *function* of the asserted preparation for grace? If it is only the product of prevenient grace, then the condemnation does not apply.

a3: When FC speaks here of love, it means the love effected as our act by the Spirit. It wishes, however, to turn our attention completely away from this love and direct us solely toward the grace of Christ pledged to us from outside ourselves. That in fact justification neither can nor may exist without love does not mean that our acceptance can be grounded on anything other than God's acquittal. This condemnation does not deny that love dwells within and must dwell within one who has faith. It rejects only the assertion that solely through the demonstration of such love does our pardon become effective.

Against this, Trent held in Canon 11 (Dz 1561): "If anyone says that people are justified (*justificari*, i.e., strictly speaking, "made righteous) either solely by the attribution of Christ's justice, or by the forgiveness of sins alone, *to the exclusion of the grace and love* which is poured into their hearts by the

Holy Spirit and abides in them; or even that the grace by which we are justified is only the good will of God: let him be anathema."

That justification occurs "to the exclusion of the renewal that occurs within us" is taught neither by the FC nor by any Reformer. There is in fact no true faith without love. Nevertheless, our justification is not to be attached to this renewal. It appeals only to God's acquittal. Love is thus not at all to be excluded as something that can be dispensed with; it is excluded as a *condition* or *ground* for our acceptance by God.

Again the decisive question is what is the *function* or *significance* of the work of God in us and thus of our renewal. That this renewal must be present is also taught by the FC. But is it the *ground* or *condition* of our pardon, or only its *product* or *consequence*?

a4: At first glance, a direct hit is here scored on the teaching of Trent.

But again the decisive question is the following: It is uncontroversial that faith (as Calvin says) has and must have two sides: the forgiveness of sins *and* repentance (or renewal). The question is the function our renewal does or does not play in our acceptance by God. According to the FC (and all the Reformers) God's forgiveness of sins and the renewal occurring within us cannot be joined together as two powers which together reach the goal.

When Trent emphasizes that grace is *effective* within us, it says nothing controversial as such. The question is only whether this love is the product of justifying grace or in some sense its condition or ground.

About a5-a7, the same is to be said as about a3 and a4.

In relation to series b, which primarily deals with the teachings of Osiander, theses 1 and 2 obviously do not concern Roman doctrine. The exegetical question taken up in thesis 3 cannot here be investigated. Thesis 4 in the form stated does not address Catholic theology. Agreement exists concerning thesis 5. This condemnation is of special importance because it shows that the FC does not view our renewal or rebirth as something merely external to us, as a mere opinion or declaration of God, or as something that could be dispensed with.

The sixth condemnation addresses itself in my opinion against an all too objective and material way of speaking about "grace," as if it were a thing in itself which could be detached from the encounter with the living God.

Such ways of speaking may have crept into the Catholic tradition, particularly in some wings of scholasticism. This accusation cannot, however, be leveled at Trent (cp. e.g., Dz 1522-1524).

Article 4 (Good Works) discusses in what sense *good works* are *necessary*. Its occasion was the controversy over the theses of Major.

The *controversy* is laid out by the FC. On the *one side* stand two positions, one of which holds that without good works no one is saved because faith without love is dead, and the other of which holds that good works are necessary, but not in order to achieve salvation. On the *other side* stands the position which holds that good works are detrimental to salvation.

The FC attempts to clarify in what sense one can speak of necessity at all in this connection.

Its own *decision* is that good works are not necessary as a *condition* of justification, but they are necessary as the fruit or self-evident *consequence* of faith which flow from it according to God's order. Such good works can only occur by the power of the Holy Spirit. Nevertheless they always remain imperfect and are accepted by God only for the sake of Christ.

On this basis, an assertion of Trent is rejected, that our works serve to preserve our salvation (or faith or the righteousness we have received; SD,IV,35). Presumably, the allusion here is to canon 24 (Dz 1574) and canon 32 (Dz 1582). Canon 24 insists that good works are to be viewed not only as the fruit or sign of the reception of justification, but also that they increase the justification received.

That there is a growth of the good in the Christian was asserted by Luther many times, as also by the FC. This growth, however, constitutes no contribution to our status under grace. Good works do not effect salvation, neither before nor after justification. They do not form a supplement to the divine acquittal.

The resulting question is what is the *function* of the growth demanded by canon 24.

One could also investigate here *Articles 5 and 6*, which deal with questions about the understanding of the Law. They are of significance for our theme in so far as they make as clear as could be wished that the Law can and must be *fulfilled* by Christians.

The particular controversies, however, primarily relate to inner-evangelical battles and can therefore be left out of consideration.

Article 11 which addresses predestination should also be noted, but this theme would have to be addressed on its own and in greater comprehensiveness than is here possible. This reference must thus suffice.

The result of this examination is that the following condemnations require further clarification: Article I, condemnation 7; Article 2, condemnation 4; Article 3, condemnations a1, a3, and a4 (and in that relation, a5-7).

Chapter Nine

Luther and the Council of Trent

The Treatment of Reformation Teaching by the Council

Erwin Iserloh

1. LUTHER'S POSITION REGARDING THE COUNCIL

AFTER HIS INTERROGATION by Cardinal Cajetan at Augsburg in 1518, Luther still appealed from a pope poorly informed to a pope who would be better informed. Indeed Luther appealed to the Pope as "most holy Father and Lord," and wanted to regard his voice as the voice of Christ. But it is questionable whether Luther still expected something from the Pope. In any case Luther did not await the Pope's reaction. A month later, on November 28, 1518, he appealed from the Pope to a council before a notary and witnesses in Wittenberg. At the outset he pleads the conciliar point of view. Luther was convinced that a holy council, assembled under the Holy Spirit, represents the catholic church and in matters of faith is above the Pope. Therefore the Pope has no right to forbid such an appeal. Luther appeals to a future, legal, and free council that is to be held in a specific place and that should preserve for him a free and assured access so that he may defend his concerns.[1]

In these months around the turn of the year 1518 to 1519, Luther was advocating conciliar opinions. From 1519, however, he questioned the infallibility of the decisions of a council. In the Leipzig Disputation with Eck he allowed himself to get carried away to the point of declaring: Councils could err and have erred. He stressed: "Therefore I want to be free and to allow myself to be captured by no one, neither by the respect of a council, nor of a power, nor of the universities, nor of the Pope, so that I should not confidently confess what I have recognized as true,... whether it be approved or disapproved by some council."[2] The Holy Scripture alone (*sola scriptura*) is the binding norm for Luther. When he continued to use conciliar arguments, he was then determined by propagandistic or diplomatic motives.

When Luther appealed to a council again on November 17, 1520, in answer to the publication of the bull *Exsurge Domine*, he was submitting himself "to a tribunal whose competence he himself had denied and thereby branded his action as a pure maneuver, which placed its hopes on the conciliar views of numerous princes and dignitaries of the Imperial Diet."[3]

In his writing "On the Councils and the Churches" of 1539 Luther writes: "For me Scripture is far more reliable than all councils".[4] On the basis of this opinion, on July 13, 1530, he advised his friends at the Diet at Augsburg that they should appeal to the council. In this way there could be peace for the moment. The council would not come."[5]

The Popes helped these tactics to be successful. For they—especially Clement VII—did everything in their power to delay the convening of a council. They feared a further strengthening of conciliarism and the criticism of a thoroughgoing church reform. Also they took into consideration France, which likewise wished no council. Thus the Protestant estates, like Luther, could promote a council without having seriously to reckon with its meeting. Hubert Jedin confirms, "The world no longer believed in a council taking place."[6]

When Paul III in the spring of 1535 prepared to convene a council in Mantua and instructed the Nuntio Vergerio to familiarize the German princes with the Pope's intention, the Nuntio heard from Luther: "We indeed need no council.... But Christendom has need of a council in order to become acquainted with error and truth." He, Luther, is ready at a council to defend his teaching against the entire world.[7] The Wittenbergers wanted to attend the council. The Pope, to be sure, would not be the judge in the *causa fidei*, but they could affirm a council convened by the pope as the highest court of justice in the church.[8]

When it came in May 23, 1537, to the convening of a council in Mantua, however, the Elector of Saxony expressed doubts: A council should be a court of arbitration, to which a person submits with the acceptance of the invitation. The Elector demanded from his advisers and theologians a rationale for declining participation in the council. As a result Luther placed in the Smalcald Articles in addition to points about which there was unity and the possibility of negotiations, articles in which the parties remained divided. In this group belong especially the papacy and the mass as sacrifice. With reference to the sacrifice of the mass, Luther remarked in unyielding clarity: "we are and remain eternally divided and opposed the one to the other."[9]

Luther advised against a negative answer in order not to place the guilt for the failure of the council on himself.[10] Nevertheless the papal legate van der Vorst received a humiliating refusal to his invitation from the Protestant princes. Already at this time the politicians and not the theologians tipped the balance.

In view of the council finally summoned in Trent, Luther in 1545 repeated his point of view in his writing "Against the Roman Papacy, an Institution of the Devil," when he declared: "For ourselves we need no council. With councils nothing is accomplished."[11] Yet Luther still advises not to protest against the council in Trent. He does not want to be exposed to the charge that he is the author of the split.

Luther was not personally present in Trent. He died on February 18, 1546, just as the council was taking up its first work. Also during this first period of the council (1545-1547), the German church was practically unrepresented. In Rome, Germany in any case had been largely written off and considered lost for the Catholic faith. Since the beginning of the 1540s, Pope Paul III's motive for convening a council had been the defense against Protestant trends in Italy. The Reformation had meanwhile become an Italian affair. Protestantism had strongly spread. Many symptoms made it clear that the innovation had gained ground in Italy and serious measures were necessary. Even the highly celebrated preacher and Vicar General of the Capuchins, Bernhardino Ochino, was devoted to the new teaching. In 1542 he was able to escape the summons of the inquisition by flight to Switzerland.

Protestants were represented in Trent at the council only during the second session in 1551-1552.[12] After their defeat at the Battle of Mühlberg, they were more or less compelled by the Emperor to participate. According to their wish, an improved free conduct was given. Their further demands—the freedom of bishops from their oath of faithfulness to the Pope, the submission of the Pope to the council in the sense of the Decree of Constance, and the resumption of the negotiation over decrees already decided in Trent—neither the Pope nor the council could fulfill. That would have meant surrender.

The Protestants were thus present without having recognized the council. They avoided every direct contact with the council's legates and had contact with them only through the imperial envoys. In any case the council had already decided on a suspension in April 1552 due to war. The council had waited in vain for Melanchthon and the Wittenberg theologians, and for their sake had even postponed taking up the decree on faith. Melanchthon, on whom many of the council fathers had placed great hope, did not come to Trent.

2. THE TREATMENT OF REFORMATION TEACHING AT THE COUNCIL OF TRENT: THE MEANING AND SIGNIFICANCE OF THE DELIMITATIONS (ANATHEMAS)

L uther and Melanchthon were indeed not personally present in Trent; they were present, however, in their theology and views of the Christian life. Indeed, they stood for a time at the center of the consultations.

The question is: what material was available to the council fathers? On which sources did they base their condemnations of the teachings they imputed to the Reformers?[13] This question divides itself into five individual questions:

1. Did the council have recourse to authentic sources?

2. In what form were these sources presented—in the texts of the Reformers themselves, in citations from the writings of their opponents, or in the so-called catalogues of heresies?

3. From which years do the formulations of the teachings under objection come—from the first period, especially from 1519-25, years that were strongly characterized by polemic, or from the later years of community and confession formation?

4. Were persons or merely doctrinal opinions condemned?

5. In the same context must be asked: was the object of investigation only the *quaestio iuris*, i.e., the matter itself, or was a decision also made about the *quaestio facti*? That is, were the teachings of the church clearly set out and error as such named and condemned in view of the considerable "dogmatic unclarity" (Lortz) or "doctrinal confusion" (Jedin) reaching back to the fifteenth century, or were the Reformers, especially Luther, named and the condemned teachings imputed to them?

On question 1: Did the council have recourse to authentic sources?

From the beginning of the argument, the representatives of the church's teaching office and the theologians of the old faith sought accurate sources. The teachings under objection were documented from the writings of the Reformers. For example, Cardinal Cajetan on the occasion of the interrogation of Luther at Augsburg in 1518 took the trouble to read the Reformer's writings. In direct argument with them, he wrote out in Augsburg five questions about indulgences. Several tracts concerning the sacrament of penance, excommunication, and purgatory give witness to a close engagement of

Cajetan with Luther's writings. In a question formulated on September 9, 1518 (the meeting with Luther occurred from October 12-14), Cajetan asked whether, for the fruitful reception of penance, the penitent must have the certainty of faith that he has in fact attained the forgiveness of his sins. Of the six arguments which Cajetan first quotes for these theses, the first five are taken verbatim from Luther's sermon, *De Poenitentia* (WA 1, 323ff; AE 35, 3-22) without the Reformer being mentioned by name.[14]

Similar to Cajetan, the authors of the bull *Exsurge Domine*[15] were concerned to take the criticized sentences from the sources, i.e., Luther's writings. Already in December 1519 Hadrian of Utrecht, the Cardinal of Tortosa and later Pope Hadrian VI, had given the advice: We would like to place in the condemnation of Luther not one word other than that written by the author himself. In its concluding memorandum, the second Roman Commission, which discussed the *causa Lutheri* in February 1520, had recommended that a bull be issued against Luther's writings without mentioning him by name.[16] In a second bull, Luther should then be called upon to retract his teaching.

The third Commission, which possessed the writing of Hadrian of Utrecht, formulated the conclusion: "The articles should be formulated with the same words with which Martin formulated them, so that every evasion is cut off."[17] That is what occurred. With one exception, every sentence quoted in *Exsurge Domine* can be documented in the Latin or German writings of Luther. One could rely on the opinions from the University of Cologne and Louvain. A comparison of these opinions with the bull *Exsurge Domine* proves that the latter was closer to the original text of Luther than the opinion of Louvain.[18] Thus we can assume that the writings of Luther himself were available to this commission.

On questions 2 and 3: Were the sources available to the council in the form of the Reformers' texts, or only in the writings of their Catholic opponents or in the catalogues of heresies? From which years do the formulations of the teachings under objection come? How did these matter stand at the Council of Trent?

In the years which had passed since Luther's emergence, his writings had found a world-wide propagation and in spite of their repeated prohibition were relatively easily available to the council fathers. On the other hand, the literary enemies of Luther on the Catholic side had drawn up lists of errors. These lists offered the council fathers excerpts with which they could be content, without going back to the original writings. In 1525 Johannes Cochlaeus produced a catalogue of 500 erroneous sentences from Luther's writings.[19] In 1530

Johannes Fabri boasted that he had assembled more than 600 false teachings.[20] In his text of 1536, *Praeparatoria*,[21] presented to the Pope in view of the announced council, Fabri emphatically demanded a thorough study of the writings of the Reformers; he suggested that official compilations of the errors of Luther, Zwingli,and the Anabaptists be collected for the council. Because of the great number of Reformation writings, he suggested that this work be done prior to the council. No author is permitted to be condemned without the procurement of a more exact knowledge of his written work. Care must be taken to avoid falsely designating something as heretical. If possible, the council should limit itself to the great errors and establish the falsehood of each.[22] At the Diet of Augsburg in 1530 Johannes Eck produced a catalogue of heresies: the "404 Articles for the Diet at Augsburg".[23] He observed that this was a selection from 3000 heretical statements available to him. With this documentation he forced Melanchthon to go beyond the Torgau Articles, which justified the reform of abuses which had been carried out in Wittenberg. Out of such an apology then developed the Confessio Augstana. A twenty-one article confession of the most important truths of the faith was placed before the discussion of abuses.

For the most part the council fathers had before them in Trent lists of errors and catalogues of heresies and, to a degree, writings of Catholic theologians engaged in the controversy. Seldom did they directly engage the writings of the Reformers. The articles on original sin, which were submitted to the council fathers on May 25, 1546, made no explicit reference to the teachings of the Protestants.[24] In the discussion, however, it was suggested that the doctrines of the Lutherans and Zwinglians should be rejected in the decree, though without mentioning them by name. The question then arose whether the authors whose views were rejected must not be cited before the council to give them a hearing.[25]

These carefully critical voices were perhaps what occasioned the council's presidents subsequently to have read out a list of thirteen heresies concerning original sin, of which four were designated as the teachings of Luther and two the teachings of the Anabaptists.[26] The sources for this were the writings of Catholic controversial theologians. In the final version of the decree, Luther's teaching about concupiscence is also rejected. In addition, the rejection of infant baptism is placed under an anathema.[27] Neither Luther nor the Anabaptists, however, are mentioned by name.[28]

In connection with the decree on justification, the demand for Protestant participation was more energetically pressed. At least one must draw upon their writings and not entrust oneself without reserve to the Catholic controversialists. In relation the question of justification "on which our entire salvation hangs," Cardinal Reginald Pole implored the council fathers to read unbiasedly the books of the Lutherans and not to take the position: "Luther has said it, thus it is false." Truth often lies hidden in error; the error's success is based precisely on the truth which it contains.[29]

In the debate over the sacraments, verbatim excerpts from Reformation writings were presented to the council theologians by the council leadership for the first time. On January 17, the Council President Cardinal Cervini read out "Errors of the Heretics" relating to the sacraments in general, baptism, and confirmation. Of the "total 36 citations, almost all of which were presented in the wording of the source writings ... seventeen were taken from the writings of Catholic controversial theologians, while nineteen appear to be drawn directly from their Reformation source".[30]

Besides the council theologian Ambrosius Catharinus, who was familiar from his own literary activity with Luther's teaching on justification, the council theologian Andreas de Vega (1498-1549) is also named as one who was reasonably familiar with Luther's writings. According to Jedin, his *Opusculum de iustificatione, gratia et meritis* of May 1546 lay "on the desk of many council participants."[31] An analysis of the sentences which Andreas de Vega cited as the most important statements of Luther on the doctrine of justification indicates that he "had not himself excerpted them from the writings of Luther, but had taken them over third hand through the mediation of Catholic controversial theologians."[32] Andreas de Vega refers to the writings of Luther from 1519-1521.

Ambrosius Catharinus also received at second or third hand[33] almost all the articles of his list of errors submitted to the General Congregation of October 6, 1546.[34] In their turn, D. Soto and J.A. Delphinus are dependent on him. The material of the *Assertiones* of Ambrosius Catharinus is taken from Luther's writings of 1518-1526. "The emphasis lies on the writings of 1518-1522."[35] From this data, it is to be concluded that the Reformation opinions, collected, abbreviated, and cited in the lists of errors, were understood by the council fathers without a knowledge of their context and often not in their original sense. It also cannot be excluded that the council condemned many opinions formulated in the polemically sharp form of the years 1518-1522 which were no longer held by the Reformers. An example is canon six on justification, which condemns the teaching that evil works as well as good works, the betrayal of Judas not less than the call of Paul, were effected by God in the complete and proper sense. The position condemned here "of Luther and Melanchthon from 1520-1522 was officially corrected by Article 19 of the CA, at least modified in the meantime by Luther, and explicitly rejected and fought by Melanchthon".[36]

On question 4: Were persons or merely doctrines condemned?

In this context it is of great importance whether persons or only doctrines were condemned. Had the council really—as it states at the end of the chapters on justification—drawn up propositions (*canones*) primarily "so that all might know not only which teachings they believe and follow, but also those which they must avoid and flee" (Dz 1550), i.e., was the council's concern more the removal of dogmatic unclarity in its own sphere than the refutation of the Protestants?

The Protestants had been invited to all three periods of the council. When they were not under political pressure, as in 1550, they refused the invitation. In 1537 they did so brusquely in relation to the Nuntio Peter van der Vorst.[37] Thus they were invited. Were they also cited before the council, as heretics of the earlier centuries had been, e.g., John Hus at the Council of Constance? According to the basic principle of canon law that no one should be condemned who has not previously been heard, the bishops repeatedly proposed during the first period of council that the authors of the doctrines to be condemned be cited before the council. The Bishop of Clermont declared on February 16, 1546: "The heretics are to be summoned to the council in order to give an account of their teachings, or to confess their errors, as was done at other councils."[38] On the contrary, however, no Protestant theologian was in fact cited before the council during its entire course. But also no Reformers were condemned. Only teachings which one imputed to them were placed under the anathema, without they themselves being mentioned by name. This procedure of the council was based on instruction from the highest levels. Already in an instruction of December 31, 1546, Cardinal Farnese had drawn up the principle: We should condemn heretical teachings, not expressly named persons. This would make the process easier and also keep the way to Trent open to the Protestants.[39] This principle was once more confirmed in February 1547,[40] and it remained authoritative for the practice of all three periods of the council.

It was clear that this principle was not in harmony with most of the earlier councils. Joachim of Fiore at the Fourth Lateran Council and Wycliffe and Hus at Constance had been condemned by name. The Council of Trent, however, did not "become a tribunal," as H. Jedin has said.[41] It wished to reject errors and, in view of doctrinal confusion, to create clarity, not to condemn persons. The condemnations do not deal only with teachings imputed to the Reformers. They deal no less with Pelagian currents in late medieval nominalist theology, e.g., in the first three propositions (*canones*) on justification. Canon 1 states: "If anyone says that a person can be justified before God by his own works, done either by the powers of human nature or by teaching of the law, apart from divine grace through Jesus Christ: let him be anathema" (Dz 1551). In this proposition certainly no Protestants are condemned. On the contrary, the controlling desire here is to do justice to the basic concern of the Reformation.

The intention only to set limits to error also meant the renunciation of a decision about the unsettled scholastic antitheses within traditional theology. This intention was repeatedly stated. The council refused, e.g., to become more closely involved in the question of the mode of the sacraments' effectiveness, i.e., in the old arguments between the Dominicans and Franciscans whether a physical or moral causality is at work. It "emerges from the entire course of the debate that the intention of the council was not directed toward a decision in this well known scholastic controversy."[42]

Also in the question of the certainty of salvation, it was agreed not to decide the controversy between Scotists and Thomists over the certainty achievable in this life regarding the state of grace.[43] The case is similar in relation to communion under both forms. Here it was decided only that the communion of the chalice is not necessary for salvation and that the church has good reasons for offering only one form. The council refused to decide the controverted question whether reception of the sacrament under both forms mediates more grace than under one form. This occurred with "the clear consciousness of the fundamental difference between the teaching office and theology."[44]

In the face of error, the teaching office sets the boundaries of the field of truth. It is not accidental that the canons are formulated negatively. The task of theology is to develop the field that has been marked out over against error. Here a pluralism is possible. The teaching office claims definitively to condemn error as not compatible with revelation. That does not imply, however, that the teaching office has at its disposal sufficient arguments to establish the negatively formulated condemnation. "To set official doctrinal limits does not mean to give theologically valid answers."[45] It is the task of theology, Jedin observes, to produce more precise warrants. It is not stated that theology in every case is able to do this. If there are answers, they are in each case open to, in fact in need of, improvement.

The Council of Trent decided, for example, at the twenty-second session in 1562 that the mass is a real and proper sacrifice (Dz 1751), indeed an expiatory sacrifice (Dz 1753). As the preceding discussions and the doctrinal chapter show, the council was not able to indicate adequately that such is possible without calling into question the uniqueness of the sacrifice of the new covenant emphasized in the Letter to the Hebrews and also the full sufficiency of the sacrifice of Christ on the cross.[46]

That the decision of the council needed, indeed needs, a deeper justification is proved by the many theories of the sacrifice of the mass produced in the following centuries. These sought to specify what the sacrificial character of the mass consists in and are all rather questionable. On the basis of the exegetical, liturgical, and patristic knowledge of the last decades, we are perhaps today for the first time in a position to give a theologically appropriate answer which takes into account the concern of both sides. *The Eucharist* from the Roman Catholic/Lutheran Joint Commission and other recent consensus papers on the Eucharist are an important and encouraging step in this direction.[47]

The difference between canons and doctrinal chapters follows from the difference between decisions of the teaching office and theological explanations. Only the canons, not the doctrinal chapters presented before them, are actual definitions in the sense of infallible decisions. Since the decree on justification, these have been appended. On many occasions they have been drafted only after the basic outlines of the definition were already fixed.[48] They are indeed binding, but they do not have the magisterial significance of the carefully prepared canons; they are valid as far as their arguments go.

Evangelical theology has more difficulty drawing such a distinction between teaching office and theology. It would be useful, however, if it learns in analogy to this distinction to differentiate between that which is binding teaching of the church—e.g., what is recorded in the confessional writings— and that which is the object and fruit of theological speculation. Theology is surely useful, indeed necessary, as explication and justification of ecclesial teaching. But it must remain conscious of its serving function. In its attempt to penetrate intellectually the truths of the faith, it must not set up new fronts, either within the church or ecumenically, nor harden the existing ones. In this context my esteemed teacher, Joseph Lortz, stated on occasion that theology can be our sin. At Trent the condemnation of persons by name was renounced in order not to close finally the door to conversation. We should use this door, i.e., we should think through anew the theological questions raised in the sixteenth century by Luther and the other Reformers and examine all possibilities of convergence on the basis of the breadth of theological insight into the mysteries of faith gained in the meantime. Almost a century ago, Adolf v. Harnack could write in his history of dogma about the doctrine of justification, i.e., the article with which, according to Luther, the church stands or falls: "The Decree on justification... is in many respects remarkably well constructed; indeed, it may be doubted whether the Reformation would have developed itself if this Decree had been issued at the Lateran Council at the beginning of the century, and had really passed into the flesh and blood of the

Church."[49] If that view is correct, then we have every reason today to test whether the doctrine of justification is capable of consensus.

Notes

1. WA 2,36; R. Bäumer, *Martin Luther und der Papst* (Münster: 1985), 38.

2. WA 2, 404.

3. H. Jedin, *A History of the Council of Trent*, Vol. 1 (London: 1957), 175f.

4. WA 50,604; AE 41, 119.

5. "Appellans a minis eorum ad illud nihili et numquam futurum Concilium, ut interim pacem haberemus." (WA Br 5,470). Cf. W. Maurer, "Die Entstehung und erste Auswirkung von Artikel 28 der CA," in *Volk Gottes*. Festgabe für Josef Hofer, edited by R. Bäumer (Freiburg i.B.:1967), 389.

6. Jedin, op. cit., I,287.

7. "Hoggimai non habbiamo bisogno di concilio, quanto per noi... ma la Christianita' n'ha bisogno." *Nuntiaturberichte aus Deutschland* 1533-1559, Vol. 1 (Gotha: 1892; rpt. Frankfurt a.m.: 1968), 546.

8. Bäumer (see nt. 1), 89; CR 3, 125.

9. WA 50, 204: SA II,II,10.

10. WA Br 8, 35-38; AE 50,161 ("Therefore they would like to frighten us into refusing. Then they would feel safe and could say that we obstructed the council.")

11. WA 54,220; cp. AE 41,280.

12. R. Stupperich, "Die Reformatoren und das Tridentinum," in *ARG* 47 (1956) 20-63; H. Meyer, "Die deutschen Protestanten in der zweiten Tagungsperiode des Konzils v. Trient 1551/52," in: *ARG* 56 (1956) 166-209; Jedin (see nt 3), 359-398.

13. Cf. H. Jedin, "Historische Randbemerkungen zum Thema: Tridentinum und Wiedervereinigung," in M. Roesle und O. Cullmann, eds., *Begegnung der Christen* (Stuttgart/Frankfrut a. M. 1959), 450-461; Th. Freudenberger, "Zur Benutzung des reformatorischen Schrifttums im Konzil v. Trient," in R. Bäumer, ed., *Von Konstanz nach Trient*. Festgabe für August Franzen (Munich/Paderborn/Vienna 1972), 477-601; V. Pfnür, "Zur Verurteilung der reformatorischen Rechtfertigungslehre auf dem Konzil von Trient," in: AHC 8 (1976) 407-428; V. Pfnür, "Das Tridentinische und die nachtridentinischen Bekenntnisse der Röm.-Kath. Kirche und die Confessio Augustana," in P. Meinhold, ed., *Studien zur Bekenntnisbildung* (Wiesbaden 1980), 84-98.

14. J. Wicks, ed., *Cajetan Responds. A Reader in Reformation Controversy*

(Washington: 1978), 47-98, 266, nt 4. In the Explicit of one small work of 1521 Cajetan expressly writes that he has not mentioned the names of his opponents because he wants to charge no one; it is for him only a question of truth: "Tacitis obiicientibu, ut nemine accusato, cuiusque in pectus, liberum habeat veritas aditum. Romae die sexto Juni 1521" (Ad Leonem decimum Pontificem maximum de septemdecim Responsionibus ad diversa praecipue obiecta, quae pro Martini Lutheri assertionibus facere videbantur; Responsio I: Super quinque Martini Lutheri articulos: Cajetan, *Opuscula omnia*, Lyon 1521, 128b); cf. J. Wicks, *Cajetan und die Anfänge der Reformation* (Münster 1983).

15. H. Roos, "Die Quellen der Bulle "Exsurge Domine" (June 15, 1520)," in *Theologie in Geschichte und Gegenwart*. Michael Schmaus zum 60. Geburtstag, edited by J. Auer and H. Volk (Munich: 1957), 909-926.

16. Op. cit.,915ff.

17. Citation according to Roos (see nt 15), 916.

18. Op.cit., 918; on the condemnation of the Sorbonne cf. F.T. Bos, *Luther in het oordeel van de Sorbonne* (Amsterdam 1974).

19. *Articuli CCCCC Martini Lutheri* (Cologne 1525).

20. L. Helbling, "Dr. Johann Fabri," in *RST* 67/68 (Münster 1941), 97; cf. *TRE* 10, 784-788.

21. CT IV, 10-23.

22. Helbling (see nt 20), 107ff.

23. W. Gussmann, ed., *D. Johann Ecks vierhundertvier Artikel zum Reichstag von Augsburg* (Kassel 1930); concerning additional collections of Reformation heresies submited in 1530, among which especially Joh. Fabri, *Antilogiarum hoc est, contradictionum Martini Lutheri Babilonia ...*, cf. E. Iserloh, ed., *Confessio Augustana und Confutatio. Der Augsburger Reichstag 1530 und die Einheit der Kirche* (Münster: 1981), 349. Concerning Fabri's catalogue of writings from 1540, cf. V. Pfnür, "Die Einigung bei den Religionsgesprächen von Worms und Regensburg 1540/41 eine Täuschung?", in G. Müller, ed., *Die Religionsgespräche der Reformationszeit* (Gütersloh 1980), 55-88, here 56 f.

24. Freudenberger (see nt 13), 584.

25. H. Jedin, *Geschichte des Konzils von Trient*, vol. II, (Freiburg i.Br.: 1957), 124; English translation II, 148.

26. CT V, 212 f.

27. CT V, 239, 26 ff., 45 ff.

28. Freudenberger (see nt 13), 584.

29. Jedin, *Geschichte* II (see nt 25), 144ff; English translation II, 171 ff.

30. Freudenberger (see nt 13), 588.

31. Jedin, *Geschichte* II (see nt 25), 142; English translation II, 169.

32. Pfnür, "Zur Verurteilung" (see nt 13), 414.

33. Pfnür, "Zur Verurteilung" (see nt 13), 421.

34. "Assertiones Lutheranorum super hoc articulo iustificationis" (CT V, 471ff).

35. Op.cit., 420.

36. Op.cit., 428.

37. Jedin, *Geschichte* I, (see nt 3) 256 ff., 368 ff. English translation I, 317 ff., 459 ff. For the following cf. Jedin, "Randbemerkungen," (nt 13).

38. CT V, 932.

39. CT X, 826 f.

40. Jedin, "Randbemerkungen," (see nt 13), 455.

41. Ibid.

42. Jedin, *Geschichte* II (see nt 25), 330; English translation II, 358.

43. Jedin, "Randbemerkungen," (see nt 13), 455.

44. Ibid., 456.

45. Ibid., 459.

46. Cf. E. Iserloh, "Das tridentinische Messopferdekret in seinen Beziehungen zu der Kontroverstheologie der Zeit," in II *Concilio di Trento e la Riforma Tridentina*. Atti del Convegno Storico Internazionale, Trento 2-6 Settembre 1963 (Rome: 1965), 401-439.

47. Roman Catholic/Lutheran Joint Commission, *The Eucharist* (Geneva, 1980).

48. Jedin, "Randbemerkungen," (see nt 13), 457.

49. A. v. Harnack, *Lehrbuch der Dogmengeschichte* III (Freiburg i.Br.: 1890), 605; rpt. Darmstadt: 1964, 711; English translation. *History of Dogma*, VII (London: 1900; rpt. New York: 1961), 57.

Chapter Ten

The Canons of the Tridentine Decree on Justification

To Whom did they apply?
To Whom do they apply today?

Otto Hermann Pesch

SOME PRELIMINARY REMARKS ON METHOD

1. . THE FOLLOWING ESSAY is the edited version of a lecture delivered and discussed at the fourth session of the first sub-group: "Justification (Faith - baptism - penance)" from September 23-25, 1983 in the Evangelical Academy at Hofgeismar. As agreed with the Study Group and the editors, it is documented here as it was delivered. This means that it has not been reworked on the basis of the viewpoints expressed in the discussion, nor has it been expanded into a total presentation of the Tridentine decree on justification. Accordingly the appended footnotes are also limited to comparatively few references. Among the participants, one could presuppose knowledge both of the historical and factual context as well as of the secondary literature decisive for the state of the discussion. For those less well informed, the selected references to the literature offer sufficient initial information to clear a path into further specialized works. Nevertheless, the objections, supplements, and continuing questions which were expressed in the discussion at Hofgeismar should not be lost. They follow, case by case, at the conclusion

of the essay in the form of short excurses. They are numbered and the figures in brackets in the text refer to them. A comparison between 1.) the details of the lecture, 2.) the possible related excursus, 3.) the further explanations of the written suggestions for improvement (*modi*) and their discussion in the "Work Report" [included in the German volume, but not here translated], and 4.) the final text as it appears in *Condemnations* would produce a fascinating small "form criticism" of the section on justification and give one some sense of the struggle all the participants engaged in over the subject matter.

2. The question asked in the Study Group, and especially in sub-group 1, was: Do the mutual condemnations of the sixteenth century, here the repudiations concerning the understanding of the justification of sinners, still apply to the churches of today? The Council of Trent in its decree on justification formulated a total of 33 canons against the Reformation teaching on justification. Each canon concludes with the formula of repudiation "anathema sit" against those who represent and hold the statements quoted in the canon. In a precise, technical form we have before us "condemnations." The task assigned to the Study Group could only be carried out if there were first an investigation of each individual canon with reference to the posed question. This could not, and cannot, be the final literary form for the emerging document, but it is only an indispensable spade-work for it. This fact explains the "stubborn" and absolutely lusterless construction of the following text.

3. The posed question contains more specifically the following four sub-questions:
1. Against whom or against whose teaching was the relevant canon at that time directed?
2. Has the canon accurately struck the intended position?
3. Does it still strike the teaching represented today in the churches of the Reformation?
4. If the answer is yes, what significance and what status does the continuing opposition have?
Each canon of the decree on justification is examined here according to the frame set by these four questions. The questions will not be repeated, but indicated by number.

4. As in the final document, each canon will be cited with its number in Dz and in ND. In the document itself, and also when necessary in the following text, the translation according to ND is not simply taken over, but is compared with the original text. Often the translation in ND must be edited—even at the

cost of a less "elegant" language—because important nuances and connotations of the Latin terminology are not sufficiently clear.

Canon 1 (Dz 1551; ND 1951)

1.-4. The canon was then and remains today what one might call a "self-starter." It does not have a direct parallel in preceding explanatory chapters. Rather it formulates, relative to justification, the quintessence, so to speak, of the decree on original sin (Dz 1510-1516; ND 507-513). The canon is important in so far as, within a document which is, according to the style of the time, oriented entirely toward defense and not, as in our ecumenical age, toward working out commonality, it describes the solid foundation of the confessed Christian faith held in common with the Reformers in reference to the unconditioned mercy of God on the sinner.[1]

Here as with all canons it should be noted that since the second preliminary draft by Seripando for the second presentation of the decree (the September draft) the canons and chapters were separated, in distinction from the decree on original sin.[2] The intention thereby was—and this also throws light on canon 1—not only to reject the Reformation teaching on justification, but at the same time, especially through the chapters, to provide preachers at least the outline of a Catholic doctrine of justification. As is well known, this led to a proposal, not accepted by the Pope, to publish the decree on justification beforehand, so that the pastors could already make use of it in their Lenten sermons in 1547. The canons and chapters retained this structure. For interpretation this means that not every statement, also not every canon, must absolutely contain a rejection of Reformation teaching. One must also consider the possibility that it simply stresses a catholic truth that the recent past had not adequately kept in mind.

Otherwise, the council concentrated its rejecting remarks especially on the Lutheran teaching, as Hubert Jedin has established.[3] The other Reformers, especially Calvin, are touched upon only lightly in the decree on justification, as the negotiations prove. Here lies a preliminary decision for the clarification of the question of the respective addressee of the canons.

Canon 2 (Dz 1552; ND 1952)

1. The canon *sounds* like the rejection of a specific position of the late scholastic teaching of grace, which had in fact in representative statements—from, e.g., Gabriel Biel[4]—put forward the thesis that the human being (the sinner) needs the grace of God only "more easily" to love God above all things, to live justly, and to merit eternal life. Historically[5] it is controversial whether the *promereri* (also in Dz 1532; ND 1935) excludes only the *meritum de*

condigno or also the *meritum de congruo*. This is by no means hair-splitting. Late scholastic theology joined this *meritum de congruo*—in opposition somewhat to Thomas[6]—to the *facere quod in se est*, which it identified with the act of loving God above all things. Even sinners are capable of this, at least for a moment, before and as God meets them with his grace and makes it possible for them to maintain this love of God beyond the initial moment. In this view, justifying grace is connected, even if by the wise ordering of God (*de potentia Dei ordinata*), to a pre-achievement of the human being, even if only for a moment. This pre-achievement establishes a merit, even if only of *congruency*, congruent namely to the so disposing wisdom of God. At least in a weakened sense human beings—sinners!—could and even must "merit" their justification by God.

2. If the *text* has these late scholastic theses in view and wants to deal with them—thus the thesis of Hanns Rückert—if *promereri* is thus only a linguistically strengthened *mereri*, then the text excludes *any* merit from the grace of justification. The canon would thereby be in complete agreement with Luther and in complete agreement with present evangelical theology, which in this regard recognizes not the slightest distance from Luther.

3. But if—thus the thesis of Heiko A. Oberman—the text does not want to exclude the late scholastic thesis, if the *promereri* thus means the *meritum de condigno* while a simple *mereri* means the *meritum de congruo*, as in fact some evidence indicates,[7] then the text of the canon only excludes an "authentic" meriting of the grace of justification, not an "inauthentic," a "merit of congruency," however that is to be understood. In this case the council would not *historically* be in agreement with Luther and contemporary evangelical theology. But definitely so in *the history of its effects*! Since Domingo de Soto,[8] a Thomist interpretation of the decree on justification has become accepted, as Oberman himself shows. This remains so up to the present. The reception of the Council of Trent by theology and the church would then have moved a step beyond the historical intention of the council fathers. Even if within the Thomist school in the two following centuries—in the dispute between the Dominicans and Jesuits—the old, late scholastic views which judged human possibilities "more optimistically" appeared in a new form, nevertheless no one need fear a complaint by the teaching office who interprets the canons of Trent Thomistically and thereby establishes agreement with Luther and contemporary evangelical theology. See Excursus [1].

4. The fourth question thus becomes superfluous.

Postscript: Personally I agree with the historical interpretation of Rückert against Oberman. The most important reason: The canon, more clearly than Chapter 8 (Dz 1532; ND 1935), denies that the *liberum arbitrium* is able to live justly *at all*. This also excludes the act of loving God above all things, which late scholasticism considered possible and as *meritum de congruo* necessary.

Canon 3 (Dz 1553; ND 1953)

1. The canon appears to be directed against the Semi-pelagians—and is thus far in complete agreement with Reformation teaching. Following Gregory of Rimini, the Augustinians, to whom also the young Luther belonged, considered the (Semi-)pelagians a living presence in the nominalists. At the outset of the conflict with Rome, Luther had made a timely discovery of his 14th-century brother of the order and led him into battle against his late scholastic opponents.[9] In any case the terminology of the canon strongly recalls the canons of the so-called Second Synod of Orange (529), rediscovered shortly before the Council of Trent (cf. here Dz 374-376; ND 1916-1918).[10]

2.-4. The answers to the questions take care of themselves. Problems first arise in connection with the following canon.

Canon 4-6 (Dz 1554-1556; ND 1954-1956)

1. Clearly intended is Luther's teaching of the "sole efficacy" of God in the event of justification. The wording of canon 4 contains suggestion of Luther's *Disputatio de homine* of 1536, especially of thesis 35 (*pura materia*) and thesis 36 (*materia Deo est*). The fathers at Trent, however, did not know this text, as is demonstrable from the history of its publication and transmission.[11] Admittedly, as the accusations within the debates leading up to the Formula of Concord show,[12] such formulations were in general circulation in polemics and in popular religious instruction. Canon 5 is a literal citation of Luther taken from the *Errores* in the excommunication-threatening bull *Exsurge Domine*, with the addition of *immo titulus sine re*, with which Luther had reacted to the citation in the *Errores*.[13] The formulation of the canon is thus, as it were, tit for tat. With Canon 6, the question arises whether an illusion is present to the teaching of the hardening of the heart in *De servo arbitrio*. It is notable that the canon has no parallel in the chapters. On the whole it is in any case discernible that the three canons aim especially at central opinions of Luther which were widely known, at least in slogan form.

2. Canon 4 misunderstands "passivity" as "apersonality." The canon stresses *assentire* by means of a negative formulation and imputes its rejection to the opposing position. Here—as already in chapter 5 (Dz 1525;ND 1929)— *assentire* is not only an intellectual "agreement" in the sense of holding something true, but an existential self-application. Those who dispute it are assumed to understand the human being as *quoddam inanime*, a "lifeless thing." Luther had often spoken in this pointed fashion.[14] He intends, or at least

never overlooks, what canon 4 wants to establish: "assent" as self involvement, allowing oneself to be grasped by God. Otherwise why the thousandfold *admonition* to faith as a "tried" (= proven, full weighted) trust in God?[15] Canon 4, read in the light of canon 3—and it must be read so and not vice versa—in any case reproduces Luther's opinion.

With canon 5 one must attend to the connection to Dz 1511; ND 508, and again the connection to Dz 371, 378 and 383; ND 504 (Canons 1, 8, and 13 from Orange). There it becomes clear: the loss of freedom is identical with the corruption of original sin. In the background stand debates which initially led to the insertion into Dz 1511 of even more verbatim citations from Orange, which clearly in the new situation required further differentiations. In order not to make the text too complicated, in the end everything was again removed and the present formulations were left.[16] Thereby becomes evident: Canon 5 does not wish to reverse the corresponding statements of Orange; it is therefore to be read in the sense of Orange. Thus the assertion of Canon 5 is: while the "psychological" *freedom of choice* is not extinguished, freedom in the biblical sense, namely the freedom from sins and for God, is extinguished absolutely, completely, and entirely. The distinction between these two freedoms is a result of the philosophical-theological discussion since the Middle Ages—at Orange there was no interest in this distinction and no occasion for it. What at Trent was and could be expected from the asserted psychological freedom of choice from a theological perspective must be seen in the context of canon 7.

Canon 6 misunderstands Luther, so far as he does not wish to relieve the sinner of responsibility for sin through the driving, total efficacy of God even in the sinner. This thesis is certainly a paradox, but no more paradoxical than the teaching of a mere "allowing" of sin by God, which defines the problem, but does not solve it.[17]

3. Contemporary Lutheran theology:

• has recognized in conversation with Catholic theology the hazards of Luther's thesis. Luther research has especially concerned itself to remove the suspicion that Luther's denial of the freedom of the will means a determinism in the psychological and philosophical sense according to which the human being sins not only with necessity, but through this necessity is absolved from the responsibility for sin.[18]

• today takes Luther's thesis of the lack of freedom with too little seriousness, rather than too much, as the reverse conclusion in the not uncommon recommendations of this teaching by evangelical Luther scholars shows.[19]

• faces the same questions regarding the problem of "God and evil" as Catholic theology.[20]

Officially, the Lutheran church has expressed itself at most in relation to the basic impulse of the thesis of the bound will, i.e., in relation to the lostness of human beings before God and to the unmerited and unmeritable act of salvation by God. It has not expressed itself in relation to the thesis' doctrinal form and certainly not in relation to *De servo arbitrio*.[21]

4. From the point of view of the relation of church to church—and not theological tradition to theological tradition—the fourth question can be dropped. Such a outcome, establishing commonality on the basis of an explicit or implicit distancing of the Lutheran church from Luther, is definitely less than satisfactory. The relaxation of the opposition which becomes possible through, on the one side, an interpretation of the canons of Trent which stresses more strongly their Augustinian imprint and, on the other, through a hesitation by Lutheran theology and churches to declare every pointed assertion of *De servo arbitrio* as the unrenounceable heritage of Reformation theology, holds promise if both sides maintain from the controversies of the past the challenge for the future. This challenge is to struggle toward a fitting way of speaking about the ever mysterious relation between, on the one side, the liberating total efficacy of God in his act of justification and, on the other, the radically dependent personal capacity of response of the human being [Excursus 1].

Canon 7-9 (Dz 1557-1559; ND 1957-1959)

1. The canons are unambiguously aimed at the teaching of Luther and of the Reformation generally that faith alone makes works, penance, and all movements of the will relating to justification good before God—and not, e.g., some quality dwelling within them, even if granted by God.

2. The elucidation of the question, whether the Reformation position is correctly addressed, would require an almost total presentation of Reformation theology, especially the theology of Luther. It is utterly doubtful that the fathers of Trent have here simply misunderstood Luther and the Reformation teaching. Canon 8 and 9 allude to quotations of Luther from the *Errores* (cf. Dz 1456, 1460, 1461, 1465; ND 1614/6,10,11).

On the other hand: the defense of the necessity and worth of "cooperation" and works, and the rejection of the idea that justification is given to the sinner *sola fide*, are two of the four "essentials" which were incontestable at every stage of Trent's debate about justification, running through them like a red thread. Any speaker in the debate who attempted in some way to step over these threads, through differentiations or advances into new territory, exposed himself to the immediate charge of being "uncatholic". (The two other "essentials" will appear in the context of canons 11 and 13f.)

For clarification, it should be noted that the council distinguishes between *gratia excitans* (canon 4) as the beginning and *gratia sanctifans* (canon 11) as the conclusion of justification. "Between" both lie all works, repentance, "cooperation" etc. (cf. Dz 1526; ND 1930), which could not well be viewed as sins, in so far as they were worked by grace. Behind this concept and its conceptual difficulties over against the Reformation position stands the desire for a kind of "psychology" of justification: A study of the process of justification in the seldom encountered by not simply invented case of the conversion of the unbeliever—as Del Monte expressly observed in the General Congregation on June 30, 1546.[22] Behind this psychological interest in turn is to be found a pastoral impulse, to make clear that which matters also to the already baptized and to serious sinners.

Luther and his followers on the contrary polemicized against works which were done *before* grace and *for* grace, thus not *quacumque* rationale facta sint (canon 7). Luther thus had in view the late scholastic doctrine of grace and "works" as self-justification, i.e., as expression of "concupiscence," understood as self-denial over against God. The same is valid for the description of the fear of hell in canon 8 (cf. Dz 1456; ND 1614/6). In the sentence condemned here, Luther was not thinking of that fear before damnation which itself is already the fruit of grace and with it a part of genuine repentance, even if not its entirety. Rather he was thinking of that repentance which pious self-analysis sets in place of unconditional trust in God. This understanding and this suspicion are connected in Luther directly with the new understanding of the sacrament of penance and indirectly with the dispute about indulgences—and, in the sense of the so-called "late dating," even with Luther's Reformation break-through itself.[23] On the other side, however, in the context of the understanding of the law, the fear of God's judgment belongs for Luther to the indispensable elements of the doctrine of justification. According to many researchers, this fear is even the decisive horizon against which alone the teaching of justification becomes understandable.

In relation to canon 9, it remains to be asked what Luther understood by faith. The fathers at Trent persistently *distinguished* faith from hope and love. They understood faith as an act of the understanding, to some extent even as the content of the objectified confession of faith, especially in the relation to the question of the certainty of salvation. It is clear that they then cannot agree with Luther. With *this* concept of faith it is a misunderstanding to impute to Luther that "nothing else is required" than faith alone to be justified. Faith, beyond which "nothing else is demanded" for justification, is significantly more than just the rational Yes to the truth of God's revelation.

3. Luther research and Lutheran, indeed Protestant, theology in general

maintains to the present day the thought and phraseology of Luther.[24] On the other hand, they can emphatically elaborate both the activation of the human being through the faith given by God and also the personal answer of the human being to God's promise, and do so as the teaching of *Luther*.[25] A Catholic doctrine of justification which regards the prescribed phraseology of the Council of Trent as indispensable would in fact strike the present partner. Otherwise the rejections in canons 7-9 can be judged to be obsolete.

4. Also important would be:

• to read canon 7-9 also strictly in the light of canon 3;

• a courageous statement on the part of Catholic theology, and best of all also by the ecclesiastical office, that the late scholastic doctrine that the grace of justification can be merited "congruently" by an act of perfect love of God is a form of speech that cannot be adequate to the present consciousness of the problem—even if in its own context it is acquitted of the charge of Pelagianism;[26]

• a judgment whether Luther's new understanding of the sacrament of penance and of the importance of absolution could receive a Catholic recognition—in the opinion of Catholic Luther researchers, such is the case;[27]

• an appreciation of the fact that the Lutheran church nowadays regularly takes positions on the question of "the works corresponding to faith," i.e., to ethical questions. Does that not mean, that in the midst of new challenges, the problem as formulated in the sixteenth century has been left behind?[28] [Excursus 2].

Canon 10-11 (Dz 1560-1561; ND 1960-1961 828-829)

1. The first half of canon 10 simply repeats canon 1. The second half has one basis among others in particular formulations in Luther's *Sermo de duplici iustitia*,[29] where Luther in fact states that the righteousness of Christ is truly our righteousness. Nevertheless, as with the earlier named *Disputatio de homine* (cf. above canon 4-6), we cannot assume that the fathers of Trent knew this text, perhaps originally preached on Palm Sunday 1518.[30] The *Errores Martini Lutheri* do not cite the sermon. The first volume of Luther's Latin writings, which appeared in 1545, does contain it, but it was not accessible to the fathers.[31] Be that as it may, *formaliter*, as understood by the fathers of Trent, blocks in any case an understanding of that which Luther thought. The fathers, in case they knew Luther's statements at least by hearsay, considered them in terms of the conceptuality of scholasticism. As a comparison with chapter 7 (Dz 1529; ND 1932) shows, the cited formula then becomes nonsense.[32]

In its first part and in its conclusion, Canon 11 strikes in its excluding formulations the wording of numerous statements of Luther.[33] As the text makes explicitly clear, the council fathers understand these Reformation formulations *exclusa gratia et caritate* according to the concept of "grace and love" bound up with a formal determination "inherent" in the soul. The decisive rejection of the exclusion of such "grace and love" in the Reformation doctrine of justification was the third essential element in all opinions expressed in the Trent negotiations.

2. From 1 it follows that Luther especially is in fact the target. In a strict textual sense, Luther did not assert that Christ is *formaliter* our righteousness, as the scholastics would have understood the word *formaliter*. He also did not assert that the forgiveness of sins is granted to us *exclusa gratia et caritate*, but only: exclusive of such "grace and love" understood as a kind of formal and qualitative determination of the continuing existence of the soul. The Council, however, was neither willing nor able to accept the counter-concept which for Luther makes this formulation unnecessary, if not objectless. In place of *formaliter* there is in Luther the thought of the "joyous exchange,"[34] in place of *gratia et caritas* there is the distinction and relation between *gratia* and *donum*,[35] or in later Lutheran theology the distinction and relation between justification and sanctification.[36] Thus we can judge: *substantively* Luther is not struck, at least not in so far as what is critical for the Council is missing in Luther, neither the newly creative power of justifying grace, nor the ethical effect, and most definitely not the decisive and strict connection between the event of justification and the saving action of God in Christ. Also in the contemporary theological discussion of the controversy, such an opposition would be seen as a too narrow determination of the difference. In contrast to the beginnings of the debate over justification, it is no longer seen as a matter for mutual denunciation.[37] For both sides, the question centers on the relative importance of their respective phraseologies: concretely, whether one's own phraseology is judged so indispensable that one cannot concede that those who do not share it in fact speak correctly about the essence of the event of justification.

3. For contemporary Lutheran theology, the formulation rejected in canon 10 and 11, especially 11, remains characteristic.[38] Lutheran theology could agree with these canons (or not reject them) only if it also saw the possibility of a relativization of its own phraseology and could concede that the subject matter could be conceptually grasped and linguistically expressed in another way with full validity and not only in a deficient manner over against the Lutheran phraseology as the only fully adequate form of speech. Nevertheless, on the whole the Lutheran teaching, now as in the past, is not struck by the condemnation in either of these canons. They yet feel themselves here attacked and in any case would never concede that they *must* view the rejected

formulations as insufficient in Trent's sense. This pressure of the formulations of Trent is not eliminated simply by the concession by Lutheran theology of the *possibility* of another conceptually and linguistically proper formulation of the witness to justification. In short: we have here for the first time a genuine occasion to ask the fourth question.

4. Important for the clarification of this problem would be:

• a consultation of New Testament exegetes who probably would relativize both conceptualities and forms of speech, even if they also might confirm the Lutheran position as fully and completely in accord with Scripture;Cf. the final text:[39]

• a general reflection on what today is and can be said about the "justification of the sinner" so that contemporary persons understand what is thereby spoken and promised to them. This would probably require that we go beyond both the Lutheran and the Tridentine levels of concept and language;

• an examination of the degree to which the pronouncements of the Roman Catholic teaching office in the last decades, in so far as they concern our theme, still use the Tridentine terminology and conceptual analysis;[40]

• and, in case they do not do so, whether that implies not only a relativizing of the Tridentine phraseology, but also a substantive adoption or recognition of Lutheran propria.[41] [Excursus 3].

Canon 12-14 (Dz 1562-1564; ND 1962-1964)

1. Here it is clear that Luther's teaching of the "certainty of salvation" is intended: faith as *fiducia*, faith in the forgiveness of sins without confusion through one's own lack of preparation and one's own subjective instability in faith, forgiveness as certainty of forgiveness. The inevitably polemical formulations here cited can in fact be read in Luther (cf. Dz 1460-1462; ND 1614/10-12).

2. Just as clearly the canons do not strike the real thought and intention of Luther. The reasons for this judgment are:

a) Faith is here understood as the temporal beginning of salvation, as its foundation and root, but not as the totality of the person's existence before God. The attempted "psychology" of the justification process in Dz 1526 and 1532 (ND 1930, 1935) here works itself out. For Luther, however, and this scarcely needs to be documented more fully, faith in each case is the total and comprehensive relation to God on the basis of God's justifying promise of forgiveness, to which faith clings and on which it depends.

b) This faith is even understood as a corpus of teaching, as the formulation "... faith into which no error can creep..." in Dz 1534; ND 1936, shows.

c) Luther connects the certainty of forgiveness to his understanding of Matthew 16:19. In countless texts, especially from the early period of the

Reformation conflict and of the dispute over the correct understanding of the sacrament of penance, Luther stresses: Because Christ has promised that what is loosed on earth will be loosed in heaven, Christ is made a liar if one then casts into doubt, for whatever reason, the unconditional validity of God's promise of forgiveness (concretely, the "absolution" in the sacrament of penance), despite all subjective instability.[42] The allusion to Dz 1460; ND 1614/10, in canon 13 shows that the fathers at Trent definitely had in mind this context in Luther's teaching. It is all the more regrettable and even incomprehensible that Trent in no way engaged Luther's central argument, his understanding of Matthew 16:19, unless one reads the first sentence of chapter 9 (Dz 1533; ND 1936) as a recapitulation of this argument (if so, a highly imprecise recapitulation).

d) The most important argument, however, for the conclusion that the Council argued past the real thought and intention of Luther is the actual substance of the doctrinal statement, especially as it emerges through the reference back to chapter 9 (Dz 1533-1534: ND 1936). The Council rejects that which Luther also took efforts to exclude as a misunderstanding of his teaching: security and an over-estimation of the self in relation to one's own standing in grace ("boasting," "complacency"), overlooking one's own weaknesses, a lack of fear of losing the grace received, feelings of comfort as the criterion of certainty, lack of moral restraint under an appeal to the certainty of salvation. On the other hand, the Council stresses the points which also for Luther are important: the reliability and all-sufficiency of God's grace in Christ, human instability and unreliability in the acceptance of grace and thus the ever-present threats against faith and salvation. [Excursus 4].

3. Contemporary evangelical theology is struck by the condemnation of Trent just as little as is Luther. In addition, in a changed situation it faces today the same problem as Catholic theology: the question of the certainty and experience of God.[43] For both it is clear that the question cannot be decided through a reference to a "body of teaching," but through reflection on the particular and unique manner in which faith creates certainty—whereby only the question remains of the contemporary meaning for Catholic theology of the statements of the First Vatican Council about the knowledge of God.[44]

4. The rejection of the certainty of salvation (certainty of forgiveness, certainty of faith) was the fourth "essential" in the opinions expressed in Trent's negotiations over the development of the decree on justification. Helpful therefore from the Catholic side would be:

• an unreserved recognition of faith as dependence on the saving God. This does not threaten the Catholic interest in the *knowledge* of faith, but presupposes it, as Luther presupposed it also.

• an explicit recognition of the basic structure of faith, according to which faith in fact occurs *within* the remaining human instability, which precisely then cannot guarantee persistence in faith;

• an explicit recognition of the insight that Matthew 16:19, as the exegesis and the history of the sacrament of penance shows, has to do with penance and not with the legitimation of papal primacy, as was uncritically presupposed at that time and long before.[45]

• an explicit recognition (with Oswald Bayer[46]) of the insight that the unconditional dependability of absolution corresponds exactly to that which the Catholic tradition means by *opus operatum.*

Canon 15-17 (Dz 1565-1567; ND 1965-1967)

1. It is unclear whether the text has Luther in mind at all. The question is raised whether this is one of the points where Calvin is "grazed" (Jedin).[47]

2. In any case, neither in formulation nor substance did Luther say what is condemned in the canons.[48] The canons do reveal how particular Reformation theses—or widespread and misunderstood popular opinions—could be pigeon-holed by the Tridentine fathers within a particular prior system of concepts. *These*, however, were not Luther's problems.

3. The canons also, in relation to Luther, take care of themselves. [Excursus 5].

4. It would be good if the long process of the revision of the doctrine of predestination[49] were appropriately supported by the ecclesiastical office, simply through an intelligent explanation of the right biblical ideas. As persons who lecture before parish audiences repeatedly experience, simple Christians in both churches still have utterly confused concepts and corresponding fears about predestination. On the other hand, an explanation by the ecclesiastical office must be possible in the light of an exegetical explanation of the true meaning of Romans 9-11 and an exegesis of Ephesians 1. The Second Vatican Council gives hints for this.

Canon 18-20 (Dz 1568-1570; ND 1968-1970)

1. The council fathers certainly *intended* Luther, or at least opinions in circulation which they believed could be traced back to Luther and which correctly represented his teaching.

2. The fathers' understanding, however, is precisely wrong.

a) In relation to canon 18, Luther says the exact opposite—namely, where he stresses that the justified person has a new desire and love for the law of God and acts correspondingly.[50] If he in fact taught what is condemned in canon 18, how could he have had the occasion to preach and to write so often as he did about the Ten Commandments? Why should he have devoted the first section of both of his two catechisms to an explication of the Ten Commandments?

b) The same holds true for canon 19. Luther, however, would see no contradiction in the fact that, nevertheless, nothing is commanded by the Gospel besides faith, because faith relates itself to love and works. In turn, their relation to faith is not additive but comprehensive. Here reference should be made to the inclusive relation between faith and works which has been long established by Luther research, even if with differing emphases of interest. This relation does not cancel their irreversible cause-effect relation, but correctly comments on it.[51]

c) The same holds also for canon 20. The formulation *absoluta promissio... sine condicione...* Luther probably would accept as a *formulation*. The true meaning would be better expressed, however, by the formulation: *unconditional* promise, but no promise *without result*. The Council, in the light of canon 3 and 4 (see above), could not have intended more.

3.-4. The third and fourth questions are superfluous. Cf. also further above on canon 7-9,4. [Excursus 6]

Canon 21 (Dz 1571; ND 1971)

1. The canon has Luther in mind.

2. The canon also strikes Luther, for Luther rejected the expression *Christus legislator* throughout his life with the strongest words [Excursus 7]. He clearly understood it, however, in a manner that the Council did not wish to advocate: that thereby the Gospel would become a signpost to self-justification, which finally would lead to despair.[52] The Council's concern was expressed by Luther through the idea he also held throughout his life of *Christus exemplum*, which on the basis of faith in the *Christus sacramentum* immediately becomes effective.[53]

3.-4. As a consequence of new reflection in Christology und more immediately on the relation of Christology to the question of God, *Christus legislator* has ceased to be a theme—apart from certain tendencies in Roman Catholic theology, especially in the context of specific ecclesiological questions. All the more, however has *Christus exemplum* become a theme—or better: *Jesus exemplum*. That is not entirely without problems, as especially the contemporary dispute over "political theology" and "liberation theology" shows.[54] The problem, however, equally engages evangelical theology. Without being able here to go into details, we can say: So long as Christology is not reduced to speaking only of *Jesus exemplum* and further questions are not programmatically presented as pointless or even dangerous, we can see in the new interest in Jesus as "model" for life and action the best modern, no longer confessionally specific, acceptance of the Tridentine concern.

Canon 22 (Dz 1572: ND 1972)

1.-4. The canon is to be read in the context of canons 14-17 and therefore along with them loses its point in so far as the clarifications given of them are sound.

Canon 23 (Dz 1573; ND 1973)

1.-4 The canon has nothing to do with Luther. Does it again, so to speak, incidentally "graze" the Begards and Beguines?[55] [Excursus 8].

Canon 24-25 (Dz 1574-1575; ND 1974-1975)

1. Both canons clearly intend Luther. Canon 25 even alludes to sentences of Luther (cf. Dz 1481f.; ND 1923/31f.).

2. Here the usual method of tearing sentences from their context and isolating them as erroneous teachings has its revenge.[56] For Luther good works are obviously the fruits and signs of justification. But in his eyes that does not stand in opposition to *conservari* and *augeri per bona opera*. Luther is in line with the Council with his concept of "faith enfleshed" (*fides incarnata*; see further above canons 18-20), of the "exercise" of faith in works, of works as indirect confirmation of the certainty of salvation.[57] Excluded for Luther is an understanding of works, even those completed in the grace of justification. as a *claim* before God. But the Council also excludes precisely that (see below).

Canon 25 hits exactly just to one side of Luther's actual teaching: The *iustus*, in *so far* as she or he is such, does not sin according to Luther also. But she or he is *iustus* first of all through God (ever anew) not reckoning to her the sins even of her highest ethical achievements.

Everything is settled (or resists settlement) in relation to the stance taken toward canons 10-11. Naturally, every expert recognizes that here Luther's thesis of the Christian as *simul iustus et peccator* is involved. It is certainly no secret that the majority of the Council could do nothing with this thesis. The Council could indeed scarcely grasp the thesis' meaning on the basis of its imprisonment in the exclusive validity of scholastic terminology, in whose framework the thesis is nonsense—although Luther strongly supports it on the basis of Augustine, whom he does not thereby misunderstand.[58] Even today Catholic theologians demonstrably have difficulties with this thesis, although one would hardly provide it with an "anathema."[59] Since Luther can summarize in this thesis his whole teaching of justification, the opinion on this formula must be seen as a test whether and how far one has really understood and moved toward Luther's Reformation teaching of justification [Excursus 9].

3. There are certain tendencies within contemporary Lutheran theology in relation to which canon 24 might be correct.[60] They are balanced within

Lutheran theology itself, however, by other "schools," which most strongly stress the importance of good works for life in justification.[61] *Sola fide numquam sola*, as Paul Althaus once formulated the point, and thereby put the true opinion of Luther.[62]

4. In view of the official positions of the evangelical church, we can proceed on the assumption that the concretization of justifying faith in ethical action represents in principle no problem. Since this concerns the new obedience toward the concrete command of God, which always needs to be better discovered and better carried out, the objective substance is expressed of that which the Council meant by *conservari* and *augeri* the grace of justification. The idea of a "claim" was as little present in the meaning of the Council as in that of relevant official representatives of the evangelical church.

Canon 26 (Dz 1576; ND 1976); Canon 31-32 (Dz 1581-1582; ND 1981-1982)

1.-2. Canon 26 defends the doctrine of merit in the *Augustinian* sense developed in Dz 1538f and 1545-1548; ND 1536f and 1946-1948. It excludes every thought of a claim and defends the doctrine of merit as an interpretation of the eschatological structure of grace. Today that is also seen by evangelical theologians.[63] Conversely, provided that the idea of claim is excluded, Luther deals more loosely with the thought of merit than is usually thought.[64] Luther can formulate the sentence: "The sons do not merit the kingdom, but the kingdom merits the sons."[65] Does this sentence state in fact anything other than the well known formulation of Augustine, to which chapter 16 so clearly alludes? One notes: the Council defends that a person is permitted to "await and hope" for reward (canon 26). The *intuitu aeternae mercedis* (canon 31) is to be interpreted on this basis, not vice-versa. And canon 32 bases the idea of merit on the "living" membership in Christ.

3.-4. If it is correct that the Council defended the thought of merit as an eschatological statement about grace while evangelical theology rejected it as a practical-ethical thought, then it is not matter of a Yes and a No to the same question. To be sure: the history of the doctrine of merit is a unique struggle to preserve eschatological thought from its practical exploitation—and we are permitted to ask whether it can ever be completely successful in view of the images the concept contains.[66]

From the evangelical side it would be necessary to examine incorrect assumptions about the meaning of the doctrine of merit and no longer to burden the discussion with them.

From the Catholic side it would be necessary:

• no longer to represent the idea of merit as implied in the biblical idea of reward (which exegetically has been worked through for a long time). This acceptance of a logical implication was demonstrably the impulse for the development of a doctrine of merit. Further it would be necessary:

• to acknowledge the long documented subordinate role of the doctrine of merit in religious instruction and in the dogmatic handbooks—occasionally no more than a longer commemoration—and not officially to enjoin what no longer shapes and illumines lived faith. The latter at any rate has ceased occur in an *explicit* form since the beginning of ecumenical conversation. The dispute over the doctrine of merit occurs exclusively in specialized theology, in which of course Roman Catholic theologians cannot simply shove the statements of the Council of Trent off the table.

Finally it would be necessary:

• to seek new phraseologies which more suitably express the substance of the doctrine of merit.[67]

Conclusion: we need not contradict the Council of Trent if, in the interest of the long present objective agreement with evangelical theology, we take leave of the *concept* and *word* "merit." Here as in other cases (perhaps in the doctrine of the sacraments) such a departure can be justified simply by reference to the at present hardly removable misunderstandings, so that a concept and word is placed on the "black list" whose substantive content can be expressed without any difficulty by other and better concepts. [Excursus 10]

Canon 27-28 (Dz 1577-1578; ND 845-846)

1. Verbally, Luther is intended and also engaged.

2. As already in canon 7-11 (see above) everything hangs on the concept of faith. *Here* we must ask: What was meant at Trent by "unbelief?" What is a *vera fides*, which is not *viva fides* and which is without *caritas*? Apparently the council fathers thought again of the *truth of faith* and adherence to the *doctrine of faith*. Thus they did not take up Luther's comprehensive concept of faith, with which the thesis condemned by Trent first begins to receive some sense.

3. Lutheran theology could contribute to an agreement if it would take more seriously Luther's express distinction between "historical" faith, which corresponds (in general) to the concept of faith formulated by Trent, and justifying faith. This latter he specifically designates as the grace of God (what at Trent corresponds to the *viva*), but he nevertheless names the historical faith "faith," like the faith of the demons. The occasionally triumphing Lutheran polemic against the distinction of "two kinds of faith" in the Catholic tradition could become a boomerang.[68]

4. Roman Catholic theology and church do not need to go back behind the *objective assertion* of canon 27f. The effort should have its common goal to

clarify the forms and degrees of faith as elements of the one salvific way of the person with God to God. [Excursus 11]

Canon 29-30 (Dz 1579-1580; ND 1979-80)

1.-4. The concern in the Tridentine statements is the defense of the sacrament of penance—these canons would properly then be the theme of the second sub-group (sacraments). [Excursus 12]

Roman Catholic theology would be well advised, in line with long present insights of research:

• itself to form a judgment about the most recent results of research on the "discovery" of the sacrament of penance by Luther;[69]

• to consider that according to Thomas Aquinas the sinner through the grace of God as a rule receives the *forgiveness of sins* long *before* the receipt of the sacrament of penance, so that this penance above all serves reconciliation with the church;[70]

• to ask what this can mean for the contemporary practice of penance;

• not to use the question of the "temporal punishment of sin" as a lever to overturn all the attained consensus in the doctrine of justification. Luther's thesis, that the pope can on earth absolve from only *ecclesiastical* punishments[71] (which ultimately imply nothing about a person's salvation), is today valid canon law.[72] About "temporal" punishment of sins after this life one would need to consult the contemporary Roman Catholic doctrine of purgatory;[73]

• to reflect seriously on Luther's thesis—one of his most original and stimulating—that the sacrament of penance is a return to the (indestructible) baptism.[74]

Canon 33 (Dz 1583; ND 1983)

1.-4. One's stance here will derive from the total result of the opinions on canons 1-32. [Excursus 13]

Excurses

[1] It is unclear whether canon 1 aims especially at late scholastic theology and its theories about the possibility of the love of God above all else by the sinner. Since the Council in any case refused either to adopt particular positions among the mutually disputing medieval schools or explicitly to reject them, but rather at most permitted an indirect recognition of its preferences by means of inclusion, we can not presume the highly general formulation of canon 1 had in view a quite particular addressee.

But, as was stressed in the discussion about this canon at the session in Hofgeismar, it is clear that the canon, in association with the pertinent chapters, shows us not only that the positive clarification of the question had priority over the negative delimitations, but also that the Council consciously sought clarification through recourse to the decisions in the dispute between Augustine and Pelagius. For this we need only compare the relevant statements of the Synod of Carthage 418 (Dz 222-230; abbreviated in ND 1901-1906). This holds even more strongly for canons 2 and 3: Unmistakably the terminology of the Council is that of the Augustinian-Pelagian controversy, notwithstanding the relation to specific questions set by late scholasticism (see above). The Council obviously did not desire in its statement of the issue to retreat behind the results of the early church controversy; rather, it wishes to decide further material issues in the light of this binding teaching tradition, once again defined here at the very outset. This is then the immovable common point of departure with the Reformers.

This insight of historical theology helped form the document's structure and guided its content (cf. page 41f). This does not mean that the representatives of the via moderna must since Trent be evaluated as heterodox. On the contrary, while a Thomist interpretation of the decree on justification prevailed in the long run, it must also be granted that, seen historically, the concern lest too much be conceded to the Reformation position has repeatedly, as late as the twentieth century, led to hidden, possibly unconscious new versions of the late scholastic theories about the capacities of the human being in relation to God. This was already pointed out in the first opinion on the document.[75] One still must state: whoever takes the results of the Pelagian controversy as the orientation point for an examination and solution to the Reformation-Catholic controversy over the understanding of justification, especially over the evaluation of the capacities of the freedom of the sinner, has in any case the full backing of the Council. They can feel themselves completely and totally "in harmony with Catholic teaching," even if within its spectrum theses are not excluded as simply erroneous to which Reformation theology could never subscribe. This certain unclarity of the margins of Catholic theology does not exceed what was possible and permissible as a "spectrum" for Reformation theology then or now. For ecumenical consensus, harmony in the wide "mid-field" is thoroughly sufficient.[76]

[2] On canon 7-9 a question arises which is "classic" in post-Tridentine Catholic theological discussion: the possibility of "natural good works." In so far as this is a question for the history of theology, no unanimous judgment could be reached in the discussion. That is not astonishing, to the degree that here one is moving within the field of tension set by the two basic types of answer and by the related interpretations of the council, as has already been mentioned (cf. [1]). This author agrees with the Catholic and Protestant interpreters who judge that works done under the impulse of *gratia excitans* no longer can be "purely natural works."[77] Such works are already elements of the event of justification—thought of as a process by the Council—at whose beginning and end stands God's grace. The formal distinction of "awakening grace" and the "proper" grace of justification is an inner Catholic problem—indeed a thoroughly momentous one, as the further unhappy development of the doctrine of "actual grace" shows[78]—in which Protestant interpreters of the council are uninterested, so long as the absolute first initiative of God controls the entire process. Thus seen, a concept of "natural good works" compatible with the teaching of the Council would be an *abstract limit statement*, securing the continuing goodness of God's creation rather than the "added value" of the grace of God beyond the "mere" cancellation of sin. *Concretely*, however, all works are either done in the grace of God or they are done out of the self-glory of the sinner and therefore are themselves sins.

[3] Canons 10-11 may be read as directed at (among others) late scholastic theories, which by *remissio peccati* understood only the eradication of the *reatus*. Moreover, the discussion made clear that one here cannot only ask whether Luther is involved. As in may other cases, when one asks about the addressees of the conciliar statements, one must think of all that was spread abroad in popular representations, e.g., in the pamphlet literature of the time.

First, the discussions had to deal extensively with the different conceptual and linguistic forms of the traditional and Reformation doctrines of justification, which are not to be explained only through reference to "misunderstandings." In the foreground of the formulations, the Reformation teaching (Luther) and the teaching of the Council of Trent cannot be reduced to a common denominator. Thus the basic hermeneutical question arises, whether the conversation partners today are ready to grant the possibility of recognizing other concepts and forms of language as expressions of the same objective truth, even if with different emphases.[79] Obviously the rules of speech cannot be simply arbitrary, but must be tested by the matter to be stated—otherwise the danger looms of a new nominalism. Here especially a look into the New Testament proves to extraordinarily helpful. In Paul alone, but even more in the entire New Testament, the tension-filled and fruitful juxtaposition of different formulations and language games become visible. On this basis it became evident that the document needed to take up related hermeneutical considerations and allow them to play an appropriate role in the work on the substantive issues. This then occurred (cf. *Cond*, pp. 15-20; 39f; 47-49).

[4] If the council fathers at Trent did not understand the meaning and basis of the thesis of the certainty of salvation—a thesis sensed by Luther's opponents from the beginning as especially new and odd and which in some cases made determined opponents out of sympathizers—then this was not just a result of obtuseness in the council hall in Trent. Rather, Luther's own formulations were also not immune to misunderstanding. This was referred to in the discussion about canons 12-14. If the astute Cardinal Cajetan in Augsburg in 1518, despite the most honest efforts to understand Luther and to meet his concern as much as possible,[80] could not concur with Luther's thesis on the basis of his own scholastic presuppositions, one cannot expect such from the overwhelming majority of the council fathers, who had to deal with this idea of Luther a generation later, without having read a line from Luther's works. So it remains up to the present, even with a calm and impartial reading of Luther's statements on this matter, precisely from the early period of the Reformation when he still hoped to be able to convince his opponents and did not, resigned and despairing, simply shoot off polemical broadsides against them. Some readers, Protestant and Catholic, find Luther's explanations illuminating and wonder how they could encounter such momentous barricades of misunderstanding.[81] Others react to these statements with almost the same fears as Luther's contemporary opponents, including the fear that Luther himself cannot take the gracious character of the forgiveness of sins as seriously as his opponents since he makes the consciously experienced and affirmed certainty of the personal forgiveness of sin the condition of the effectiveness of the justifying action of God.[82]

Opponents and friends of the Reformation teaching, both then and today, can quickly agree that for both sides it is a matter of excluding a *false* "certainty" and of stressing the specific certainty of the forgiving word of God. The decisive point of the question which still occupies us is the *treatment of the uncertainty of each within the commonly stressed certainty*. Appropriately, the discussion in the Study Group group was on this point especially intensive. Up to the last day, so to speak, the discussion did not result in a unanimity which would have made an end of the controversy over the certainty of salvation a "self-starter." The final formulation in the study document[83] allows this remainder of disagreement clearly to ring through and seeks to take it into account by permitting the arguments and counter-arguments, the perspectives and counter-perspectives in the working out of the theme, to emerge as exactly as possible. Whoever was involved, however, could hardly have received the impression that, even for those whose reservations were not removed, the remaining dissent *here* still could have a church-dividing significance, justifying mutual condemnations.

[5] It may be otherwise for Calvin and the Reformed tradition. The sub-group on justification was not successful in its attempt to receive a competent opinion from the Reformed side. Here again the real absence of the involvement of Reformed theologians in this sub-group had its effect.[84] In the plenary discussions of the entire Study Group, however, Reformed theologians from the other sub-groups did not criticize the submitted formulations on this aspect of the theme in a way that called into question the basic statements of the text.

[6] In the background of the three canons stands the fear that Luther's doctrine of justification could lead to ethical licentiousness. In reaction to the presentation in this essay, it was (rightly) admonished that canon 20 not only mentions the commandments of *God*, but also those of the *church*. This raises the question of church discipline in Luther and the other Reformers against the background of the discussion with the Antinomians. The document takes up this question in the context of the excursus about the sacrament of penance.[85] Independent of this, the question of church commandments in relation to the reception of the sacrament is even on inner-Catholic presuppositions a dogmatic and moral-theological problem.[86]

[7] The assessment of this essay, that Luther *all his life* rejected the expression *Christus legislator*, must in limited in view of the end of Conclusio III in the "Resolutiones," where Christ for Luther is "without doubt" "divine Lawgiver" and his teaching "divine law".[87] Luther here

is making an argument ad absurdum against his opponents in the indulgences dispute. If Jesus' demand for penance, contrary to [Luther's] first thesis on indulgences and in agreement with the opinion of his opponents, aims at sacramental penance and thus at satisfying works of penance, but the pope on the other side has full authority to modify these, then this means that the pope disregards divine law. Here Luther still does not wish to assert this of the pope, but rather to think out to the end the absurd consequence to which the defenders of the practice of indulgences are forced if they deny Luther's first thesis.

Historically, it should be noted that we are dealing here with a Luther text from the spring of 1518. The genuine Lutheran-Reformation distinction of Law and Gospel is clarified only in the further course of the dispute over indulgences and becomes a technical term at the latest in the "Small Galatians Commentary" of 1519—and then with the consequence that Christ no longer can or may be understood as "Lawgiver."[88]

[8] The discussion in the sub-group at first produced no further clarity over the addressee of this canon. The text from the Schmalcald Articles, which the study document quoted in another context,[89] could justify the hypothesis that the addressees of the canon are to be sought somewhere among the "Schwärmer." The substantive content of the canon would once again be for Luther a foregone conclusion.

[9] Even beyond the presentation of this essay, canon 24 appeared in the discussions of the sub-group as most in need of interpretation. The idea of a growth in goodness as a result of justification appeared to the representatives of the Lutheran tradition as very problematic. Since the opinion of Luther research on this topic is highly divergent in its emphasis,[90] it can here only be stated that in this respect the Lutheran members of the sub-group represented *one* voice in the chorus of Luther research. On the other side, it was conceded by the Catholic members that the opposition intended by the Council between "fruit" and "cause" is murky. To the expression "sign" (of justification) the question was raised whether the Council here alludes to the famous *syllogismus practicus* of the Reformed tradition or even consciously wished to allude to it.[91]

It was established that Canon 25 was occasioned by the extremely paradoxical statement of Luther in the Heidelberg Disputation, which is clearly directed against the late scholastic understanding of the natural preparation (*ex puris naturalibus*) for the reception of grace. In the evaluation of such statements the literary genre of the disputation theses must be taken into account: they should shake opponents out of their reserve and are by nature *not* the final opinion of their author on the matter—although they usually are claimed thus by the other side. Luther substantively and in part verbally distinguished "sinful acts" and the "lasting sin". In the Heidelberg Disputation Luther speaks of the latter, of lasting sin. On the other hand, Trent is definitely thinking of sinful acts and in so far the Council teaching does not strike Luther, regardless whether the fathers at Trent have misunderstood Luther's concept or wished only to inculcate the Catholic teaching, without committing themselves to a clarification of the counter-position.

[10] In the essay I had fully consciously introduced my thesis, present for some time in several publications, of the dispensability of the concept of merit for theological and faith language and the possibility of preserving its only legitimate meaning without the burdened word.[92] In no way did I need to feel misunderstood if the discussion in the sub-group then spoke of my "banning" the concept of merit. Important for me in this connection was the reference that the implication of the concept of merit in the concept of reward—"if reward, then also merit"—was introduced into theological thought by Tertullian through the turn from the New Testament understanding of reward to his new understanding in the framework of a legal way of thinking.[93]

[11] With these two canons, the discussion in the study group revolved around two questions. First, what is the meaning in Luther of *peccatum mortale*? and as a variant of this question: what is the sin "against the Holy Spirit"? The second question concerned once again the relation between *fides vera* and *fides viva*. There was unanimity, that for Luther a *fides vera* always *simultaneously* is a *fides viva* and vice versa. For him therefore the Tridentine distinction is meaningless. Because all was bound up with different conceptions of faith, they spoke at cross purposes and could not understand one another. The final formulations of the study document attempted to work through this blockade of understanding—here it really was such—and to show that, despite the intention of the opposing parties at that time, the one conception need not judge the other.[94]

[12] In the deliberations of the study group it was not at first adequately clear whether and how the problematic of the sacrament of penance should be addressed and worked through in the document's subsection on the justification of the sinner. In view of the extremely intricate historical, liturgical, dogmatic, and pastoral-theological problems relating to the sacrament of penance and the ecclesial shape of penance in the churches concerned, an understandable hesitation prevailed to take this problematic in hand. In the end, an ever stronger material necessity won out, especially in view of the fact that all the decisive positions of Luther's Reformation doctrine of justification were developed in the dispute over the meaning and form of the sacrament of penance.[95] On the other hand, this topic could not simply be "finished off" by a few side remarks in the framework of the other explanations, while all the other sacraments were handled in detail in the document's sub-section on sacraments. One finally chose the form of a longer excursus and placed it at the historical and also substantive intersection point of the question of the sacrament of penance and the doctrine of justification: after the section on the certainty of salvation. Both in the sub-group and especially in the plenary deliberations, this excursus became an object of intense, at times frankly vehement, discussions and repeated reformulation. This is a clear sign how the described historical connection, even under the conditions of a completely changed practice in all the concerned churches, still works as a theological impulse. In addition it revealed how extensively the concerned churches, usefully frightened by the abuses of the late Middle Ages, have in the meantime restructured their practices of penance, so that now it cannot rightly be expected of them that they suspend these with a light heart. The problematic of the sacrament of penance became and is a classic case of the question the study faced: non-condemnation, mutual recognition, *without convergence* in teaching and practice.

[13] Again it must be first pointed out that the absence of an effective involvement by Reformed theologians had a limiting effect on the work in the sub-group. Important references to the Reformed tradition—especially, e.g., in the question of ecclesial penance (see [12])—arose first in the deliberations of the plenary, where Reformed theologians and Catholic experts on the Catholic-Reformed conversation were present.

In Hofgeismar, after only a short discussion, the subgroup envisaged the following construction of the section of the document on justification:

1. A kind of preamble—somewhat on the relation between Christology and justification.

2. A rough outline description of the former controversies over the doctrine of justification, which in a slogan-like and stereotyped simplification would show how these controversies have defined the confessional oppositions far into our century.

3. Hermeneutical reflections on why the former controversies are today represented in other ways and have lost their confessional and theological obviousness. To these hermeneutical reflections belong the assessment of new historical-theological insights as well as perspectives of the newer theological discussion in both churches about the epistemological and ecclesiological importance of dogmatic and/or confessional formulations in connection with the present insights of linguistic philosophy.

4. Theological reappraisal of the heretofore controversial points listed under 2 in the form of a threefold organizing question:

a) Where were there simply misunderstandings?

b) Can the irreconcilable oppositions of that time be mediated in a new way today in light of the preceding hermeneutical reflections?

c) Are the remaining oppositions still church-dividing?

This sketch was essentially retained, as is immediately evident from a comparison with the final text, in spite of all sorts of rearrangements in detail. In the plenary deliberations, however, it soon became apparent that the foreseen "introduction" worked out by sub-group 3 contained a hermeneutical section about the change in the dialogue situation with reference to the old oppositions. The hermeneutical meditation developed by study group 1 and foreseen as section 3 (see above) was consequently almost verbatim taken into the introduction and stands now as section 1 of the entire document. Statements of the corresponding draft from study group 3 were incorporated, as far as they contained additional statements. Thus a common hermeneutical introduction is now given in the text's "Introduction," which then is applied at the corresponding place in the subsection on justification almost point for point to the special problems of this topic.

It remains to be noted that in sub-group 1 doubts repeatedly arose (and could not be completely settled even up to the end) whether it was a good idea to begin with a slogan-like description of heretofore "differentiating doctrines." The focus of the doubt was whether the later individual reappraisals would make up for the presentation of the old oppositions. The overwhelming majority of the sub-group and of the plenary found this doubt to be groundless in the final text. Nevertheless the difference in procedure compared with other sections is clear. While they treat point by point first the old opposition and immediately afterwards its present resolution, the section of the document on justification first presents a connected list of heretofore oppositions and then, interrupted by the hermeneutical meditation, a similarly structured attempt at a re-appraisal. Repeatedly decisive for this procedure in the sub-group and in the plenary was the argument that study group 1, unlike the two other sub-groups, could not draw upon a (in some areas significant) number of preliminary works in other "consensus documents" and then simply balance them. It had to work through its thematic area almost from square one. It is significant, and this also underscores the special importance of this study document, that the clearly central theme of the Reformation and thus the central controversy between the Roman Catholic Church and the churches of the Reformation in contrast to all other controversies only most recently has been given a fundamental consideration in official church-to-church commissions. The Study Group has consciously accorded the central and pre-eminent position in the document to the theme of "justification," as is its due.

Notes

1.　The echo of this mutuality resounds in the document of the official Lutheran/Roman Catholic US Dialogue Commission on the theme justification—the first comprehensive convergence document on this theme altogether. Cf. H.G. Anderson et al. ed., *Justification by Faith*, Lutherans and Catholics in Dialogue VII (Minneapolis: 1985), paragraph 156, Thesis 1, cited in *Condemnations*, 36.

2.　The following is a list of the most important and bibliographically helpful items on the Decree on Justification from Trent. In the following they are referred to only on special occasions:

　　　History: H. Jedin, *Geschichte des Konzils von Trient*, 4 volumes in 5 (Freiburg i.Br.: 1950-1975) (partially a new edition), II, 104-268; English translation II (London: 1961), 125-165; O. de La Brosse/J. Lecler/H. Holstein/Ch. Lefebvre, *Lateran V und Trient* (1 Teil = Geschichte der ökumenischen Konzilien X), (Mainz: 1978), 290-355; G. Alberigo, "Das Konzil von Trient in neuer Sicht", in: *Concilium* 1 (1965) 574-583 [an overview of the newer tendencies in the writing of the history of councils]; R. Bäumer, ed., *Von Konstanz nach Trient. Beiträge zur Kirchengeschichte in den Reformkonzilien bis zum Tridentinum* (Paderborn: 1972), in which esp. Th. Freudenberger, "Zur Benutzung des reformatorischen Schrifttums am Konzil von Trient," 577-601; same, ed., *Concilium Tridentinum* (Darmstadt: 1979) [report on research, documentation of important contributions, bibliography]; A. Forster, *Gesetz und Evangelium bei Girolamo Seripando*

(Paderborn: 1963); K.J. Becker, *Die Rechtfertigungslehre nach Domingo de Soto. Das Denken eines Konzilsteilnehmers vor, in und nach Trient* (Rome: 1967); St. Horn, *Glaube und Rechtfertigung nach dem Konzilstheologen Andreas de Vega* (Paderborn: 1972); J. Martin-Palma, *Gnadenlehre. Von der Reformationszeit bis zur Gegenwart* (Freiburg i.Br.: 1980) (= Handbuch der Dogmengeschichte III/5b), 7-66; E. Iserloh, "Luther und das Konzil von Trient (1984)", in: the same, *Kirche - Ereignis und Institution.* Aufsätze und Vorträge, 2 volumes (Münster: 1985), II, 181-193; cf.also the contribution of Iserloh in this volume; J. Raitt, "From Augsburg to Trent," in Anderson, ed., Ibid., 200-217. Brief presentations naturally are in the handbooks of church history and in the relevant lexicon articles.

Catholic Interpretation without ecumenical interest, rather with a polemically limited intention, in the traditional handbooks of Catholic dogmatics. Cf. A Hasler, *Luther in der katholischen Dogmatik. Darstellung seiner Rechtfertigungslehre in den katholischen Dogmatikbüchern* (Munich: 1968).

Catholic Interpretation with ecumenical openness: H. Volk, "Die Lehre von der Rechtfertigung nach den Bekenntnisschriften der evangelisch-lutherischen Kirche," in E. Schlink/H. Volk, eds., *Pro veritate. Ein theologischer Dialog*, Festgabe für Erzbischof Lorenz Jaeger und Bischof Wilhelm Stählin (Münster/Kassel: 1963), 59-96; H. Küng, *Rechtfertigung. Die Lehre Karl Barths und eine katholische Besinnung* (Einsiedeln: 1957); on this book, F. Barth, "Römisch-katholische Stimmen zu dem Buch von Hans Küng, "Rechtfertigung"," in: *MdKI* 11 (1960) 81-87; K. Rahner, "Fragen der Kontroverstheologie Über die Rechtfertigung," in: the same, *Schriften zur Theologie* IV (Zurich: 1960), 237-271; H. Küng, "Zur Diskussion um die Rechtfertigung," in: *ThQ* 143 (1963) 129-135; the same, "Katholische Besinnung auf Luthers Rechtfertigungslehre heute," in *Theologie im Wandel*, Festschrift zum 150jährigen Bestehen der katholisch-theologischen Fakultät der Universität Tübingen 1817-1967 (Munich: 1967), 449-468; P. Fransen, "Dogmengeschichte Entfaltung der Gnadenlehre," in: *MySal* IV/2 (1973), 631-763; 712-727; more general but relevant for the decree on justification; the same, *Hermeneutics of the Council and other Studies* (Louvain: 1985), 69-286; O.H. Pesch/A. Peters, *Einführung in die Lehre von Gnade und Rechtfertigung* (Darmstadt: 1981), 169-209; C.J. Peter, "The decree on Justification in the Council of Trent," in Anderson, ed., ibid., 218-229.—Concerning some special questions: A. Stakemeier, *Das Konzil von Trient über die Heilsgewssheit* (Heidelberg: 1947); St. Pfürtner, *Luther und Thomas im Gespräch. Unser Heil zwischen Gewissheit und Gefährdung* (Heidelberg: 1960), esp. 11-44; E. Schillebeeckx, "Das tridentinische Rechtfertigungsdekret in neuer Sicht," in *Concilium* 1 (1965) 452-454 [in reply to Oberman, see below]; H.-P. Arendt, *Bussakrament und Einzelbeichte. Die tridentinischen Lehraussagen über das Sündenbekenntnis und ihre Verbindlichkeit für die Reform des Bussakramentes* (Freiburg i. Br.: 1981.)

Catholic Dogmatics at the present ecumenical standard: M. Schmaus, *Katholische Dogmatik*, 5 vols in 8,III/2 (Munich: 1956); the same, *Der Glaube der Kirche*, 2nd revised ed., 6 vols. in 13 (St. Ottilien: 1979-1982), VI/1; M. Flick/Z. Alszeghy, *Il Vangelo della grazia. Un trattato dogmatico* (Florence: 1964); J. Auer, *Das Evangelium der Gnade. Die neue Heilsordnung durch die Gnade Christi in seiner Kirche* (= J. Auer/J. Ratzinger, Kleine katholische Dogmatik V) (Regensburg 1970), see index "Trient"; P. Fransen, "Das neue Sein des Menschen in Christus," in *MySal* IV/2 (1973), 921-982.

Evangelical Interpretation, historical: H. Rückert, *Die Rechtfertigungslehre auf dem tridentinischen Konzil* (Bonn: 1925); against this, H.A. Oberman, "Das tridentinische Rechtfertigungsdekret im Lichte spätmittelalterlicher Theologie," in *ZThK* 61 (1964) 251-282, printed also in: Bäumer (ed.) *Concilium Tridentinum* (see footnote 2), 301-340; in response, again Rückert, "Promereri. Eine Studie zum tridentinischen Rechtfertigungsdekret als Antwort an H.A. Oberman," in *ZThK* 68 (1971) 162-194, printed in the same, *Vorträge und Aufsätze zur historischen Theologie* (Tübingen 1972), 264-294; concerning which again Oberman, *Werden und Wertung der Reformation. Vom Wegestreit zum Glaubenskampf* (Tübingen: 1977), 135f, nt. 186.

Evangelical Interpretation, sceptical of ecumenical consensus: E. Kinder, *Die evangelische Lehre von der Rechtfertigung*. Selected and with introduction by E. Kinder (Lüneburg: 1957); W. Joest, "Die tridentinische Rechtfertigungslehre," in *KuD* 9 (1963) 41-49; also H. Vorster, *Das Freiheitsverständnis bei Thomas von Aquin und Martin Luther*, Göttingen 1965, 15-18, 71f, 97f, 313-327.

Evangelical Interpretation in ecumenical openness: P. Brunner, "Die Rechtfertigungslehre des Konzils von Trient," in: Schlink/Volk (eds.) (see above under Volk), 59-96, printed in the same, *Pro Ecclesia. Gesammelte Aufsätze zur dogmatischen Theologie*, 2 vols. (Berlin 1962/1966), II, 141-169—informative to read in comparison with the contribution of Joest; A. Peters, "Reformatorische Rechtfertigungsbotschaft zwischen tridentinischer Rechtfertigungslehre und gegenwärtigem evangelischem Verständnis der Rechtfertigung," in *LuJ* 31 (1964) 77-128; G.A. Lindbeck, "A Question of Compatibility: A Lutheran Reflection on Trent," in Anderson (ed.), ibid. 230-240.

Brief but instructive overviews: B. Lohse, *Epochen der Dogmengeschichte*, (Stuttgart: 1974), 189-196; G. Greshake, *Geschenkte Freiheit. Einführung in die Gnadenlehre* (Freiburg i.Br.: 1977), 73-81; G. Müller, *Die Rechtfertigungslehre. Geschichte und Probleme* (Gütersloh: 1977), 69-76. See also the selection of literature by K. Lehmann for sub-group 1 on pp. 368-371 of the German of this volume [not here translated].

3. *Geschichte* (see footnote 2), II, 260; English translation, II, 307-309.

4. Cf. G. Biel, *Collectorium in quattuor libros Sententiarum*, II d. 28: qu. un art. 3 dub. 1 (L); dub. 2 (N): W. Werbeck/U. Hoffmann, 4 volumes in 5, (Tübingen: 1973-1974), II, 539 f, esp. 540, 16, 540-543, esp. 542, 26f; 543, 57-60. References also in L. Grane, *Contra Gabriel. Luthers Auseinandersetzung mit Gabriel Biel in der Disputatio contra scholasticam theologiam 1517* (Copenhagen: 1962), 203f, 211f.

5. Cf. the controversy between Oberman and Rückert in the writings cited in footnote 2.

6. On Thomas, cf. Pesch/Peters (see footnote 2), 57-63, 103-107—with references to additional specialized literature. On late scholasticism ibid. 112-117—with literature ibid. 110, footnote 2. As a supplement, see D.R. Janz, *Luther and Late Medieval Thomism. A Study in Theological Anthropology* (Waterloo: 1983); the same, *Luther on Thomas Aquinas* (Stuttgart: 1989); J.L. Farthing, *Thomas Aquinas and Gabriel. Interpretation of Thomas Aquinas in German Nominalism on the Eve of the Reformation* (London-Durham: Dubuque University Press, 1988).

7. Cf. Oberman in the texts cited in nt. 2, e.g., in *Werden und Wertung*, ibid.

8. This is the thesis of Oberman. More on Soto in Becker (see nt. 2), esp. 141-153, 266-273 (see also the index under meritum) in agreement with the description of

the position of Soto in Oberman; cf. H. de Lubac, *Die Freiheit der Gnade* (= a German translation of Surnaturel according to a much altered second edition, Paris 1965), 2 vols. (Einsiedeln: 1971), I, 169-194.

9.   Cf. WA 2, 399,10; 408,3; also 288,1; 394,33-395,17. On Luther and Gregory cf. L. Grane, "Gregor von Rimini und Luthers Leipziger Disputation," *STL* 22 (1968) 29-49; the same, *Modus loquendi theologicus. Luthers Kampf um die Erneuerung der Theologie (1515-1518)* (Leiden: 1975), 135-138; H.A. Oberman, ed., *Gregor von Rimini. Werk und Wirkung bis zur Reformation* (Berlin 1981); also the same, *Werden und Wertung* (see nt. 2), 86-93, 130-133. Oberman's thesis of a "via Gregorii" at the end of the later Middle Ages is certainly disputed; the titles available to me of the lively discussion are collected in O.H. Pesch, "Theologische Überlegungen zum 'Subjektivismus' Luthers. Zur Frage: Über Lortz hinaus?," in R. Decot/R. Vinke, eds., *Zum Gedenken an Joseph Lortz (1887-1975)*. Beiträge zur Reformationsgeschichte und Ökumene (Stuttgart: 1989), 106-140: 110, nt. 18.

10.   On the canons of Orange and their rediscovery, cf. the summary of the state of historical knowledge in Pesch/Peters (see nt. 2), 34-40; for their effect on the teaching of grace by the scholastics and for the Council of Trent cf. ibid. 55-68, 176-184.

11.   Cf. WA 39, I, 177,3: *Quare homo huius vitae est pura materia Dei ad futurae formae suae vitam* (*Disputatio de homine*, 1536, Th. 35); American ed. 34, 137-144. Over against the WA there is a critically edited text of the entire disputation in G. Ebeling, *Lutherstudien* II: *Disputatio de homine*, 1. Teil: Text und Traditionshintergrund (Tübingen: 1977), 15-24 (with German translation). There also, on pp. 1-15, a description of the origin and transmission of the theses and with it parenthetically the proof of the high degree of improbability that the council fathers of Trent knew this text.

12.   *Condemnations*, 32, 46.

13.   Cf. Dz 1555 with 1486. Luther had already in the Heidelberg Disputation said that the *liberum arbitrium* is a *res de solo titulo*. When Rome listed this sentence in the *Errores Martini Lutheri*, Luther repeated the thesis in his answer and strengthened it through the addition: *...immo titulus sine re* (WA 7, 146,3) and repeats it also in the writing against Erasmus of 1525: WA 18, 756, 1-8; American ed. 33, 3-295.

14.   E.g.: "Er ist der zimerman, wir sind das holtz dazu... Hie zimmert und arbiet an uns, hofelt [hobelt] und schnitzet uns, das er den alten menschen inn uns also volkomen bereite, das wir seine newe Creatur seyen" (WA 31, I, 419, 5; Explanation of Ps 111,1530); American ed. 13, 351-387. Cf. also WA 7, 575, 8; American ed. 21, 297-358: Wir sind "nur die werckstat darynnen ehr wirckt" (Magnificat Commentary, 1521). On the context as well as the state of the discussion of Luther research cf. O.H. Pesch, *Theologie der Rechtfertigung bei Martin Luther und Thomas von Aquin. Versuch eines systematisch-theologischen Dialogs* (Mainz 1967), 283-317.

15.   Above all in the context of the constantly assaulted certainty of grace. Outline of the problem and literature in O.H. Pesch, *Hinführung zu Luther* (Mainz: 1983),

116-122. The word "tried" (*erwegenen*) faith: WA DB 7, 10, 16. The many-layeredness of the concept of faith for Luther, which does not invalidate its unity, but eludes any comfortable formulation, cannot be sufficiently stressed, cf. Pesch (see nt. 14), 195-282.

16. Summary of these events in Brunner (see nt. 2), 61f.

17. Cf. Pesch (see nt. 14), 106-109, 379-382, 510-516, 846-849.

18. Cf. the exemplary commentary of H.-J. Iwand on *De servo arbitrio* in *Martin Luther. Dass der freie Wille nichts sei. Antwort D. Martin Luthers an Erasmus von Rotterdam* = H.H. Borcherdt/G. Merz (eds.) *Martin Luther. Ausgewählte Werke*, 6 volumes, with 7 additional volumes (Munich: 1948ff), additional volume 1 (1954), 253-315, esp. 280f; on the interpretation of WA 18, 632,3-641,26; American ed. 33, 3-295; G. Ebeling, *Luther. An Introduction to His Thought* (Philadelphia, 1970), 218f.

19. Cf. again the exemplary Iwand (see nt. 18), 253-255; the same *Um den rechten Glauben*. Gesammelte Aufsätze, edited with introduction by K.G. Steck (Munich: 1949), 14f., 248; Ebeling (see nt. 18), 239-258; and recently M. Brecht, "Moral und Gnade. Der Vermittlungsversuch des Erasmus und Luthers Widerspruch," in: O.H. Pesch (ed.), *Humanismus und Reformation. Martin Luther und Erasmus in den Konflikten ihrer Zeit* (Munich/Zurich und Katholische Akademie Freiburg i.Br.: 1985), 71-90, esp. 88 ff.; in the same sense, the same, *Martin Luther*, Vol. 2, Ordnung und Abgrenzung der Reformation 1521-1532 (Stuttgart: 1986), 210-234, esp. 230 f.; further literature in Pesch, *Theologie der Rechtfertigung* (see nt. 14), 106-109; the same, *Hinführung zu Luther* (see nt. 15), 176-188.

20. Cf. Pesch (see nt. 14), 379-382, 846-849; documentation for this is also T. Koch, "Das Böse als theologisches Problem," in *KuD* 24 (1978) 285-320; and W. Pannenberg, *Anthropologie in theologischer Perspektive* (Göttingen :1983), 109-116 in the context of 77-150; in certain respects Pannenberg argues on the line of *De servo arbitrio*, without a mention of Luther's writing or the concept of the "bondage of the will".

21. Cf. characteristically the documents of the Assemblies of the Lutheran World Federation in Helsinki (1963) and in Evian (1970) as well as the preliminary studies (to which also belongs the work of Joest mentioned in nt. 2) and the relevant statements of the Leuenberg Concord and the Malta Report. Overview, index of sources, and evaluations in Pesch/Peters (see nt. 2), 331-338. Cf. also: *All Under One Christ: Statement on the Augsburg Confession by the Roman Catholic/Lutheran Joint Commission*, 1980, para. 14 in: H. Meyer/L. Vischer (eds.), *Growth in Agreement*: Reports and Agreed Statements of Ecumenical Conversations on a World Level (New York/Geneva: 1984), esp. 243.

22. Cf. Jedin II (see nt. 2), 152; English translation II, 181-182.

23. On the limitless discussion about Luther's "Reformation breakthrough" and also the relation to it here suggested, cf. O.H. Pesch, "Zur Frage nach Luthers reformatorischer Wende. Ergebnisse und Probleme der Diskussion um Ernst Bizer, Fidex ex auditu," in *Catholica* 20 (1966) 216-243, 264-280; the same, "Neuere Beiträge zur Frage nach Luthers 'reformatorischer Wende'," in:

Catholica 37 (1983) 259-287; 38 (1984) 66-133. The first research report is included in the documentation volume by B. Lohse (ed.), *Der Durchbruch der reformatorischen Erkenntnis bei Luther* (Darmstadt: 1968), 445-505; the second in the continuation volume: B. Lohse (ed.), *Der Durchbruch der reformatorischen Erkenntnis bei Luther. Neuere Untersuchungen* (Stuttgart: 1988), 245-341, followed by three more recent contributions by J. Mehlhausen, R. Schwarz, and R. Staats as well as a selected bibliography 1966-1987. Of special interest is the essay by Staats, "Augustins *de spiritu et littera* in Luthers reformatorischer Erkenntnis," in *ZKG* 98 (1987) 28-47; in Lohse (ed.), loc. cit. 365-384: Tower experience/Reformation breakthrough in winter, 1518/19, but before 2. February 1519.

24. Most emphatically in the "school" of Gerhard Ebeling. Cf. *pars pro toto*, Luther (see nt. 18), 178-197; the same, *Dogmatik des christlichen Glaubens*, 3 volumes (Tübingen: 1979), I, 79-110; III, 194-248.

25. Most emphatically—in Germany—in the "school" of Paul Althaus and generally in the "Erlangen school". Cf. *pars pro toto* the same, *Die Theologie Martin Luthers* (Gütersloh: 1963), 195-218; and W. Joest, *Gesetz und Freiheit. Das Problem des tertius usus legis bei Luther und die neutestamentliche Parainese* (Göttingen: 1968); the same, *Ontologie der Person bei Luther* (Göttingen: 1967). On the substantive issue—and on similar tendencies in Scandinavian Luther research!—cf. Pesch, *Theologie der Rechtfertigung* (see nt. 14), 66-76, 283-317; the same, *Hinführung zu Luther* (see nt. 15), 154-175.

26. This last point Heiko A. Oberman and Leif Grane especially stressed against such Catholic critics of late scholasticism as Joseph Lortz, Erwin Iserloh and Peter Manns; a report about this discussion in Pesch (see nt. 14), 708-714; and in Pesch/Peters (see nt. 2), 110-118.

27. Cf. W. Schwab, *Entwicklung und Gestalt der Sakramenttheologie bei Martin Luther* (Frankfurt/Bern: 1977); H. Jorissen, "Die Busstheologie der Confessio Augustana. Ihre Voraussetzung und Implikationen," in *Catholica* 35 (1981) 58-89.

28. Here especially one should consider the "Denkschriften der Evangelischen Kirche in Deutschland." Cf. also O. Bayer and others, *Zwei Kirchen—eine Moral?* (Regensburg: 1986).

29. WA 2, 145-152, here esp. 145, 9-146, 35: *Igitur per fidem in Christum fit iustitia Christi nostra iustitia ...* (146, 8). *... qui credit in Christo, haeret in Christo, estque unum cum Christo, habens eandem iustitiam cum ipso* (146, 14); American ed. 31, 297-306.

30. Thus especially K. Aland, *Der Weg zur Reformation* (Munich: 1965), 103-105. Most recently disputed by Staats with considerable, but in my opinion not *totally* convincing reasons (see nt. 23), 44-46, in Lohse (ed.), Ibid (see nt. 23) 381-383. According to Staats the "sermon" is not an example of preaching, neither for Palm Sunday 1518 (where the underlying text, Philippians 2:5-11, is the assigned text, of which Luther only treats the verses 5-7) nor for 1519 (according to the older research), but it is a speech given at some point in the winter 1518-19 at an academic occasion.

31. On page 68-70b; cf. the index provided by Rolf Schäfer, "Zur Datierung von Luthers reformatorischer Erkenntnis," in *ZThK* 66 (1969) 151-170: 165-170, here 165, in Lohse (ed.), Ibid., 148. Freudenberger's investigations reveal that the sermon is to be found at most on indices of Reformation writings of those who in vain sought to document a foundation of the council's discussions in the literature of the Reformers. To only a few of the fathers in the debate about justification (Salmeron, Ambrosius Catharinus, Seripando) could one ascribe a rudimentary knowledge of the sources. Only in the debate over the sacraments were the Reformation texts more throughly studied in order at least to be able to produce a "list of errors"; cf. Freudenberger (see nt. 2), 584-587.

32. Luther underscores—see the cited texts from *Sermo de duplici iustitia* as representative of numerous others—the *identity* between the righteousness of the justified sinner and that of Christ—only thus does he see all "works righteousness" on the basis of the persons's own possession and achievement as excluded. Since the righteousness of the sinner is none other than that of Christ, the latter is its *being* or *essence* [*Wesen*]. Expressed in scholastic terms that means: Christ's righteousness is *formaliter*, according to the form of its essence, the righteousness of the justified sinner. Since the beginning of the 13th century, however, the concept *formaliter* had expressed the essence of the righteousness of grace as an inner reality *within* the person; ironically for the same reason as Luther: in order to exclude every self achievement of the human being in the event of justification. The opposite position understood the righteousness of grace not as *forma*, but (in an Augustinian manner) as movement of the soul, thus unavoidably with its participation. In order to safeguard that grace is foundationally prior to all human activity (Peter Lombard: "As the rain to the fruitfulness of the earth", *Sent.* II d. 27, 3), it is conceived according to the conceptual model "form" (or *qualitas*), the communication of which the human soul can only passively suffer and not support through an active contribution. An overview and special literature, *pars pro toto*, in Pesch (see nt. 2), 42-54. The development of the doctrine of grace in late scholasticism (and its pastoral application!) was such that Luther believed that only by contesting that righteousness is an *innerhuman* reality in any sense could one escape from the theoretical and practical danger of works righteousness. For the scholastics, on the other hand, the righteousness of grace as an innerhuman reality was self-evident and not a question; it needed only to be safeguarded against any Pelagianizing misunderstanding and this happened through a kind of further development of the Augustinian doctrine of grace by Aristotelian means. The blocking of understanding resulted because the council fathers at Trent with few exceptions (Seripando!) felt no impulse to doubt that all Pelagian misunderstandings had been successfully excluded by the Aristotelian categories. Understanding was blocked in the reverse direction in that the Reformers no longer perceived the original impulse behind the development of the concept of grace as form. Proof: the reproof by Catholic controversial theologians addressed toward Melanchthon at and after the Diet of Augsburg that he had fired at a straw man version of the scholastic doctrine of grace—see Pfnür, *Einig in der Rechtfertigungslehre? Die Rechtfertigungslehre der Confessio Augustana (1530) und die Stellungnahmen der katholischen Kontroverstheologie zwischen 1530 und 1535*, (Wiesbaden: 1970), 329f, 350—and the accusation even today made by Lutheran theologians that the scholastic conception amounts to an "ethicizing of grace"—see texts such as Ebeling, *Luther* (see nt. 24), and K.-H. zur Mühlen, *Nos extra nos. Luthers Theologie zwischen Mystik und Scholastik* (Tübingen: 1972), esp. 152-155.

33. *Pars pro toto* cf.: WA 1, 140, 11 ff.; 56, 347, 10; 10 I 1, 281, 16 (on the *imputatio iustitiae Christi*, to this also belong the texts which speak of the righteousness of Christ as our righteousness as well as our justification *propter Christum*); American ed. 51, 26-31;—WA 56, 284, 20, 7, 23, 1; 39 I, 83, 37 ff.; 97, 17 f.; 40 III, 350, 4 (on the *sola remissio*); American ed. 25, 4-525.—WA 2, 511, 15; American ed., 32, 137-260; 8 106, 10; American ed. 27, 153-410 (on grace as favor Dei). On the substantive question cf. Pesch (see nt. 14), 170-195. It is striking that the earlier Lutheran Confessions, especially CA and the Apol, use but do not stress the threefold terminology (for instances BSLK 175, 26-39, No 75 f.), on the other hand the Formula of Concord verbally nails in place all three formulas; cf. in the index of the BSLK the indicated passages under the terms Christsus B II c), Gerechtigkeit des Menschen, 3 and 4 paragraphs, Rechtfertigung a) and c). Reaction to our canon 11? On the substantive issue, cf. the contributions of Vinzenz Pfnür and Friedrich Beisser in this volume.

34. "Classically" in "On the Freedom of the Christian", WA 7, 25, 26-26, 12 ("Zum zwölften"); American ed. 31, 333-377. Further material from all periods of Luther's teaching and literature in Pesch (see nt. 14), 144, 234 f., and—cited for its collection of text material, not for its judgments—Th. Beer, *Der fröhliche Wechsel und Streit. Grundzüge der Theologie Martin Luthers* (Einsiedeln: 1980), 15-30.

35. Cf. E. Iserloh, "Gratia und Donum. Rechtfertigung und Heiligung nach Luthers Schrift 'Wider den Löwener Theologen Latomus'," in *Catholica* 24 (1970) 67-83 (= Kirche—Ereignis und Institution [see nt. 2] II, 70-87; and, with the mentioned qualification, again Beer (see nt. 34), 64-174.

36. Details in Pesch (see nt. 14), 283-289 (literature there cited).

37. Cf. O.H. Pesch, " 'Um Christi willen...' Christologie und Rechtfertigung in der katholischen Theologie. Versuch einer Richtigstellung," in *Catholica* 35 (1981) 17-57, esp. 18-43; now in: the same, *Dogmatik im Fragment. Gesammelte Studien*, Main 1987, 115-150, esp. 116-138.

38. Cf. *pars pro toto*, two Lutheran theologians from opposite "camps": P. Althaus, *Die christliche Wahrheit. Lehrbuch der Dogmatik* (Gütersloh: 1952), 231-237, 280 f., 596 f., 600-607; G. Ebeling, *Dogmatik* III (see nt. 24), 196-242.

39. *Condemnations*, 46-49.

40. Only two obvious references: The Second Vatican Council alludes only seldom and rather casually to the terminology of the Tridentine teaching of justification, for instance DV 5 (no faith "without the anticipating and helping grace of God"), or GS 25,3rd Section ("...the impulse to sin, which only through strenuous effort with the help of grace can be overcome"). In the encyclical *Redemptor hominis* John Paul II in paragraphs 7-10 and 13—where it must be, if at all—does not quote Trent once, but rather the Bible and the Second Vatican Council and expresses himself on the meaning of the mystery of salvation using their linguistic range.

41. In a more general manner, but yet also with special reference to the doctrine of justification, however, astonishing steps have been taken in the present

pontificate, partially by the Pope personally, in the direction of a recognition of Lutheran basic statements. Cf. O.H. Pesch, "Erträge des Luther-Jahres für die katholische systematische Theologie," in Peter Manns (ed.), *Zur Bilanz des Lutherjahres* (Stuttgart: 1986), 81-154, here: 132-141; there also the summary of the judgments of these events. Nevertheless, one must warn against optimism. For instance Gottfried Maron in his critical book: *Kirche und Rechtfertigung. Eine kontroverstheologische Untersuchung, ausgehend von den Texten des Zweiten Vatikanischen Konzils* (Göttingen: 1969), does not see the silence on the theme of justification at the Council as accidently determined by the order of the day. According to his judgement, the witness to justification is replaced out of theological conviction by the thought of *participatio ecclesiae*—with unbearable consequences in the view of Reformation theology. Cf. also the relevant discussion report in O.H. Pesch, *Gerechtfertigt aus Glauben. Luthers Frage an die Kirche* (Freiburg i. Br.: 1982), 13-55, here esp. 15-42. Recently Werner Löser has renewed the old accusation of controversial theology in programmatic form: Reformation theology in its doctrine of justification illegitmately made one statement of the total biblical witness into the standard for everthing and thus narrowed the catholicity of the ecclesiological tradition into confessionality: "Was gilt in der Kirche? Katholische Fragen an die evangelische Kirche," in *Jahrbuch des Evangelischen Bundes* 30 (1987) 49-67.

42. The grounding of the certainty of salvation in the impossibility of declaring in faith that Christ is a liar is *the* stereotyped argument of the early-Reformation Luther in this matter. This has been incontestably worked out—in the context of the new understanding of the sacrament of penance—by O. Bayer, *Promissio. Geschichte der reformatorischen Wende in Luthers Theologie* (Göttingen: 1971), 164-202; and in W. Schwab, (see nt. 27), 77-144.

43. Characteristic, e.g., is the way the line of thought in Ebeling in the passage quoted in nt. 38 runs in this exact context. Cf. also Pesch, *Hinführung zu Luther* (see nt. 15), 128-133.

44. It concerns especially Dz 3008:ND 118. The problem seems of lesser weight as the reproach of "an intellectualized" concept of faith" is made by many: In the Catholic and in the Reformation view, "faith" at the core means to depend on God, because God is God and is therefore dependable. In the contemporary Catholic theology, the Vatican definition of faith is strikingly seldom perceived as a problem, although no one any more simply takes over this definition. Cf. O.H. Pesch, "Glaube als Lebensweisheit. Zum Glaubensbegriff in der gegenwärtigen katholischen und evangelischen Theologie," in W. Baier/St. O. Horn, and others (eds.) *Weisheit Gottes—Weisheit der Welt*, Festschrift Joseph Cardinal Ratzinger (St. Ottilien 1987), 453-492, here esp. 468-491; specially on Vatican I cf. P. Walter, *Die Frage der Glaubensbegründung aus innerer Erfahrung auf dem I. Vatikanum. Die Stellungnahme des Konzils vor dem Hintergrund der zeitgenössischen römischen Theologie* (Mainz: 1980.)

45. Here a summary reference to the well known work on the history of dogma by Bernhard Poschmann and Karl Rahner can be sufficient. Summary of the discussion (including exegesis) now in H. Vorgrimler, *Busse und Krankensalbung*, HDG IV/3 (Freiburg i. Br.: 1978), 3-92.

46. Bayer coins the formulation that the sacraments are effective *ex verbo dicto*: "Die

reformatorische Wende in Luthers Theologie," in *ZThK* 66 (1969) 115-150, here 127.

47. See nt. 3. I have not been able to discover who is intended in these three canons, though there might be new source studies not available to me. The previous normative work on the sources, also especially of the Tridentine negotiations, namely Jedin, Lecler (in: de la Brosse and others), Fransen, and Martin-Palma (see nt. 2), oddly enough do not give an opinion on this question—apart from a very general reference to Calvin in Lecler, ibid., 344. A working through of the state of the discussion yields the following fixed points: a) The Reformation teaching of the "certainty of salvation" to begin with produced at the Council a violent internal discussion among the relevant traditional school positions. b) Scotus' teaching of a certainty of grace resting on the grace of God and supported through the sacraments was still so strong that it prevented the rigorous dispute of *every* possibility. c) The psychological and ontology-critical interest of the Augustinians neutralized itself through their nearness otherwise to the Thomist position in this matter, that a certainty of grace is possible only as a special divine privilege. d) This Thomist line essentially prevailed because it permitted the dividing line from the Reformation position to be drawn most clearly—in light of which the inner-catholic open possibilities of a diversity of opinion had secondary importance in doubtful cases. e) This dominating interest in demarcation did not allow the difference between certainty of salvation/certainty of grace and certainty of predestination even to become a question. An illuminating insight into the motives of the Council fathers born from the same fears is found in G. Müller/V. Pfnür, "Rechtfertigung - Glaube - Werke," in: H. Meyer/H. Schütte, *Confessio Augustana. Bekenntnis des einen Glaubens. Gemeinsame Untersuchung lutherischer und katholischer Theologen* (Paderborn/Frankfurt a.M.: 1980), 106-139, here 126-129 (with literature). Despite apparently rigorous formulations—a most depressing collection in a remote place is O. Kuss, *Der Römerbrief*, Dritte Lieferung (Röm 8,19 - 11,36) (Regensburg: 1978), excursus: on the problematic of "predestintion", 828-934, here 880-889—present Calvin research is of the conviction that the common opinion of an *arbitrary* "double predestination" (*praedestinatio gemina*) was and is a chronic misunderstanding of the teaching of Calvin, even if an obvious one of great historical effect: see the specialized literature in the excellent contribution by M. Löhrer, "Gottes Gnadenhandeln als Erwählung des Menschen," in *MySal* IV/2, 767-824, here 790-793.

   Cf. further moreover the monograph by G. Kraus, *Vorherbestimmung. Traditionelle Prädestinationslehre im Lichte gegenwärtiger Theologie* (Freiburg i. Br.: 1977), 157-187. Kraus says nothing about the Council of Trent.

48. Description in Pesch (see nt. 14), 269-274, 382-393; and in the same *Hinführung zu Luther* (see nt. 15), 244-263; specialized literature there as in Löhrer (see nt. 47).

49. For the exegesis, reference should be made to the more recent commentaries on Romans (Kuss, Schlier, Käsemann, and most recent of all Wilckens); for systematic reflection—without the new approach in Karl Barth, KD II/2, unthinkable—cf. Löhrer (see nt. 47) and Kraus (see nt. 47) as well as most recent the long article "Erwählung" in TRE, esp. the systematic section by Traugott Koch. Cf. Second Vatican Council, LG 2f, 16; DV 14. A new and unique interpretation, which appears no longer to be conscious of the classical problems,

is by L. Weimer, *Die Lust an Gott und seiner Sache oder: Lassen sich Gnade und Freiheit, Glaube und Vernunft, Erlösung und Befreiung vereinbaren?* (Freiburg i. Br.: 1981), 401-428.

50. Two "classical" passages from many: WA 7, 26,22 f. - 30,15-30 (On the Freedom of the Christian Person); American ed. 31, 333-377. WA 6, 514, 19-21 (De captivitate Babylonica); American ed. 36, 11-126. Numerous further quotations in Pesch (see nt. 14), 294 f.

51. This is always the special concern of Paul Althaus; cf. in summary: *Die Theologie Martin Luthers* (see nt. 25), 213-218; further Joest, *Gesetz und Freiheit* (see nt. 25); A. Peters, *Glaube und Werk. Luthers Rechtfertigungslehre im Lichte der Heiligen Schrift* (Berlin/Hamburg: 1962); but also Ebeling (see nt. 18), 157-197; and from Catholic Lutheran reserach, especially P. Manns, "*Fides absoluta—fides incarnata. Zur Rechtfertigungslehre Luthers im Grossen Galaterkommentar*," in E. Iserloh/K. Repgen (eds.), *Reformata Reformanda*. Festgabe für Hubert Jedin, 2 volumes (Münster: 1965), I, 265-312, now printed in the same, *Vater im Glauben. Studien zur Theologie Martin Luthers* (Stuttgart: 1988), 1-48. Further Lutheran voices and description in Pesch (see nt. 14), 283-317.

52. A collection of relevant texts in Pesch (see nt. 14), 54 f. Cf. also further under excursus [7].

53. Survey of findings in E. Iserloh, "Sacramentum et exemplum. Ein augustinisches Thema lutherischer Theologie," in: Iserloh/Repgen (see nt. 51), 247-264; now in the same, *Kirche - Ereignis und Institution* (see nt. 2), II, 107-124.

54. Here one scarcely needs to provide documentation and details. It is simply a matter of the following problem: While political and liberation theology recalls the word and action of Jesus—the historically known Jesus—as impulse and guiding principle of Christian and ecclesial action and complains of the irrelevance of *mere* Christological orthodoxy, its opponents fear a humanistic and ethical reduction of the church's confession of Christ—and both sides have difficulty taking seriously the concerns of the other, even though they both protest that they have preserved completely and entirely, in harmony with its original meaning, that upon which the opposite side lays all weight.

55. Dz gives this indication in a note to canon 23 under reference do CT 5, 449,26. Lecler (see nt. 47), 344, thinks he can establish a teaching of Calvin as the item addressed in the council statement, but he gives no documentation. For Luther the canon is self-evident; cf. further under excursus [8].

56. Cf. *pars pro toto* the reference given in nt. 51 to Althaus and Peters.

57. Also on this point, Althaus (see nt. 51); cf. also Pesch (see nt. 14), 279-283.

58. The formula is only meaningful on the basis of the teaching of the non-reckoning (*non-imputatio*) of sins and the reckoning of the righteousness of Christ (see the reference in nt. 33 on this), thus in the framework of a relational understanding of the righteousness of the justified sinner. For the origin of this teaching in Luther cf. Pesch (see nt. 15), 314 and the literature quoted there.

59. A presentation of the issue with consideration of these "difficulties" as well as the relevant research literature in Pesch (see nt. 15), 189-202; *Theol. der Rechtfertigung* (see nt. 14), 109-122, 526-537. Cf. further J.F. McCue, "Simul iustus et peccator in Augustine, Aquinas, and Luther: Toward Putting the Debate in Context," in *Journal of the American Academy of Religion 48* (1969) 81-96.

60. Wherever "works" are so understood (whatever else may be true of them, including their ethical significance), that faith relates to them only as source of freedom for them and as standard of judgement about them, but any reverse effect of works on the act of faith itself is, even if not excluded, simply left unthought. It is unavoidable here again to mention Gerhard Ebeling; cf. *Luther* (see nt. 18), 187-197; the same, *Dogmatik* III (see nt. 24), 244-246.

61. For example, Paul Althaus and Albrecht Peters in the passages quoted in nt. 51. Cf. also Pesch/Peters (see nt. 2), 156-166.

62. Cf. P. Althaus, "*Sola fide numquam sola*. Glaube und Werke in ihrer Bedeutung für das Heil bei Martin Luther," in *Una Sancta* 16 (1961) 227-235.

63. Especially P. Brunner (see nt. 2), 95 f.; in relation to Thomas and the Augustinian tradition: U. Kühn, *Via caritatis. Theologie des Gesetzes bei Thomas von Aquin* (Berlin (DDR)/Göttingen 1964/65), 216-218, 262f. It is not the problem of the Council if other Lutheran theologians base their criticism on the mere use of the term *meritum*, understanding it as they were earlier taught to understand it, without regard to the interpretation given it in the council texts themselves. A disappointing example of such unfruitful criticism is W. Härle, "Lehrverurteilungen—kirchentrennend in der Rechtfertigungslehre?," *MD* 38 (1987) 123-127:127—even with an appeal to me; cf. nt. 66 and excursus [10].

64. Cf. Pesch (see nt. 14), 317-322; and the documentation of texts in Beer (see nt. 32), 145-161.

65. WA 18, 694, 27 (*De servo arbitrio*, 1525—in connection with Matthew 25:34); American ed. 33, 3-295.

66. Cf. O.H. Pesch, "Die Lehre vom "Verdienst" als Problem für Theologie und Verkündigung," in: L. Scheffczyk/W. Dettloff/R. Heinzmann (eds.), *Wahrheit und Verkündigung*. Festschrift für Michael Schmaus zum 70. Geburtstag, 2 volumes (Munich/Paderborn: 1967), II, 1865-1907; now in the same, *Dogmatik im Fragment* (see nt. 37), 377-416; and the same, *Frei sein aus Gnade. Theologische Anthropologie* (Freiburg i. Br.: 1983), 389-410.

67. I have attempted this in the places cited in nt. 66.

68. Cf. Brunner (see nt. 2), 75-82; Joest (see nt. 2), 61-68; zu Mühlen (see nt. 32), 79 f.; G. Ebeling, *Das Wesen des christlichen Glaubens*, Tübingen 1959, 153 f., 162; the same, "Einfalt des Glaubens und Vielfalt der Liebe. Das Herz von Luthers Theologie," in: the same, *Lutherstudien* III (Tübingen: 1987), 126-153f; the same, *Luther* (see nt. 24), 195f. On the question in Luther cf. Manns (see nt. 51), 279-288; Iserloh (see nt. 35), 80-83 (= *Kirche - Ereignis und Institution*, II, 83-87; summary in Pesch, *Hinführung zu Luther* (see nt. 15), 163-165; and with Pesch/Peters (see nt. 2), 191-195.

69.   Cf. the reference to the work of Oswald Bayer in nt. 42 as well as to Wolfgang Schwab and Hans Jorissen in nt. 27. There the further specialized literature.

70.   *STh* III, 84, 7 ad 2; 1; 86,2c. 6c. ad 3; cf. *De veritate* 28, 8 ad 2; *Quodl.* IV 10 (qu. 1 a. 1).

71.   Cf. WA 1, 233,18: 234,15; 235,3; 236,20 (Theses 5, 20, 34, and 61 of the Theses on indulgences); 534,20-538,35; 567 26-570,33; 590,33; 615,17-616,9 (Resolutions on the theses); 243-246 (sermon on indulgences and grace); American ed. 31, 25-33, 83-252; and 6, 63-75 (sermon on the excommunication; American ed. 39, 7-22. To this context cf. the impressive contribution of V. Vajta, "Die Kirche als geistlich-sakramentale communio mit Christus und seinen Heiligen bei Luther," in *LuJ* 51 (1948) 10-62, here 39-41.

72.   This position did not first appear in the present day. It is connected with the development in the understanding of excommunication, which—even in *Exsurge Domine* and notwithstanding all ritual forms—already prior to Luther was no longer understood as expulsion from fellowship with *God* or as the assertion of such. Cf. the article "Kirchenbann" in *LThK*. The theological foundation of ecclesial disciplinary law cannot be a topic here. An ecclesial punishment, although an appeal to the conscience of the delinquent and binding *in foro interno*, nevertheless cannot and does not wish to be a determination of the situation of this *forum internum*. This emerges from the following facts: a) Despite adherence to the thought and practice of "retributive punishments," "deterrent punishments" (and thus the "medical" purpose of the punishment) have the clear priority, quantitatively and objectively. b) Only those can be punished who have *intentionally* or *carelessly* in a *seriously imputable* way *externally* violated a law or a command of authority (CIC, Canon. 1321). c) The "imputability" can only be determined on the basis of *external* criteria, especially the stubbornness and unteachability of the delinquent in all preceding admonitions and pastoral efforts, as prescribed by law; the law can neither exclude on the basis of some other quality of the situation which depends on purely internal factors, not can it include these in its rules—ergo! This all is valid in an unlimited way for the new canon law, although unfortunately—cf. K. Walf, *Einführung in das neue katholische Kirchenrecht* (Zurich: 1984), 229—the quotation, unusually long for a law book, from the reform decree of Trent (sess. XIII, de ref., cap 1) in Can 2214 of the 1917 code, which in evocative language set forth punishment as the *ultima ratio* within the *pastoral* action of the church, in Can. 1311 of the 1983 code fell victim to a concern for brevity. The result is that, in a formulation far more unlimited than that of 1917, now the reference is *only* to the "innate and proper" *right* of the church to punish. For the commentator of Can 1311 in: J. Listl/H. Müller/H. Schmitz (eds.), *Handbuch des katholischen Kirchenrechts* (Regensburg: 1983), 923-929 (Richard A. Strigl), it would have been fitting to enjoin this theological clarification of the limits of the ecclesial right of punishment, rather than selecting formulations (esp. 923f) which again suggest the identity of legal excommunication and exclusion from fellowship with God.

73.   Cf. the most recent catholic eschatologies, thus for instance; *MySal* V (1976), 855-864 (the editor Wilhelm Breuning, manages completely without the concept of "purgatory"!); D. Wiederkehr, *Perspektiven der Eschatologie* (Zurich: 1974). 258-266 (he manages likewise without "purgatory"!); J. Ratzinger, *Eschatologie. Tod und ewiges Leben*, Kleine katholische Dogmatik, ed. by J. Auer & J

Ratzinger (Regensburg: 1978), 179-190; H. Vorgrimler, *Hoffnung auf Vollendung.
Aufriss der Eschatologie* (Freiburg i. Br.: 1980), 163-165; F.-J. Nocke,
Eschatologie (Düsseldorf: 1982), 130-134; M. Kehl. *Eschatologie* (Würzburg:
1986), 285-289, in connection with 131-133, 239f, 266-269; and K. Rahner,
"Über den "Zwischenzustand"," in: the same, *Schriften zur Theologie*, XII,
(Zurich: 1975), 455-466; the same, "Fegfeuer," ibid., XIV (Zurich: 1980), 435-
449; and most recently G.L. Müller, " 'Fegfeuer'. Zur Hermeneutik eines
umstrittenen Lehrstücks in der Eschatologie," in *ThQ* 166 (1986) 25-39. On the
attitude of Luther including his blockade of understanding (for which he cannot
be blamed), cf. the noteworthy and ecumenically courageous contribution of W.
Thiede, "Luthers individuelle Eschatologie," in *LuJ* 49 (1982) 7-49. The
controversial topic "purgatory" could in fact be evaluated as settled if Tiede's
serious attempt at an "evangelical teaching about purgatory" at the end of his
essay were to find Lutheran assent. According to my judgement this attempt is in
complete accord with, on the one hand, Luther's Reformation discoveries and, on
the other, the most recent eschatological positions of Catholic theology.

74. Esp. LC, IV,80-82: but also already WA 6, 529,22-34 (De captivitate Babylonica);
     American ed. 36, 11-126.

75. Cf. P. Hünermann, "Theologische Kriterien und Perspektiven der Untersuchung
     zu den gegenseitigen Lehrverwerfungen des 16. Jahrhunderts," in W.-D.
     Hauschild and others, *Ein Schritt zur Einheit der Kirchen. Können die
     gegenseitigen Lehrverurteilungen aufgehoben werden?* (Regensburg: 1986), 43-
     66. It is a historical fact that the Augustinian, anti-Pelagian decisions in the
     doctrine of grace, taken up again decisively by Thomas, were in no way the
     dominant form of thought in late scholasticism and in the time of Luther. They
     cannot stand before us as the "great" catholic-ecclesial tradition. For the period
     after Trent cf. the glimpse in Pesch/Peters (see nt. 2), 213-219. This point, most
     recently repeated by Hünermann, I have never disputed, cf. *Hinführung zu Luther*
     (see nt. 15), 168.

76. The Roman Catholic Church and theology have a unique possibility to remove the
     suspicion that it is playing here with false cards: a rehabilitation of the radical
     Augustinianism of the 16th and 17th centuries (Baius, Jensenius, Pascal and
     others) and likeminded mystics (Fénélon!) who at that time, along with others, fell
     under the verdict of the church because of anti-Reformation fears. Cf.
     Pesch/Peters (see nt. 2), 209-212, 217-219; and the rehabilitation (which in
     principle has already occured) of de Lubac, *Die Freiheit der Gnade* I (see nt. 8).
     These fears continued far into our century and were apt to hinder catholic-
     theological doctoral work with undesired results; cf. P. Manns, "Begegnungen
     eines katholischen Theologen mit Martin Luther (1986)," now in: the same, *Vater
     im Glauben* (see nt. 51), 242-440:427; cf. also ibid. VIII nt. 6.

77. Cf. Schmaus (see nt. 2), III/2, 274 f.; Küng, *Rechtfertigung* (see nt. 2), 186-188;
     K. Rahner, "Was ist eine dogmatische Aussage?," in: the same, *Schriften zur
     Theologie*, V, 54-81, here 69f; Brunner (see nt. 2), 84 f.; Joest (see nt. 2), 52-56.

78. Cf. Pesch/Peters (see nt. 2), 187-191.

79. European, especially German, evangelical theologians demonstrably have much
     difficulty with the thought of theological and confessional formulations as

"linguistic rules" and fear a relaxation and weakening of the Reformation *proprium*; cf. a brief stock-taking with references to additional literature in O.H. Pesch, "Rechtfertigung und Kirche. Die kriteriologische Bedeutung der Rechtfertigungslehre für die Ekklesiologie," in *ÖR* 37 (1988), 22-46; 23-28. Anglo-saxon Lutheran theology is different. Cf. the in this aspect programmatic book by G.A. Lindbeck, *The Nature of Doctrine, Religion and Theology in a Postliberal Age* (Philadelphia: 1984) and the test cases in the two evangelical contributions mentioned in nt. 1, in: Anderson (ed.), *Justification by Faith*, as well as the entire document. For the relevant question under the aspect of ecclesiastical doctrinal decisions, cf. Richard Schaeffler, "Abgrenzungen und Verwerfungen. Sprachphilosophische Überlegungen zu einem theologischen Thema" in the German of this volume [here not translated].

80. On Cajetan and especially his position on Luther's teaching of the certainty of salvation, cf. B. Lohse, "Cajetan und Luther. Zur Begegnung von Thomismus und Reformation," in *KuD* 32 (1986) 150-169; B. Hallensleben, *Communicatio. Anthropologie und Gnadenlehre bei Thomas de Vio Cajetan* (Münster: 1985), esp. 462-498; in both works, the incorporation of the considerable number of new Cajetan-studies, which all seek a theological and human rehabilitation of the great opponent of Luther over against the older disparagement. On the work of Hallensleben cf. also the discussion by B. Lohse, in: *ThRv* 83 (1987) 286-289.

81. Cf. as examples the already several times mentioned works of Oswald Bayer und Wolfgang Schwab. I count myself here; cf. *Hinführung zu Luther* (see nt. 15), 103-111.

82. Cf. Hallensleben (see nt. 80); and especially P. Hacker, *Das Ich im Glauben bei Martin Luther* (Graz: 1966), esp. 104-151, here 141 ff.

83. Cf. *Condemnations*, 53-56.

84. Reformed theologians were appointed to all three sub-groups as well as to the plenary assembly. Through a sum of coincidences, however, in sub-group 1 there was no continuous Reformed collaboration.

85. Cf. *Condemnations*, 56-72, here 65.

86. Cf. R. Baerenz, *Das Sonntagsgebot. Gewicht und Anspruch eines kirchlichen Leitbildes* (Munich: 1982), 31-48.

87. WA 1, 533, 15-34; American ed. 31, 83-252.

88. Cf. Pesch, *Gerechtfertigt aus Glauben* (see nt. 41), 59-74, esp. 67 f. and the same, *Theologie der Rechtfertigung* (see nt. 14), 54 f.

89. Cf. *Condemnations*, 55 f.: Reference to SA III,3,42: in comparison with WA 6,529,11-13 (cf. Dz 1540, 1637).

90. Cf. nt. 56f.

91. Cf. Heidelberg Catechism, Q. 86, brief information on this passage, with literature, in Pesch/Peters (see nt. 2), 163-166. In reference to Calvin, one would

need to supplement Kraus (see nt. 47), 172 f.

92.   Cf. the reference in nt. 66.

93.   Cf. here also, J. Burnaby, *Amor Dei* (London: 1947), 219-252 and in the "Werkstattbericht" in the German of this volume [not here translated], the discussion of *Condemnations*, 66-69.

94.   Cf. *Condemnations*, 47-53.

95.   Cf. above on Canon 12-14.